Competition in Theory and Practice

Revised and updated

T. Burke, A. Genn-Bash and B. Haines

London and New York

First published 1988
by Croom Helm Ltd

First published in the USA by
Croom Helm in association with Methuen, Inc.

This revised and updated edition published 1991
by Routledge
11 New Fetter Lane, London EC4P 4EE

This edition simultaneously published in the USA and Canada
by Routledge
a division of Routledge, Chapman and Hall, Inc.
29 West 35th Street, New York, NY 10001

© 1988 and 1991 T. Burke, A. Genn-Bash and B. Haines
Printed in England by Clays Ltd, St Ives plc

British Library Cataloguing in Publication Data
Burke, Terry
    Competition in theory and practice.
    1. Competition
    I. Title   II. Genn-Bash, Angela   III. Haines, Brian
    338.6′048   HF1436
    ISBN 0–415–05292–0

Library of Congress Cataloging in Publication Data
Burke, Terry, 1942–
    Competition in theory and practice / T. Burke, A. Genn-
    Bash, and B. Haines.
        p.   cm.
    Bibliography: p.
    Includes index.
    ISBN 0–415–05292–0
    1. Competition.   I. Genn-Bash, A. (Angela), 1951– II.
Haines, Brian, III. Title.
    HD41.B87   1988
    338.6′048 – dc 19   87-30321

Contents

Preface   vii

Introduction   ix

1. The Dilemmas of Competition   1
2. Classical Views of Competition   27
3. Modern Models of Competition   49
4. Competition in Business Strategy   85
5. The Rules of the Game: UK, EEC, USA, Japan   118
6. A Practical Guide to Anti-competitive Practices   151
7. Four Study Areas   170
8. Competition Theory Revisited   202
9. Policy Conclusions   219

Bibliography   236

Index   247

Preface

Our motive for writing this book is to explain some of the ambiguities and confusions over the meaning of the word 'competition', given its importance in modern Western culture. We look at competition from a multidisciplinary viewpoint, consider its importance to business people in formulating strategy and to officials charged with implementing competition policy. We also consider reasons why competition often fails to take place and the economic and social effects of anti-competitive behaviour.

Our intention is to build tentative links between quite different disciplines so, over time, broadening the intellectual basis of business studies and providing some additional common ground for practitioners of different aspects of commercial activity. We readily acknowledge the dangers of wandering into other people's specialisms, but we travel in the hope of tolerance and in the interests of better managerial capability to tackle the problems of the next generation.

The book arose from a research project undertaken at the Polytechnic of Central London relating to UK competition policy during the period November 1983 to September 1986. The research team consisted of Geoffrey Killick, Brian Haines, Angela Genn-Bash and Terry Burke. The authors wish to thank Geoffrey Killick for his helpful suggestions and criticisms concerning material to be included in the book.

In addition, our thanks go to Len Shackleton for writing the section 'Austrian Economics and Competition' in Chapter 3. We are most grateful to him for developing an expertise in the field of Austrian economics.

We should also like to thank the students at PCL for patiently listening to our views on competition and for providing us with valuable feedback. Finally, thanks to Terry Haines and Les Bash for their valuable comments and encouragement.

The book, while rooted in economics, has an interdisciplinary approach, and should be highly recommended reading for the following:

(i) 2nd and final year mainstream undergraduate courses in applied and pure economics plus business strategy/policy courses (BA Business Studies, BA Social Science and BSc Economics).

(ii) Graduates on MBA programs and business diplomas.

(iii) Law students with an interest in economics.

(iv) Undergraduates and graduates on European Studies courses.

(v) Final year BTEC/HND students.

The prerequisite for understanding this book is an open mind and on that basis is accessible to anyone interested in business and the social sciences.

In addition to UK students, we hope it will also be of interest to EEC, US, Japanese and Australasian students since, although we have mostly used UK examples set in an EEC context, the theoretical expositions have international validity, and we have examined the different approaches to competition policy within the UK, EEC, USA and Japan.

Since the book's original publication in January 1988, two major policy proposals have been introduced and the MMC has published its report on the Beer industry. Where possible we have revised or made additions to the text to reflect these developments.

Introduction

Western society is organised on the assumption that firms freely compete for markets for goods and services, for access to factors of production and for the ownership of other less efficient firms. In this competitive game, there are high rewards for successful players and a promise of ever rising standards of living for all the spectators.

Despite its apparent attractions, we find there are many critics of competition who claim that it leads to a shoddy, acquisitive and unfair society. We also find that governments have to intervene to keep the players playing – they seem all too often to avoid competition, laying the players themselves open to charges of inefficiency and exploitation of consumers.

For many competition raises issues of values, just as much as those of efficiency. Societies not only make judgements by comparing likely outcomes of alternative courses of action – they also judge possible actions against ideals.

These points were explored in an early essay by Frank Knight, 'The Ethics of Competition' (Knight, 1923, pp. 579–624), where he observes that these ideals are part of the culture of a society. This culture sets, for its age, a series of minimum requirements for life, for health and for comfort.

The existence of these minima raises questions of who sets them and by what means. Different groups of decision-makers using different methods will produce very different scales of social values. Knight observes that different kinds of economic systems will tend to generate and nourish different kinds of wants. The competitive economic order is, in a major way he says, responsible for making emulation and rivalry the outstanding qualities of the Western peoples, who have adopted and developed it.

He also suggests that giving the people what they want ends up by corrupting popular taste. The competitive market, through the price mechanism, lines up resources in such a way as to satisfy consumer needs to the greatest possible extent in magnitude, but in the process has to attract the greatest number of customers, by pursuing the lowest common factor.

Competition is said, by its advocates, to place each productive resource in the precise position where it can make the greatest possible addition to the total social dividend. Competition is an excellent, tough and no-nonsense means of getting things done, of matching consumer needs to producer resources.

The actual activities of those engaged in business are the means by which we deliver the fruits of competition. Knight writes that business activity has taken on the nature of a game, in which the desire for wealth reveals itself as a desire to capture an opponent's piece or card.

In such a competitive game it is absurd to talk of equality as an ideal – success is in terms of the right to consume more, to control more, to enjoy greater power and status. In the struggle towards inequality luck plays a crucial part. Luck works cumulatively, so that those that do well in the early rounds gain progressively and differentially as the game proceeds, while those who do badly may not even remain in the game. To do well it is imperative to get a good start, either by luck or through initial endowments.

The business game, in Knight's essay, dominates life. Millions are forced to live by it and be judged by its rules. 'To play the game' means to accept; the 'good sport' has replaced the 'good man'. The greatest virtue is to win, by whatever means; the lesser is to exit quietly having lost; to protest is at best bad form, at worst blasphemy. To break the rules does not really matter so long as you win and are not publicly detected. Once the rules are successfully broken, there is no going back; the game takes a new and dirtier form.

We can develop further the debate concerning ethics and efficiency by briefly considering the alternatives to competition – coercion and co-operation. Coercion involves the imposition of the will of one party on another; co-operation involves the voluntary blending of many wills into a single corporate will; competition involves each individual freely following their own will, without regard to the general consequences.

Each of these three approaches has its advocates, its critics and its own rationale. We offer three broad tests.

(i) Is the approach in accord with our natural, or genetically given, inclinations, drives and abilities? Is it in tune with the deeper structures underlying human behaviour and hence with the societies erected thereon? If it is not in tune, then in the end it will not work, or at least, will only do so as a result of a continuing expenditure of mental and other effort.

(ii) Is it efficient in getting things done? Is it materially beneficial to society as a whole and to the individuals who make up that society?

(iii) Is it ethically neutral – or is it to be judged on criteria other than those of naturalism and utilitarianism?

All three approaches can under certain conditions pass the first two tests – it is in the ethical domain that distinctions may be made between them.

Ethics, to return to Frank Knight, is concerned with choices between different kinds of life. Competition may provide an added pleasure to an activity, especially to the winner, or during the progress of the game, to those who still stand some chance of winning. Compulsory games, however, are not fun for all.

Human happiness might, Knight suggests, depend more on spiritual resourcefulness and affection for one's fellow creatures. Co-operation, if only it would work, might teach people to like, rather than beat one another.

The strong ethical case for competition is that it encourages an alert and striving society, provides space for liberty and prevents the exploitation of consumers by manufacturers.

We observe, day in day out, in an allegedly competitive society a universal drift towards monopoly, checked only by the problems of monopoly organisation. The drift stems in part from the existence of economies of scale, in part from individuals realising that they can often gain more, materially and mentally, by co-operating than by competing and in part from individual players in the business game removing, without replacement, other players' pieces from the board.

In searching for the roots of competition and in exploring its impact on economic society, this book ranges widely over the fundamental ideas of the past – Adam Smith, Darwin, Marx and Freud and over mainly post-war economic thinking on competition.

It reviews the 'rules of the game' with reference to the UK, the EEC, Japan and the USA. Then, by way of case histories, it looks at ways in which real-world firms react to competitive pressures.

The book concludes with an examination of how firms can modify their behaviour to take advantage of changes in the competitive environment and how governments can intervene in the workings of competition in the public interest.

1 The Dilemmas of Competition

WHAT DO WE MEAN BY 'COMPETITION'?

The concept of competition carries within it the notion of rivalry for the possession of a not easily divisible object or the achievement of an exclusive outcome. So we have a picture of more than one person, or group of persons, wanting, at the same time, something that cannot readily be shared. Each contestant tries to gain the desired object, while denying it to the rivals.

At this early stage in our discussion of competition we assume away a number of important real-world features which, deriving from technological considerations, are likely to modify substantially the competitive process. These excluded ideas would include problems of access to knowledge and the existence of economies of scale and of minimum efficient sizes for plants. These factors would tend to reinforce rather than weaken any tendencies towards the concentration of capital and centralisation of ultimate control.

HOW TO READ THIS CHAPTER

In this chapter we set out to make you think afresh about competition. You may believe that competition is the essential ingredient, the vital yeast, which makes for economic growth and efficiency. Or you may feel that competition is an integral part of our alienation from our surroundings, from our work and from our fellow human beings, our co-existents.

Whatever your perspective, read this chapter in an active way – using it to challenge your own ideas. Use it to get you thinking about competition – its place in business, in the provision of goods and services, in our own lives and in those of our fellow citizens.

INTRODUCTION

The idea of 'competition' has had, for two centuries or more, a powerful influence on the way we think about our society, the way we organise things and on the ways in which we conduct our own economic and personal lives. There is, however, little agreement on what competition really entails – let alone whether it is a good or bad thing. To help organise our thinking on competition we identify five key issues, which we present in the form of five paradoxes of competition and invite the reader to explore the underlying ideas, learning to spot common oversimplifications and contradictions.

We then pay a visit to the mythical land of Competania, where a freedom to compete is everyone's birthright, yet where slowly over the decades this right is reduced by the build up of legal case law until the re-establishment of competition requires positive political action. The purpose of this section is to surface links between rights, the law and political actions. We then extend this analysis to encompass neighbouring Rivalaria.

In the final section of this opening chapter we present the metaphor of a great game to help organise our thinking and resolve some of the apparent contradictions of competition. Businesses and individuals are said to be playing in a game, with a complex set of rules, in which they can adopt defensive or offensive strategies, according to the relative costs, risks and rewards.

The chapter concludes with a proposal for a descriptive model linking our basic drives to our economic behaviour and thence to the conduct of business and government.

FIVE PARADOXES OF COMPETITION

1. Competition is the pursuit of happiness; through competition individual selfishness leads to universal happiness.

A selfish shopkeeper in order to attract trade gives a better service than the next shop. If all shopkeepers are equally selfish, then the shopper will get the best of all possible deals.

2. Competition simultaneously creates wealth and poverty – competition has made possible the enormous material progress of the past 200 years, by unlocking the energies of society, yet it has spelt misery for the tens of millions of workers involved in the creation of that wealth.

Historically, Britain, and northern Europe, saw a basically low-density rural population transformed into a high-density urban one, in order to provide the concentrated workforce required for the new industrial factories. This process, which took place under conditions of free competition, created a new working class. This new class suffered appalling depredations, while the overall material wealth of the country doubled and redoubled.

3. Competition means that you as a person can *have* more but *be* less. What *does* it profit a man if he gaineth the whole world yet suffer the loss of his soul?

In any competition, winners are rewarded with prizes. In Western society everyday status attaches to the external trappings of wealth – the house, the car, etc. We are all too often judged on what we own, rather than on what we do.

4. Businesses compete in order to reduce competition; modern economic society is built through a process of competition rather than within a framework of competition.

In a new market aggressive firms go for market share. Firms are soon sorted into winners who grow larger, and losers who, in time, will exit from the game. After a time there will be so few players left that there will be little trace of the original competition.

5. In the sphere of politics, while both the right and the left have a rhetoric for competition against monopoly profits, neither tries very hard to translate words into actions.

Politicians, to the right of centre, base their philosophy on the virtues of competition, yet are funded by firms and individuals enjoying super-normal profits. Similarly politicians of both left and right, whatever they say about competition, need the efficiency that comes with scale. On the left politicians may have a preference for collective endeavour, yet dislike collusion between big businesses.

COMPETITION AND PURSUIT OF HAPPINESS

The promise of unlimited progress has sustained the hopes of generations since the beginning of the new industrial age. Industrialisation has progressively involved the substitution of mechanical and electrical energy for animal and human energy and more recently for human computational powers. In this process of industrialisation, competition has dissolved the feudal chains and, at least for the upper, and possibly the middle, classes it has augured in an age of apparent personal freedom. Production plus freedom might be said to be the twentieth-century formula for unrestricted happiness.

Modern industrial society is distinguished by being more explicitly competitive than its feudal and mercantalist forerunners. Business, as a specialised function, is more clearly marked off, or differentiated, from other economic, social and political activities.

The rights of individuals as against those of the community, are more sharply defined in modern Western states as opposed to the more traditional pre-industrial societies. Individuals make decisions for themselves, seeing themselves largely independent of custom. In these choices individuals try to maximise their own happiness subject only to the limits of time, money and opportunity.

Any standard intermediate economics textbook will demonstrate that this budget-constrained pleasure maximisation by individuals, with the associated profit maximisation by firms, leads not only to consumers getting the goods and services they want at lowest possible prices, but also to the most efficient distribution of resources throughout the economy. It can also be shown that the volume and the growth of goods and services produced in such an economy will always be at a maximum. The essential precondition for this happy state of affairs is, however, that the world is one of full and untramelled competition.

In a famous quotation Adam Smith (*Wealth of Nations*, 1776, pp. 26–7, 1.ii.2) makes the point that we are driven by self-love to serve others: 'It is not from the benevolence of the butcher, the brewer, or the baker that we expect our dinner, but from their regard to their own interest.' The ideas of Adam Smith, and others, are explored in the next chapter which looks at some of the seminal ideas concerning competition.

The essence of our first paradox of competition is that it is selfish behaviour, not altruism, which leads to universal happiness.

WHO PAYS THE COSTS OF COMPETITION?

Alfred Marshall, the late Victorian and Edwardian economist, whose work dominated economic thinking for a generation or more, in his *Principles of Economics* (Marshall, 1920, pp. 4–8) mused on the negative connotations evoked by the word competition, which had gathered about it an evil savour, and had come to imply a certain selfishness and indifference to the well-being of others.

However, he saw that competition released energy and encouraged resourcefulness. It led to a cheapening of commodities and acted as a curb on excessive profits. Marshall suggested the term 'competition' was badly suited to describe the characteristics of modern industrial life. He proposed replacing it with 'economic freedom'; an idea still worth pursuing in order to add a new dimension to the politics of competition policy.

However, he also saw the sudden increase in economic freedom associated with the early days of the Industrial Revolution as the source of much evil (Marshall, 1920, p. 621).

> Now first are we getting to understand the extent to which the capitalist employer, untrained to his new duties, was tempted to subordinate the wellbeing of his workpeople to his own desire for gain; now first are we learning the importance of insisting that the rich have duties as well as rights in their individual and in their collective capacity; now first is the economic problem of the new age showing itself to us as it really is . . . But however wise and virtuous our grandfathers had been, they could not have seen things as we do; for they were hurried along by urgent necessities and terrible disasters. We must judge ourselves by a severer standard.

These concerns led Marshall to conclude (1920, p. 622) that 'gradually we may attain to an order of social life, in which the common good overrules individual caprice . . . unselfishness then will be the off-spring of deliberate will; and freedom: a happy contrast to the old order of life in which individual slavery to custom caused collective slavery and stagnation, broken only by the caprice of despotism or the caprice of revolution.'

So in Marshall we find that while competition is a liberating force, which has enabled us, to our material benefit, to break out of the prison of tradition, it needs to be complemented by a conscious and deliberate concern for the common good, presumably obtained through a political rather than an economic process.

Writing a generation earlier Karl Marx and Frederick Engels in the *Communist Manifesto* (1844) point to the importance of competition to the new bourgeoisie who in 'scarce one hundred years has created more massive and more colossal productive forces than have all preceding generations together'.

Yet, according to Marx and Engels, the modern labourer instead of rising with the progress of industry sinks deeper and deeper through competition into isolation and poverty (Marx and Engels, 1844, p. 48). Their solution was for the individualistic competitive capital owning bourgeoisie to be replaced by the proletariat, who would apparently centralise production in the hands of the state.

The essence of the second paradox is that, historically, competition has led to its benefits accruing to one group, while its costs are borne by another. For some the lesson is that competition should be controlled or even superseded; for others that there should be compensation through redistribution for any ill effects resulting from competition; and yet for others that the forces of competition have hitherto been insufficiently strong to maximise total well-being.

COMPETITION AND INDIVIDUAL HAPPINESS

Underlying the march to happiness have been two psychological and economic premises:

(i) The aim of life is the realisation of maximum pleasure, the satisfaction of all desires and subjective needs.

(ii) The underlying driving force is competitive acquisition, which if allowed full and unrestricted play leads to harmony and peace and the successful achievement of universal happiness.

The search for unlimited pleasure is nothing new – it was indulged in by the elite of ancient Rome, with their supposed taste for orgies, by the great Renaissance princes of Italy, by the aristocracy of eighteenth-century France and England. What is new is that this search has now become the universal and underlying justification for Western industrial society.

In practice, in the West, an intermediate goal, that of amassing great wealth, has displaced the direct search for present happiness. The search for money and profit is assumed to be the object of the individual members of society and of their commercial institutions.

This search for money as the intermediary of happiness itself throws up a minor paradox. Work is seen by many as something 'bad', which must be undertaken in order to purchase the 'goods' of leisure and pleasure. The pleasure, status and security that people undeniably derive from their work is lost from sight and at best is converted into psychic income, which has the intrinsic disadvantage that it, unlike real money, cannot be used for the purchase of pleasure. Real money is, however, acquired through competitive activity at work.

Modern society still has traces of an ethical social code that governed actions in the world before economic competition. People still have ideas of a fair or 'just' price or wage in some echo of Thomas Aquinas. Sometimes traders talk of sharing custom between them and leaving something for the next person. Publicly owned and co-operative enterprises may put social goals of fairness and public service before ones of profit. Or we may observe work seen as a vocation, a source of purpose and personal dignity rather than simply money income. Or displays of altruism between fellow trade union members. And so on.

However, this older more organic society has been substantially replaced by an autonomous economic machine, which runs according to its own natural 'laws' and stands outside and superior to the society which created it.

The economic machine not only appears to work, for most of the time, but, being based on acquisitiveness and aggression can apparently be justified in terms of being in accord with nature. Charles Darwin, or more properly Herbert Spencer, suggested that struggle for survival is man's natural condition and that through struggle we obtain mastery over nature and the elimination of the weak and the unfit.

If the economic machine and its laws are rooted back in some primeval instinct, then it is hardly surprising that from time to time it reveals a double nature, showing a face like that of Kali the Indian goddess of destruction. Thus believers continue to worship and to sacrifice to the economic machine in good times and bad.

After Darwin observers could claim that competition was not only found widely in nature, but was also an innate human drive, the satisfaction of which was itself right and necessary for human happiness. It may, however, be that the innate competitive or aggression drive is more problematical than many nineteenth-century writers believed; in fact we regularly observe that individuals, if free to choose, often prefer a sheltered and slightly inefficient existence to one of exposure to the unforgiving icy winds of competition.

Some observers, however, have a very different reading of the rise of competition. Erich Fromm in *To Have or to Be*? (Fromm, 1979) sees the competitive search for material prosperity as little short of catastrophic in terms of both individual well-being and the socio-economic development of the world. We are in his terms in a 'having-mode', built on possessions and power and driven by greed, envy and acquisitiveness. He offers an alternative 'being-mode', concerned with active living and shared experiences. Fromm fears that the having-mode has dangerously overlain our most basic instinct for survival.

Perhaps, at risk of an overcrude simplification of a very subtle argument, we can put at the centre of his thought the idea that 'I am what I have' has substantially replaced 'I am what I experience', and experience itself has been reduced for many to a process of acquisition of things.

In contemporary society the having-mode of existence is assumed to be rooted in human nature and hence virtually unchangeable. People are assumed to be basically lazy and will do nothing unless driven by either the incentive of material gain – or hunger or the fear of punishment. In this perspective people are assumed to be selfish and greedy, although the assumption of natural laziness is at odds with the assumption of natural competition.

Can we make some kind of sense of these conflicting propositions? Human beings stand, in relation to the rest of the animal kingdom, at the point of minimum reliance on instinct and maximum development of intellect: self-awareness, logic and imagination. In this exposed state, with our absence of built-in guidelines, we need some internalised framework, or reference map, to give order to chaos, to give certainty to our ideas about the world.

The psychological function of this internal map is to provide a semi-automatic guidance system. The map may well change from historical age to historical age; it may be in parts defective, but it is never wholly wrong. It gives life a reason and a reasonableness. Our current map indicates that competition between people is natural and necessary. Fromm is suggesting that this need not be so and there may be other and better maps.

The essence of our third paradox is that success in competition enables us to be more important, to have more possessions, but leaves us less space to experience each other and to explore life's potentials. The having-mode results in us using people, regardless of their own well-being, for our own acquisitive ends, thereby reducing ourselves as human beings. In these terms competition is seen to diminish even its winners.

WHAT DO BUSINESSES DO ABOUT COMPETITION?

People in business usually subscribe, both intellectually and financially, to an ideology of competition. They, however, spend their working days reducing the actual level of competition to be found in the economy. Firms, quite reasonably, work hard to encourage in their customers loyalty for their goods and services. In this way firms are shielded from the full strength of the competition.

In this competitive process, firms try to build into their goods and services qualities which will reduce people's sensitivity to their own and other peoples' price changes. This process of product differentiation leads to a greater emphasis being placed by firms on satisfying customers' less economic needs.

If successful, the firm erects a small protective wall around its own market, behind which it either extracts some degree of monopoly profit or relaxes into a less than full efficiency posture. In the end, rivals will be drawn into the market and, often at considerable expense, will batter down the barriers to entry. The effect of such barriers to entry is to slow down the workings of the market, causing a misdirection of efforts and resources for possibly very long periods indeed.

Traditional economic theory stresses price as the main thrust of competition. In practice we observe that most businesses put greater emphasis on product performance, presentation and on selling effort. Price cuts are held to be ruinously expensive and counter-productive, in that they can be matched almost immediately by rival firms selling identical products, in the process wiping out the profits to be gained in that part of the marketplace.

A good example of competition through product innovation can be found in the US automobile industry, where concentration of biannual style changes made it impossible for small firms to match the pace of change of the big sellers. (Menge, 1962, pp. 632–47).

The behaviour of managers in favouring product over price changes is facilitated by the ever growing technological base of society and by consumers' greater spending power, which enables them to experiment and discover new tastes. For a full discussion of the many forms of non-price competition see A. Koutsoyiannis (1982).

Product differentiation, normally supported by advertising, is only one of the tactics available to the modern manager. There are a number of valuable legally enforceable protective devices, such as patents and copyright, licences and exclusive contracts. In addition firms may prefer to resort to directly non-competitive actions, such as taking over a rival or entering into a restrictive cartel.

Somewhere along the spectrum of protective actions, which stretches all the way from painting green lines round a product to give it some kind of identity to employing tactics associated more with the Mafia than with business, society is likely to intervene and declare such actions anti-competitive and therefore unlawful.

From the above we might expect the practising manager to develop an explicit strategy for dealing with (i.e. reducing) the competition. It is likely to be under four major headings:

Product development and differentiation.
Allocation of funds and other resources to maintain and enhance
   specific competences.
Development of a strong presence in the distribution systems.

Possible reactions to actual and potential actions by current and future competitors.

The manager, by his or her use of resources for investment in product, plant and people, for promotional activities and for the attainment of a more secure distribution system, is, as a person, competing strongly and energetically. However, every success makes it harder for someone else to enter, or remain, in the market. In this way the drive to compete results in a diminution of the level of competition.

The essence of the business paradox of competition is that rivalry in business has as its aim the elimination, or curtailment, of competition. This diminution of competition occurs naturally and automatically, without resort to physical growth through mergers and take-overs.

POLITICAL RHETORIC

There has similarly been no shortage of ambiguities in the conduct of the Conservative government, elected in 1979 and led by Mrs Thatcher. One, probably unplanned, effect of the privatisation programme may have been for the government to create a series of privately-owned monopolies, which are effectively outside the competitive process – just the sort of thing Adam Smith railed against in *Wealth of Nations*.

If the right is in a muddle over competition so too is the British left, which, although it may have a rhetoric concerned with lambasting the top 'monopolies', has, with its location in production, a practice of enshrining unions as 'countervailing' power and of replacing privately-owned monopolies with state-owned ones. This convergence of labour and capital in eschewing competition may be seen as evidence of a conspiracy against the sovereign consumer or of a wise consensus as to the relatively small role which can sensibly be left to competition in a modern industrial society.

We look for roots of political views on competition. Where are they to be found? In our history? In our own personal and social make-up? Or should the explanation be sought at the more fundamental Darwinian level of the living organism? Or even further back at the level of the gene as some readings of the socio-biology literature might suggest?

Different political positions have implicit or often explicit ideas concerning the origin of competition.

Then there is the problem of trying to isolate what is meant politically by competition. What, for example, is its antithesis – is it monopoly or co-operation? And beyond the questions of what is competition, there are the questions of what uses are in practice made of the concept by entrepreneurs, by politicians and by opinion formers.

COMPETANIA

In our exploration of the five paradoxes of competition, we posed a number of riddles concerning the desirability and the effectiveness of competition. Let us, for the moment, put these on one side and draw out Marshall's notion of economic freedom (see above).

Let us visit the Republic of Competania, where men are born free to trade – and where they take an eighteenth-century approach to natural rights. Let us imagine a country in which everyone is born with full economic freedom, a right to compete. Each individual has a legally enforceable right to enter into any area of economic or other endeavour and there to practise without let or hindrance, without the say so of any existing occupants.

This right to compete has in Competania a similar status to that often ascribed in other countries to freedom of speech. Like the much vaunted freedom of speech, we find in our imaginary land that there would be many obstacles in the way of its exercise.

But all is not lost. This, remember, is a legally enforceable right and let us assume that we have a system of courts and judges, which, upon petition by the wronged party, can order others to respect the right of competition and presumably to pay compensation for its infringement.

The presumption in law would be that any interference with the right to compete, by the state, or by other individuals, would have to be justified before a court by the existence of a pressing social reason. It might, for example, be argued that public safety demanded that surgeons should be licensed in some way before they were allowed to practise, or that the state should be given a monopoly in defence or in the administration of justice. In such a society we would expect economic freedom to be the widely accepted norm.

One difficulty with this approach is that, if Competania is anything like Britain, judges prefer to rule on the particular facts of the case before them and to rely on an historically accumulated body of rulings to give guidance as to the permitted limits to a freedom; rather than be bound by grand general principles.

This reliance on judicial sense and precedence tends over time to obscure any simplistic and transparent notions – such as a creator given individual freedom to compete – and to provide a bank of legally sanctioned anti-competitive practices. Over time access to the courts becomes increasingly difficult and unrewarding until, for the individual, the right to compete becomes as illusory as any other unenforceable right.

So in this imaginary land, where men (and presumably women) are born free to compete, where we rely on a civil legal process to enforce that freedom, we are likely to find that competition is eroded over time as precedents are built up and pressing social needs discovered. Our visit to Competania suggests that the maintenance of competition has to be 'constantly looked to, constantly laboured for' (Abraham Lincoln, Springfield Speech, 1857) and requires the existence of an active agency to prosecute abuses and by legal and political means to reverse the growth of anti-competitive case law.

Before we leave our imaginary world we need to ask why might we posit a given inalienable right to compete and why should we urge agencies to maintain that freedom. Is freedom to compete one of those useful truths which are self-evident, such as '. . . that all men are created equal, that they are endowed by their Creator with certain inalienable Rights, that among these are Life, Liberty and the pursuit of Happiness' (Thomas Jefferson, Declaration of Independence, 2 August 1776) ?

An inalienable right to compete might be seen, not as divinely given, but as something we are born with – an innate capacity or drive to compete, the fulfilment of which is an integral part of the pursuit of happiness. So we move from an intellectually conceived right, to the idea of the drive to compete as much part of human nature as the capacity of speech – an idea trailed in Adam Smith's *Wealth of Nations* (1776).

For Smith an important aspect of human nature, which in his view we should be free to indulge, is our 'propensity to truck and barter'. This propensity he suggests is the 'necessary consequence of the faculties of reason and speech' (Smith, 1776, 1976, II.1 p. 25).

This idea takes us tantalisingly to the work of Noam Chomsky, who argues that we are all born with a capacity for language, which includes a built-in generative grammar. The deep structures of language are thus innate, genetically transmitted and located in the physical organisation of the human brain (Chomsky, 1965).

If we accept that we are born with language grammars built into our unconscious mind and we use our active intelligent conscious mind to create an apparently limitless series of sentences, then it is a short step to positing that we are born with other behaviour grammars, which give shape, form and intelligibility to our actions. One of the possible forms of behaviour, which our behaviour grammar is capable of generating, might be competitive trading as opposed to co-operative sharing. In this world, Competania has chosen to elevate one possible form of behaviour into a legal right.

THE RIGHT TO FREE TRADE

But just as we imagined a single country with a universal right to trade and compete, we can by act of imagination extend our view to a world level. Here each country would have an absolute right to enter any market and there to trade on equal terms with those already in occupation. *Laissez-faire* and its partner Free Trade are formal theories of international competition, which too have their defenders and their critics.

While within a single country it is relatively easy to construct a legal system to defend and enforce the right to compete – it is much more difficult to construct such a system at a supranational level, although there does exist a complex set of treaties to promote Free Trade and to vanquish its enemy Protectionism.

Unsurprisingly we discover that theories of *laissez-faire*, with their internationalist rather than nationalist stance, were pioneered in Great Britain in the eighteenth and nineteenth centuries during the years of the creation, growth and consolidation of the world-spanning British Empire. However, having a theory of a right to free trade was one thing, enforcing it was quite another.

One of the more dramatic incidents of the assertion of free trading rights is to be found in the British-Chinese 'Opium War' in the early 1840s, when the monopolistic East India Company persuaded the British government to use the British Royal Navy to ensure a continuing free trade in opium into China, which the emperor had sought to ban. While the war did not really revive the banned opium trade, it did give Britain Hong Kong and forced the Chinese into more general trading relations with the Western world by way of the famous six treaty ports of 1842.

The pursuit of free trade is rather less dramatic today. The 'General Agreement on Tariffs and Trade' (GATT) exists to try to reach an internationally agreed commercial policy, which, amongst many complex exceptions, limits protection and encourages free trade. GATT embodies a set of rules restricting the use of tariffs and other barriers to trade. It also provides a forum where nations can progressively negotiate away barriers to trade to the general advantage.

The theory underlying the expected benefits of trade, the Principle of Comparative Advantage, we owe to David Ricardo, writing in 1821. The ideas encompassed in the Principle have in fact a much wider application than just in a consideration of foreign trade and can usefully be taken to an organisational and even personal level, to show that specialisation and exchange (trade) increase total well-being.

Let us now return to Competania and to its neighbour Rivalaria. Just as there is a right to compete within Competania, so there is full and free competition between the two countries. The first thing we note is that over time there will be a tendency towards profit rates being equalised in all sectors in both countries. This is simply because the owners of capital will over time move their wealth from low to high profit areas, discouraging the one and encouraging the other.

If one of the products of Rivalaria is, for whatever reason, cheaper to purchase than its equivalent in Competania, we would expect the citizens of Competania, other things being equal, to switch from home produce to imports. In the process, capital and labour would be freed, which would move to Rivalaria or into Competania's most successful product.

Ricardo writes (1951, p. 132):

It is quite as important to the happiness of mankind, that our enjoyments should be increased by the better distribution of labour, by each country producing those commodities for which by its situation, its climate, and its other natural or artificial advantages, it is adapted, and by their exchanging them for the commodities of other countries, as they should be augmented by a rise in profits.

Under a system of perfectly free commerce, each country naturally devotes its capital and labour to such employments as are most beneficial to each. This pursuit of individual advantage is admirably connected with the universal good of the whole. By stimulating industry, rewarding ingenuity, and by using most efficaciously the peculiar powers bestowed by nature, it distributes labour most effectively and economically: while, by increasing the general mass of productions, it diffuses general benefit, and binds together by one common tie of interest and intercourse the universal society of nations throughout the civilized world.

It is this principle which determines that wine shall be made in France and Portugal, that corn shall be grown in America and Poland, and that hardware and other goods shall be manufactured in England.

Ricardo proceeds by way of numerical example to show that each country should do what it is relatively best at. We can intuitively reach the point by considering an aeroplane disaster movie – the pilot has collapsed; the air hostess has a comparative advantage over the passengers when it comes to flying the aircraft. She should fly the plane and leave the cabin duties to others, even though she may also be a better cabin steward than any of them, but is, relatively speaking, because of her general aviation experience, an even better tyro pilot.

Or, in terms of produce, we could imagine that Rivalaria was better than Competania at growing both dates and grapes, but could produce the date crop more easily than the grape. It makes sense for Rivalaria to specialise in date production both for domestic use and for export while Competania concentrates on growing grapes for both markets.

The basis of trade is that a country should export those goods which it can produce relatively, to its other goods, more cheaply, and import only those goods which it produces relatively more dearly.

Reactions to this theory, which may be said to have suited the then dominant nation, Great Britain, can be typified by the work of Friedrich List (1789–1846). List, who was driven out of Germany for his liberal ideas, lived in America from 1825 to 1830, where he was engaged in the extraction and transportation of coal. He left a legacy of protectionism to be developed by other American economists and politicians, whose voices can be heard to this day.

Returning to his native Germany, List devoted himself to the cause of German unification, advocating the removal of internal tariffs and the extension of the railway system. Unappreciated in his own lifetime List committed suicide while on holiday in the Tyrol. Subsequently his ideas had a powerful influence on the rise of Germany to European eminence.

List denied Adam Smith's proposition that the national good was the sum of all the individual goods. Smith took the view that in seeking his own advantage the individual

> naturally, or rather necessarily, [is] led to prefer that employment [of his capital] which is most advantageous to the society . . . by directing that industry in such a matter as its produce may be of the greatest value, he intends only his own gain, and he is in this, as in so many other cases, led by an invisible hand to promote an end which was no part of his intention (Smith, 1976, pp. 454, 456).

List believed that the nation had a higher existence than did individuals; that the national good came before the good of the individual. For List the nation was a people united by 'language, customs and manners' rather than the result of a geographical historical accident. He believed that each nation should find its own best development path.

Both Germany and America were, at that time, predominantly agricultural nations. List wished to see a better balance between agriculture, manufacture and commerce. His reasons, for Germany, were partly to do with national defence and survival in a potentially hostile world, partly to do with wishing to equal or overtake their arch rival Britain and partly to do with the needs of what List saw as the German national character.

To obtain this balance List was willing to rely on free trade for the agricultural sector, but required protection for the infant production industries. He recognised that this protection would in the short run involve national sacrifices as German citizens would no longer be able to buy the cheapest goods, but in the long run he saw great benefits arising for Germany.

List felt that Germans had been humbled and reduced to the position of hewers of wood and drawers of water for their neighbours the Britons. He believed his nationalistic approach to economics would change all that.

List was aware of the dangers of protectionism and believed that once a nation had achieved the desired balance then all sectors should be exposed to the rigours of free trade in order to guard against national decadence.

The ideas of List can be traced, by devious routes, through to the modern dependency literature which, in various forms, points to the difficulty a Third World country has, while remaining linked through a competitive market to more advanced nations, in building up its own industrial or commercial base. Some authors advocate a partial disengagement, some a concentration on the country's 'natural economy', some, however, are profoundly pessimistic about the future of the more peripheral dependent nations.

A key work on an aspect of this problem is W. A. Lewis's *Principles of Economic Planning* (1951). One of Lewis's most fruitful ideas was to divide an underdeveloped economy into two sectors – a central modern competitive one, and a backward peasant rural one. An increase in productivity will then have quite different effects in the two sectors, due to different degrees of competition for products and labour. There are clear echoes of List in the use of this approach to working out how best to rebalance a dependent economy.

S. Amin in *Unequal Development* (1978) in his Marxist analysis of unequal exchange in effect restates Lewis's two-sector model with a more pessimistic conclusion. What Amin and many other development economists have in common is a concern at the meeting, under a competitive relationship, between advanced and non-advanced systems, in which the more advanced appear to gain at the expense of the less advanced.

A typical counterview to the free trade free-for-all would be that a sensible strategy for a relatively weak country to adopt would be consciously to develop its own internal capacities, possibly in friendly partnerships, or possibly under conditions of autarky, until it was strong enough to go it alone on the world stage.

This view implies a degree of internal political decision-making and direction. There must be a political decision to disengage from competitive relations with the rest of the world. There must be a political process to ensure, during the period of total or partial isolation, the maintenance of a healthy internal market, the gathering of sufficient foreign earnings to fund development and a comprehensive industrial strategy, to produce and deliver the right goods at the right times in the right places and at the right prices; the task normally, left under capitalism, to the marketplace.

In other words protectionism does not just apply to external relations – it has a profound effect on the internal structure of a country, since to some extent the internal free competitive market is displaced by central direction by government, based on a political as opposed to a competitive economic process.

The addition of Rivalaria to Competania on our map of the world led to an initial presumption that there should be full free trade between the two to their harmonious and mutual benefit. Problems would arise if one country refused to trade, even though individuals within it might wish to do so.

This discussion has raised among other things the important question as to whether nations were simply the sum of individuals, or whether we can identify something called the 'national interest' which overrode individual interests. In other words do nations and states have rights which individuals do not, and, if so, from where do they derive? If nation states, rightly or wrongly, exercise such rights, they may also diminish economic freedom elsewhere. But it is not obvious that this action gives other nations the right to impose universal economic freedom by force.

THE METAPHOR OF THE GAME

We saw in the last section, in our visit to Competania and in our discussions of relations with its neighbour Rivalaria, that the assumption of the right to compete, whatever the origin of that right, did not guarantee that the resultant world would be a fully competitive one. Quite apart from any technical considerations, the form and extent of competition will depend critically on the actions of others and on the agreed rules governing economic behaviour. All of which puts us in mind of a useful metaphor for competition – that of sport and games.

In fact mass televised sport provides many of us with a vicarious experience of competition, the thrill of the struggle, the sweetness of victory, in the process compensating us for the deprivation of the dole and the drudgery of the workplace.

Sport provides in the public mind a means of making sense of modern society. We are invited to 'play up and play the game'; we wish to be known as good 'sports'. Competition in business, and in its popular surrogate sport, recognises two kinds of virtue – winning (often by dubious means at the edge of the rules) and losing (then retiring quietly and without fuss).

In sport, as in business, only the best and fittest survive the various rounds – the weak and the less fit are eliminated in the competition till only the world's best grace the field of competition. The stylised competition found on the playing field and the games table may provide us with the basis of a useful meta-theory to set the agenda for this book.

The world explored in this book can be likened to a vast game, with four elements:

1 A set of rules defining all the possible outcomes and administered by a referee.
2 A set of players, or active agents, that is firms, individuals and even nations, who may be said in some sense to have objective functions, which consciously or unconsciously they wish to maximise – that is they desperately wish to win or, if wet, to be 'excused games'.
3 A set of non-players, or spectators, whose own fortunes, depending on the rules of the game, may or may not be affected by the outcomes.
4 A passive player, whom we might describe as 'nature' or the 'state of the world' and a random process, itself governed by the rules, which can administer shocks to the system.

The rules, which substantially determine the course and conduct of the games may be either timeless and system independent (i.e. the law of entropy) or may be social constructions, often specific to a given economic system (i.e. the law of patent). Armed with an understanding of the rules and some knowledge of human behaviour, the business or policy analyst may predict outcomes and advise businesses, individuals and governments on desirable outcomes and suggest how they might best be achieved.

In order better to explore some of the ideas underlying our use of the concept 'competition', let us imagine a visit to 'The – It's More Fun to Compete – Electronic Game of Life'. Imagine, in a crowded amphitheatre, the players, each with a computer keyboard and VDU screen, sit around a darkened arena.

Suspended above the players in a black gondola is a gowned referee, with immediate access to a panel of wise advisors seated high above the crowd in a tiered box.

Around the amphitheatre sit the spectators. Depending on the rules of the game, as called from time to time by the referee, the spectators find themselves winning and losing. Their own fortunes may be affected by the actions of the players, either by way of what economists call externalities, or by a direct transfer of wealth from non-players to players. In some games the referee may allow some of the spectators to leave the terraces and join the game if they see it as being to their advantage.

At a signal from the referee, the players enter their moves and a central computer calculates the outcome. Some of the losers are led away; others remain, weakened but allowed to stay for another round; while yet others are credited with greater resources, giving them better chances of winning out in the next and subsequent rounds.

The game continues until only a small number of players are left, who may then be expected to collude together to ensure that no one fails and to share out the monopoly profits gained at the expense of the non-players.

The extent to which collusion is allowed depends on the actions of the referee and the advisors. From time to time, if collusion is tolerated, one of the players will decide to break ranks in the hope of a big bang win, which will either knock out the other players or reduce them to impotence. If the move either fails or is blocked by the referee, we may expect the players remaining in the cartel to collude to punish the rebel. This punishment may or may not be tolerated by the referee.

The referee has the power to change the rules, either in response to pressures from the players, from the spectators or on the advice of the wise men and women in the panel.

The outcome of any game depends, not just on the rules, but on the skills and intentions of the players, particularly the players' mutual awareness of each other's possible strategies. 'Game Theory' provides a formal framework for the analysis of such interdependent situations.

So, in addition to rules we need players, for what good is a game without players? Our players, if they play in the strip of *homo oeconomicus*, are deemed to be fully rational, maximising a known and specified objective function. Such paragons of rationality may be rarely found in nature, where we often observe a very different class of player, who, perhaps baffled by the complexity of things or maybe just for the fun of it, appears to choose at random, acting on the spur of the moment.

Between these two pole positions of full rationality and impulsive behaviour, we can identify a number of player types:

The 'conservative' player who assumes that the future will be like the past and follows existing custom and practice until proved wrong (in formal language this is described as having 'adaptive expectations').

The 'smart' player who is fully wise to the game and plays the game in the expectation that winning strategies will be pursued and will succeed (in formal language this is 'rational expectations') .

The 'maverick' player who deliberately selects a non-standard strategy in order to scoop the pool. The successful maverick either simply catches the other players napping or follows a winning strategy, which had been previously unobserved. Such mavericks, or entrepreneurs, are the active agents who carry the game forward from one situation to another.

Associated with the rules and diverse actions of the players, we can imagine a 'pay-off' matrix – a table which displays all the penalties and pay-offs attached to the various possible strategies and outcomes. In the real life game, of course, the details of the pay-off matrix are only dimly comprehended and are in any case subject to external random shocks delivered by 'nature' and dependent on the 'state of the world'.

The problem facing any real world player in pursuit of an optimal strategy is that the situation is in essence incapable of rational resolution, since both the rules and the outcomes are known only imperfectly. In any real world game the moves and counter-moves lying ahead soon run into tens of thousands, making any evaluation of alternative strategies literally incomprehensible to the conscious human brain and probably beyond the capacity of all but the very largest computer systems.

Faced with this bewilderment, players might be forgiven for choosing according to some private rule – tossing a coin, saying 'yes' if the coffee arrives with the spoon on the left, or even consulting and astrologer. In practice, when we observe the actions of a large number of players, we are able to detect patterns, which, in general, can be associated with theoretically rational solutions.

In line with Milton Friedman in his *Essay in Positive Economics* (Friedman 1953, pp. 20–21) we may say the players behave 'as if' they understood what they were doing. This is the equivalent to saying that human agents have an unconscious mind, which has the capacity to analyse in a rational way all the most likely outcomes and this unconscious mind attempts to regulate human behaviour independently of the conscious mind.

An alternative to a fully rational unconscious might be an automatic group learning mechanism, which echoes the Darwinian story of evolution through natural selection. Individual agents try out strategies at random – the majority fail, often fatally for the player; some are broadly neutral in their impact, while others offer real benefits in terms of playing in subsequent rounds.

Provided agents learn from experience and repeat successful, rather than unsuccessful, strategies, only those players will survive who pursue rational strategies; in other words the observed world behaves 'as if' the players are fully rational, since, all those who followed the 'non-rational' strategies have been eliminated along the way.

The purpose of introducing the idea of sport, or of a great IT-based game, at this stage has been to provide a metaphor for business competition. We are familiar with the notion of people wanting to win at games and doing everything they can, more or less within the rules, to carry away the prize. We next need to focus our thoughts on two things – why they want to win so much and where the rules come from. (See Chapter 2).

But first to get the most out of our sporting metaphor we need to explore some of the ideas involved in a branch of mathematics known as 'game theory'.

GAME THEORY

In this book we treat game theory as a metaphor, rather than a mathematical exercise. Readers who wish to explore game theory in a more formal sense are directed to the classic formulation by John von Neumann and Oskar Morgenstern, *Theory of Games and Economic Behaviour* (Princeton, NJ, Princeton University Press, 1944) and to the large number of excellent texts that have derived therefrom.

The simplest games are those with known, or at least knowable, unambiguous winning strategies. An example is the game of Nim, where a number of matches are laid out in rows and the players in turn pick up some or all of the matches from a single row, the object being to force the other player to pick up the last but one match. The peculiarity of the game is that whoever moves first must win provided they know the secret of the winning strategy. The game is barely a game and is extremely boring except when used by the unscrupulous to impress the unenlightened.

In technical game theory language Nim is:

finite – meaning it has a definite ending

two person – meaning only two players

zero sum – meaning that what one player wins the other loses, the wins and the losses summing to zero

with perfect information with an optimal strategy – meaning there is a known strategy which, if followed, must lead on to victory for the player making the first move regardless of the actions of the opponent.

Such a game is far too simple to capture real world economic events, where optimal strategies cannot be known with any degree of certainty, where other players' actions can affect the result and the outcomes themselves are subject to unpredictable external events. Games, which are both more lifelike and more fun, have a range of possible winning strategies, each, depending on the actions of other players, with differing potential pay-offs.

Two famous games, which can be used to highlight the mutual interdependence of the players, are the 'Tragedy of the Commons' (Hardin, 1968, pp. 1243–8) and the widely described 'Prisoners' Dilemma'.

In the 'Tragedy of the Commons' we have a finite number of players who have the right to graze cattle on some common land. The game starts with all players having an equal number of cows – their aim is to maximise the weight of their beasts for sale at the end of the game, their wealth being proportional to the weight of their beasts.

All goes well until one player decides to increase the size of his or her herd by one. The result of this is that the common is now marginally overgrazed and so all cows lose weight. The rogue player is better off, while all the rest are worse off.

It clearly pays the other players to increase their herd sizes in order to make up the lost weight. But each increase in total herd sizes increases the level of overgrazing and reduces the weight of the individual cows, thus at the end of the game all players are worse off than at the start. The competitive behaviour of the graziers has reduced their total welfare – they either needed to trust one another to restrict their herd sizes in the interest of the common good, or to appoint an external 'referee' to police herd sizes. Presumably in repeated games they would learn to do one or the other.

By way of numerical example let us assume there are six farmers, each owning one cow, weighing 1000 lb. The common, or pasture, can sustain six cows without overgrazing. For each additional cow introduced the weight of all cows drops by 100 lb. It is rational for any farmer to add a second beast so that his or her total wealth in cows becomes 2×900 lb = 1800 lb. This action will be copied by the others and will continue until all farmers own two cows, each weighing only 400 lb, giving a total wealth of 800 lb each. Thus all the farmers are now worse off than if they had agreed to maintain the *status quo*.

Examples of persistent over-grazing or over-fishing are common enough and have involved the EEC and other international institutions in tortuous negotiations to limit and ration catches. Here it is the benefice, or nigardliness, of nature which sets the limits to the total catch.

In the famous 'Prisoners' Dilemma' (a game invented by Merrill Flood and Melvin Dresher in the 1950s and subsequently formalised by A. W. Tucker) we have a good example of the interdependence of decision-making in ignorance.

Imagine two alleged criminals have been arrested and are being held in separate interview rooms. The police in turn make each prisoner an offer: confess and inform on your colleague and you will be rewarded by the judge for your public spirited action; continue in your refusal and the judge will be most severe in sentencing you, since you will surely be found guilty.

The problem facing the prisoner is that he or she knows that without a confession the police have little or no chance of obtaining a conviction. The dilemma facing each prisoner is whether to confess or not. If both continue to deny their involvement in the crime, they will both get off scot-free, if both confess then both will be sentenced to say three years, while if one confesses and the other does not, one will be financially rewarded and the other given, perhaps, a stretch of seven years.

The apparent best strategy is the selfish one of confessing in the hope that the other continues to deny the crime; if this goes wrong and both confess then both prisoners face relatively short terms of imprisonment.

Interestingly in repeated games, which are unlikely to be permitted by the police, the two prisoners would learn to trust one another and both deny the crime.

This and other games have been investigated by Andrew Colman in *Game Theory and Experimental Games* (1982), where using the methods of experimental psychology he compares behaviour predicted by game theory with that observed in the laboratory. This stimulating book points to an important junction between psychological and economic behaviour.

Robert Axelrod in *The Evolution of Co-operation* (1981, pp. 27–54) describes a computer tournament staged in the United States where contestants were invited to devise a computer program to play out repeated games of the Prisoners' Dilemma.

The winning program, entitled 'Tit for Tat', was one in which the programmed player was essentially friendly and co-operative, simply doing back was what done to it. Tit for Tat, an essentially trusting and co-operative program, outperformed its more competitive rivals. A second tournament was held with the challenge of beating Tit for Tat. The result was that, while once again, Tit for Tat won the competition, overall the co-operative programs outperformed the more competitive ones.

This would suggest that at quite blind and unthinking levels, such as the gene material, the genes following co-operative strategies will outperform, in terms of survival, those pursuing competitive strategies. We would thus expect that human agents will have capacities both for co-operation and competition, and that in many areas of life co-operation is more likely to lead to system survival than competition.

Observation suggests that a great deal of human conduct, even in the economic sphere, owes more to co-operative than competitive behaviour. We should note that the decision to co-operate can itself be a selfish one – 'in order to get my own way I have little choice but to throw in my lot with the others'.

An interesting discovery is that more than one strategy can co-exist in a given population. This is described by John Maynard Smith for the field of biology in his *Evolution and the Theory of Games* (1982). The interesting point, for us, is, not whether it is legitimate to jump from biologically to socially driven situations, but that theory predicts the survival of groups adopting different strategies. We can observe in business, markets where quite different types of firms, following quite different strategies, can survive for quite a number of years.

Game theory thus not only provides us with a useful metaphor, encompassing both the players and the rules by which they play, but also with a prediction, both in terms of mathematical logic and of human behaviour, that in any society we will find both competitive and co-operative strategies being successfully pursued – either separately, or possibly even co-existing.

WHAT LESSONS CAN WE DRAW FROM ALL THIS?

1. Individuals, whether in their private capacities or as parts of organisations, are assumed, in line with conventional economic thinking, to wish to maximise their utility, by seeking pleasure and avoiding pain.

We take as given, an interior drive, or mental energy, which finds its outlets via some innate unconsciously held 'grammar', which is capable of generating an enormous range of structured behaviour outcomes. The individual will select outcomes to record with an internalised 'map', which has been derived, or learnt, from the surrounding socio-economic environment.

2. Included among the possible and acceptable outcomes, agents can adopt a defensive or an offensive strategy in their dealings in the surrounding environment. In practice, in society, we observe, that these two types of strategy can co-exist together.

3. A defensive strategy can be characterised as one where the agent avoids risk and protects a secure and possibly privileged position. Such a strategy is essentially cautious and fearful of change. This will often involve co-operation and collusion with others.

4. In an offensive strategy the agent is cast in a more heroic mould, willing to leave the safety of the known and, undeterred by risks and dangers, sets out to conquer. The offensive players are strong, confident and self-assertive.

5. The choice of strategy by individual agents will depend on their own character structure (which we have assumed to be a combination of underlying instinctual drives, innate behaviour generative 'grammars' and an internalised 'map' of what is right) and on the surrounding socio-economic structure (that is the 'rules of the game' and importantly the behaviour of the other players); the two structures being interdependent. That is, the character of individuals is partly personal (inheritance and experience based) and partly social. The society we live in will, in part, be a result of economic and political forces and, in part, through their behaviour, be a reflection of the characters of its members.

6. While we are not concerned with predicting how any single individual will behave, we may wish to make statements about how agents overall will behave – what proportions are likely to adopt which types of strategies. Regardless of the individual character structures,

the *proportions* electing for a defensive (low risk) and for an offensive (high risk) strategy will depend essentially on the costs, risks and rewards involved.

This suggests some form of indifference curve analysis in which agents can choose between offensive and defensive strategies, or mixtures of the two. The slope of the 'budget line' will be set by the relative net rewards of adopting a totally defensive or totally offensive strategy. Changes in the slope of the budget line will result in changes in the optimal (to individuals) mix of offensive and defensive strategies. This will be reflected in the overall structure and level of competition found in society.

7. The cost-reward structure is an aspect of the total socio-economic structure – the 'rules of the game' referred to above. But this structure will not only determine the proportions of players opting for a competitive process, it will also determine the likely outcomes of those processes. In other words if we knew what the rules of the game were, and how they were set, we could predict the level of competitive activity in an economy, know where we could expect it to be channelled and with what outcomes.

8. The rules of the game can, for heuristic purposes, be partitioned into two parts – those which are imminent – that is generated within the physically active system: the so-called economic laws, the limits set by the actions of the other players – and those which are transcendent – that is set externally by politicians, lawyers, priests, writers and other ideologues. The interaction of these two types of rules, which in varying degrees are mutable, determines the kind of economic society we live and trade in.

The purpose of the rest of this book is to extend the reader's understanding of these complex relationships in order to enrich personal, social and economic decision making.

2 Classical Views of Competition

In this second chapter we delve into some of the economic, political and social ideas which are firmly embedded in Western consciousness in an attempt to isolate some of the issues underlying the answers to four key questions concerning competition:

1 Is competition or regulation the right and proper basis for the organisation of civil society?
2 Is competition or co-operation the more 'natural' way for people to behave?
3 Do we realistically have any choice whether or not to compete and would such forced competition be likely to be beneficial?
4 Is competitive behaviour compatible with the widely observed social or group behaviour?

In our search for answers we explore four sources of ideas about competition, all of which have powerfully shaped the ways in which we view the topic and which in turn have affected our own behaviour, both as individuals and as members of corporate organisations.

The first set of ideas is drawn in the main from Adam Smith, whose *Wealth of Nations* (1776) provides for many the *fons et origo* of contemporary competitive capitalism. It also introduces a problem apparently built into his economic system – in which the scope for competitive behaviour is progressively reduced with economic development. To Smith we add some specific thoughts on the importance of economic and other liberty drawn from J. S. Mill.

Our second source is the *Origin of Species* (1859) by Charles Darwin, which in the popular mind is associated with the idea of the survival of the fittest. The Darwinian ideas of competition are followed through to those of the sociobiologists, whose work is captured by the brilliant metaphor – the Selfish Gene – which perhaps suggests that we are born to co-operate as well as compete.

Our third source of seminal ideas is Karl Marx. For Marx, competition provides the source of the blind forces which drive capitalism forward in its erratic progress, in a permanent clash of creative and destructive impulses. On pain of extinction, the capitalists are forced into a titanic competitive struggle.

The fourth source takes as its starting point the psychoanalytic stance of Freud, but is rapidly enlarged in scope to a much wider social psychology perspective, in which competition is seen as something both determined and as something learned. Here we discover that individual behaviour can be seen as a product of both personality and environment; a formulation which, without too much distortion in translation, can be applied to business behaviour. In the course of this section stress is laid on the importance of the group.

ADAM SMITH

Simultaneously there exists in the late twentieth-century society an almost religious belief that more competition will cure the ills of society and an equally firmly held conviction that competition is the very devil itself. Economic society, based on competition, so goes the second creed, is wasteful, deeply materialistic, anti-humanitarian and forms a justification for an unjust *status quo*.

More competition is seen by the one as synonymous with less (harmful) state interference and by the other as an increasingly heartless exploitation of fellow beings, which must be moderated by social intervention.

The roots of this antagonism can in part be traced to an eighteenth-century debate as to how a competitive society might develop sufficient co-operation for civil institutions to perform their necessary functions. The philosophers of that period had seen the feudal society based on mutual obligation give way to one based on trade.

Hobbes in *Leviathan* in his explanation assumed an original state of atomistic competition and selfishness in his 'bellum omnium contra omnes' – the war of all against each. From this continual war, Hobbes deduced the emergence of a strong and awesome interventionist state, which through fear would drive men and women to forsake their natural competitive activities and build a civil society based on stable reciprocal relationships.

This Hobbesean pessimistic view of civil society born out of an authoritarian state, which itself was the desperate product of a world enfeebled by strife, was substantially modified by Locke and subsequently by Adam Smith himself.

Locke saw the natural state of humankind as one not of perpetual struggles, but of harmony. This harmony would, however, be disturbed as society ran up against the constraints set by the 'niggardliness of nature'. The role of the state for Locke was a protective one – to regulate conflicts over resources in order to ensure the continuance of the natural and benevolent order of things.

Adam Smith, who was often more concerned with liberty than with competition as such, carried forward self-interest as the mainspring of his economic system – provided each individual was free to strive to maximise their own benefit, and so behaved, then, through the working of an 'invisible hand', the outcome would be the overall maximisation of social wealth.

Adam Smith wrote of a world fully mercantilist, but not yet quite capitalist. He writes as dawn breaks on day one of the new age. The division of society into owners of labour and owners of capital had yet to be fully realised; work rather than ownership of capital was seen as the source of reward. Competition between workers is invoked by Smith as the mechanism which brings market prices into line with 'natural' prices, which at least in one section of his work are linked to labour inputs.

Price adjustments resulted from the movement of artisans into trades where prices and profits were high, and out of those where they were low. Prices were in the process adjusted to the level at which they would just support those in that trade and no more. (Smith, 1763, Oxford, 1896, p. 176).

True, in the *Wealth of Nations* (Smith, 1776, 1976), Smith at one stage makes the independent labourer, and his freedom to change jobs, the centrepiece of his story. Smith is here concerned that no outside agency – government or labour or employer organisation – should interfere with the free right of someone to sell their labour.

The property which every man has in his own labour, as it is the original foundation of all other property, so it is the most sacred and inviolable. The patrimony of a poor man lies in the strength of dexterity of his hands; and to hinder him from employing that strength and dexterity of his hands, in what manner he thinks fit, without injury to his neighbour, is a plain violation of this most sacred property. It is a manifest encroachment upon the just liberty both of the workman, and of those who might be disposed to employ him (Smith, 1776, 1976, I.x.c.12, p. 138).

Smith, however, saw in Britain in the latter part of the eighteenth century, that competition was increasingly between nascent capitalists, who now employed labour at a wage, and who sought out the most profitable investment opportunities, rather than between artisans looking for remunerative trades.

The independent producer was already fading from the picture 'in every part of Europe, twenty workmen serve under one master for one that is independent'. The level of wages resulted from a bargain – 'The workmen desire to get as much, the master to give as little as possible. The former are disposed to combine in order to raise, the latter in order to lower the wages of labour' (Smith, 1776, 1976, I.viii.11, pp. 83–4). In this unequal struggle the advantage lay with the masters, since they were relatively few in number, so could combine more effectively, had longer purses and enjoyed the basic support of the legal processes.

The capitalist mode of organisation of work not only reduced wage costs, but was able to achieve an extremely fine division of labour, thus realising previously unthought of levels of productivity. 'Initially small-scale owners of stock, or capital, bring workers together, organise the division of labour within the enterprise, provide the best machinery and fund the stock of materials for the whole production process' (Smith, 1776, 1976, VI.5, pp. 65, 6).

The division of labour is the main plank in Smith's argument, which, as his title suggests, is mainly concerned with discovering the source of the wealth of the nation. The individual artisan, who once covered the whole range of a trade, becomes a specialist. This specialisation increases his or her productivity, by concentrating on a limited range of skills, which can then be perfected, by reducing the time lost moving between different tasks and by introducing specially designed tools and machines. In this process the capitalist eliminates a whole range of competitive negotiations formerly carried out between the independent artisans.

A world based on capital accumulation is bound to supersede one based on exchange between artisans. Feudal production was principally devoted to satisfying the consumption needs of the aristocracy, whose wealth and position were based on the ownership of land. These needs were expressed not only in things – fine clothes, fine food and fine houses – but also in people – whole armies of essentially unproductive servants and liverymen living-off surplus created elsewhere in the economy.

Feudalism thus had a built-in tendency to reach a production ceiling. Capitalism enabled society to break through this barrier as the aristocratic drive to ever greater expense was replaced by first the mercantilist and then the capitalist drive to accumulate.

The fine division of labour – its fineness achieved through large-scale manufacture and limited only by the extent of the market – required a complex social organisation to hold it all together. Smith's insight was that these intricate relaionships could best be achieved through reliance on market mechanisms.

This raises an interesting logical problem of considerable practical importance. In practice the division of labour takes place within the firm in the form of hierarchical or co-operative rather than through exchange relationships. The need for exchange is thus mainly between firms rather than between individuals, who enter the story only as sellers of labour and buyers of finished products. None the less Smith's own analysis is based on self-seeking individuals entering into exchange relationships. These exchanges are quite natural, since, according to Smith, we are all born with a propensity to truck and barter.

'Whether this propensity be one of the original principles of human nature, of which no further account can be given, or whether, as seems more probable, it be the necessary consequences of the faculties of reason and speech, it belongs not to our present subject to inquire' (Smith, 1776, 1976, II.2, p. 25). What had apparently started as an exchange of ideas had become an exchange of things.

To the topics of productivity increases through the division of labour and efficient allocation through exchange, we add Smith's other fundamental proposition that the pursuit of personal happiness would lead to universal well-being. The argument ran as follows – it is in the interest of each individual to specialise, since this increases personal productivity and yields more goods for exchange.

Since all parties are similarly engaged, the total wealth of society is maximised, provided we give full and free play to our natural inclinations to exchange goods and ideas. The central drive in this society was competition between artisans for customers.

Unlike Hobbes' lonely individual, whose hand is turned against all men, Smith has a gentler vision, in which from motives of self-love we seek each other out for mutual benefit in a state of natural harmony.

Smith's ideas on economic freedom, for which he is principally remembered today, are concentrated in Book IV and relate mainly to issues of overseas trade. They are none the less of more general importance as they reveal the likely effects of government interference on the free movement of profit-seeking capital.

Protection, which has the effect of conferring a monopoly on a domestic industry, leads to labour and capital being drawn into that industry in the expectation of an easier and softer life. This leaves other more productive industries short of resources and leads to an overall reduction in national income. The national interest would be better served, according to Smith, if individuals invested freely according to the best natural rates of return.

Smith considers, and rejects, the infant industry argument – that a domestic industry may need protection for a period to allow it to grow strong enough to face international competitive forces. Smith's case depends on the resultant misallocation of resources, lowering national income, savings and hence investment. Smith states that the overall misallocation effect would outweigh any benefits deriving from the growth of the single industry.

Smith does, however, allow for two possible exceptions to his unyielding defence of free trade. The first is concerned with the need to carry British goods in British bottoms, so as to preserve a basis for the naval defence of the country.

> The defence of Great Britain, for example, depends very much upon the number of its sailors and shipping. The Act of Navigation, therefore, very properly, endeavours to give the sailors and shipping of Great Britain the monopoly of trade of their own country, in some cases by absolute prohibition, and in others by heavy burdens upon the shipping of foreign countries (Smith, 1776, 1976, IV.ii.24, p. 483).

The other possible exception relates to help for excess workers who find themselves in a once protected industry. Smith suggests prudence in lifting prohibitions in such a case although suspects that the difficulties of a return to free trade may too easily be exaggerated.

The basis of Smith's distrust of protection lay in a belief that it made economic sense to import whatever was cheaper than could be produced domestically. This proposition, as refined by David Ricardo, is better stated as free trade is beneficial where there is a divergence between comparative costs between countries. In the extreme case where a country has an absolute advantage over another in all branches of trade, it will none the less pay it to concentrate on those industries where its advantage is relatively strong and trade where it is relatively weak.

It would be quite wrong, however, to conclude that Smith believed that a world left to business people would be one of free competition. He noted that deliberate concealment of information would prevent the free flow of capital into industries enjoying, in secret, excessive profits (market price above natural price, as Smith puts it). Similarly secrets in manufacture permit extraordinary gains to be harvested for even longer periods (Smith, 1776, 1976, I.vii.21–22, p. 77).

His attack on monopoly was based partly on the misdirection of funds, the excessive prices charged and the restriction on output, but also on its being an enemy of good management. 'Universal competition forces everybody to have recourse to good management for the sake of self defence' (Smith, 1776, 1976, I.xi.b.5, p. 163).

We close this section with two of Smith's bitter observations, which point ahead to the difficulties which law-makers will have in ensuring that firms do in fact compete.

People of the same trade seldom meet together, even for merriment and diversion, but the conversation ends in a conspiracy against the publick or in some contrivance to raise prices. It is impossible to prevent such meetings, by any law which either could be executed or would be consistent with liberty and justice. But though the law cannot hinder people of the same trade from sometimes assembling together, it ought to do nothing to facilitate such assemblies, much less render them necessary (Smith, 1776, 1976, I.x.c.27, p. 145).

And perhaps less well known:

To expect, indeed, that the freedom of trade should ever be entirely restored in Great Britain, is as absurd as to expect Oceana or Utopia should ever be established in it.

Not only the prejudices of the publick, but what is more unconquerable, the private interests of many individuals, irresistibly oppose it. Were the officers of the army to oppose with the same zeal and unanimity any reduction in the number of forces, with which master manufacturers set themselves against every law that is likely to increase the number of rivals in the home market; were the former to animate their soldiers, in the same manner as the latter enflame their workmen, to attack with violence and outrage the proposers of such regulation; to attempt to reduce the army would be as dangerous as it has now become to attempt to diminish in any respect the monopoly which our manufacturers have obtained against us.

This monopoly has so much increased the number of some particular tribes of them, that, like an overgrown standing army, they have become formidable to the government and on many occasions intimidate the legislature. (Smith, 1776, 1976, IV, ii, 43, p. 471).

JOHN STUART MILL

The *Wealth of Nations*, as we have noted above, can be read as a call for liberty rather than a prescription for efficient production. The theme of liberty as a good in itself is, perhaps, best expressed by John Stuart Mill who in *On Liberty* (1859) puts the pursuit of liberty ahead of that of happiness. Provided no other is harmed, then 'over himself, over his own body and mind, the individual is sovereign' (Mill, 1859, 1974, p. 69).

Happiness, the utilitarian goal – which approximates to Smith's 'self-love' – had to be approached indirectly by way of the cultivation of feelings and reason (poetry, art, music and other activities pursued for their own sakes) and a concern for the happiness of others (Mill, 1924, pp. 100–1).

Mill was not, in defending liberty, primarily concerned with external tyrants and despots, who imposed their will on an unwilling majority. Rather his concern was closer to home and far more modern. Society itself was the tyrant, penetrating deeply into every aspect of life, private and public, leaving few means of escape.

Public opinion dictated what was to be thought, how people should behave and worse still how they should feel. Mill feared the death of the individual and sought to reassert the doctrine of liberty, which he felt was becoming lost in an increasingly conformist world.

Although Mill separates economic freedom from individual liberty, his arguments run closely together. Cheapness and quality flow from the exchange between buyers and sellers. Although he admitted a possible need for public control to prevent fraud or to limit danger, he felt that in general it was better to leave people to work things out for themselves rather than attempt to control economic behaviour.

Mill accepted that in the pursuit of legitimate personal ends there would be winners and losers, for example in a competitive examination or in a business venture. Provided the game had been a fair one, Mill felt the losers had to live with the result.

Society admits no right, either legal or moral, in the disappointed competitors to immunity from this kind of suffering, and feels called on to interfere only when means of success have been employed which are contrary to the general interest to permit – namely fraud or treachery and force (Mill, 1859, 1974, p. 164).

Exceptionally, Mill granted society the right to exercise power over others in order to prevent harm. The tension between the free self and the need to protect society continues to this day to challenge the liberal conscience, which simultaneously promotes a person's freedom to be themselves and the need to intervene for the good of society. Mill's own position was slightly different – he held firm views on the necessity for, as well as the form of, private morality and only tolerated public intervention to prevent harm, rather than to do good.

Mill was fairly robust, for example about the sale of dangerous items, such as poisons and other harmful substances – and felt that provided they were clearly labelled and traded in such a way as to inhibit their use in pursuit of crime (i.e. recorded in a book or sold in the presence of witnesses) then it was not the business of society to interfere. 'Speaking generally there is no one so fit to conduct any business, or to determine how or by whom it shall be conducted, as those who are personally interested in it' (Mill, 1859, 1974, p. 180).

In detail Mill's attempt to define the boundary line between individual liberty and the right of the state appears quirky to the modern reader who lives happily with areas of freedom and with restrictions which were unknown to Mill. His general line of thought, however, is crystal clear – people should be free to conduct their own business, free to experiment, not tied to a universal bureaucracy, proceeding according to a set of fixed rules.

Not for Mill the conscious and planned organisation of production and distribution. Mill wanted the 'greatest dissemination of power consistent with efficiency' and the 'greatest centralisation of information and diffusion of it from the centre' (Mill, 1859, 1974, p. 185). Although Mill's strictures were aimed against government enforcement of social rules, one is tempted to speculate how acceptable Mill would have found the, admittedly more anarchic, assertion of social norms through the supremacy of large commercial firms.

CHARLES DARWIN

If Smith is principally, if inadequaely, remembered for his advocacy of free competition, Darwin is associated with the idea of the survival of the fittest. It is true that in the *Origin of Species* Darwin writes of a condition where species run up against some resource frontier, where only the fittest might survive; but his main interest, as we shall see, was in variation in nature. The idea of the struggle for survival we have already met in Locke above. However, its best known, and, for our purposes, most significant expression is to be found in Thomas Malthus.

Malthus intended his *Essay on the Principle of Population as it affects the Future Improvement of Society* (1798) as a counter to the

French Revolution and to the then current ideas on the perfectability of man and society. His argument was that man's appetite for basic food and shelter would, through uncontrolled population expansion, always outrun his resources, leading to a continuing struggle for the barest means of survival. He wrote:

> The power of population is indefinitely greater than the power in the earth to produce subsistence for man. Population when unchecked increases in a geometrical ratio. Subsistence increases only in an arithmetical ratio . . . This implies a strong and constantly operating check on population from the difficulty of subsistence (Malthus, 1926, pp. 13–16).

The fact that the two ratios on which Malthus relied so heavily had no particular theoretical or empirical basis did not prevent the *Essay* achieving immediate acceptance by the ruling landowning classes, who no doubt warmed to his assertion: 'The truth is that the pressure of distress' on the lower classes of society 'is an evil so deeply seated that no human ingenuity can reach it' (Malthus, 1926, p. 95), thus obviating the need for reform.

In an equally chilling passage, which appeared only in the second edition (1926, pp. 531–2), Malthus wrote:

> A man who is born into a world already possessed, if he cannot get subsistence from his parents on whom he has a just demand, and if society do not want his labour, has no claim of right to the smallest portion of food, and in fact has no business to be where he is. At nature's feast there is no vacant cover for him. She tells him to be gone, and will quickly execute her own orders, if he do not work on the compassion of some of her guests.
>
> If those guests get up and make room for him, other intruders immediately appear demanding the same favour . . . The guests learn too late their error, in counteracting those strict orders to all intruders, issued by the great mistress of the feast, who, wishing that all guests should have plenty, and knowing that she could not provide for unlimited numbers, humanely refused to admit fresh comers when her table was already full.

History relates that Malthus' fears of the population explosion swamping the world resource base were misplaced, since he underestimated the potential of the technological response to changing environmental conditions, since people, unlike plants and animals, are producers rather than gatherers and therefore have the power to reorder the way things are done. In the nineteenth and twentieth centuries the principal re-ordering agent has been the search for profitable outlets for capital, boosted from time to time by the dictates of war.

Darwin's theory of evolution, based on the struggle for survival and natural selection, provides another intellectual source for competition in modern political and economic thought. The line of argument we have so far traced from Hobbes's totally atomistic competitive struggle of all against all, through to the Malthusian frontier, where the population outstrips its resource base. Here at the margin of existence, according to Darwin, only the fittest plants and animals can survive long enough to reproduce themselves, so transmitting their genetic superiority down the generations.

The first Darwinian idea we explore is one of change – of evolution. Nature – and by extension human society – will, according to its own rules, metamorphose from one form to another. Such an idea was profoundly shocking to an age brought up on the biblical notion of a specific and complete creation, the details of which were to be found in Genesis, the opening chapter of the Bible, which told of the creation of the world and all the species contained therein in a single 'day'.

Archbishop Usher, a seventeenth-century cleric, had calculated to the day that the world was only 6,000 years old. Apart from the great changes wrought by the Flood, there had been too little time in the brief history of the world for any significant variation. But even the Flood did not change the nature or mix of species since Noah rounded them all up, two-by-two, so they could ride out the Flood in the comfort of the Ark.

The Creationist paradigm was, even before Darwin, running into trouble. Evidence was accumulating of lost species, of changes in species and the discovery of new species in remote non-biblical lands, such as Australia.

Observations suggested variations within species were relatively common. The animal breeders of the seventeenth century had consciously modified their livestock, changing its form by selective breeding. Similarly parts of the original homogeneous population in the wild, which had become geographically separated, had developed into distinctive subgroups, even where environmental conditions were broadly similar.

Where the environment had changed, the development of species was even more dramatic. Species suited to one condition had either to adapt or to expire. The metaphor used by Darwin was of an irregularly branching tree – from the parent stem, new species would branch off and in their turn divide again, even though the original parent stem might itself have ceased to grow and to bear fruit.

Species were thus seen to descend from a common ancestor, transmuting from form to form over time – the greater the distance from the parent stem, the more likely the variation from the original norm.

The idea of a fixed order had a natural appeal to a traditional hierarchical society in which each individual knew the place to which they had been born. The Creationist story, however, fitted less well the social turmoil of the Industrial Revolution, which itself was, in its technological aspects, the result of treating nature as malleable, of separating the divine from the scientific.

The late eighteenth and early nineteenth century had discovered that the pursuit of science led to prosperity, while the pursuit of God to poverty. God was not abandoned by the new industrial rich, rather he was increasingly confined to a celestial sphere.

A second aspect of the Creationist argument was that God was to be seen as the great designer of the world. The elements of nature so brilliantly fitted their purposes that only a conscious designer, and not blind chance, could so have fashioned their perfection. Bishop Paley in his *Evidence of Christianity* argued that an intelligent divine creator was the most plausible explanation for the beautiful fitness for purpose revealed in Nature.

One thing which shines through Darwin's work is the insistence that variation and difference are the stuff of nature, while permanence and stability were illusions. If variation was Darwin's central concern, he also required a mechanism to account for evolutionary change.

So long as a species bred true, sexual reproduction ensured variety at the level of the individual, some of which would be passed from generation to generation. The amazing fertility of nature ensured that the population would constantly run up against resource frontiers. In this extreme condition any individuals with a more favourable variation, would have an improved chance of surviving to transmit the variation on to the next generation, where the process of blind competition would be repeated, until the modified and improved individuals had replaced the unmodified.

Darwin's proposition was that the environment was in a state of change, that populations tended to expand to the limit of their resources and that sexual reproduction ensured a supply of inheritable variations, some of which favoured survival, some of which did not. We can express this by saying that the outcome depended on a combination of chance biological changes and a changing environment, the whole process driven by blind competition for increasingly scarce resources.

For this mechanism to work we have to accept that relatively minor novelties accumulate over time to yield a decisive advantage, either by an incremental process, in which the species adapts better to its environment, or by introducing a discontinuity, whereby cumulative change triggers off a major functional reorganisation, enabling the species to occupy a new and different evolutionary niche.

A rather different mechanism for evolution, which was from time to time adopted by Darwin, was that of J. B. A. P. de Monnet Lamark, who suggested that characteristics acquired by individuals in one generation could be transmitted genetically to the next. A linked aspect was Lamark's assumption that over time organisms tended towards greater complexity in the process of moving progressively to higher developmental states, the gaps at the lowest levels being filled by spontaneous generation of new organisms.

Although the evolutionary debate has been unkind to Lamark, his contribution to the Victorian vision of the world was a powerful one and was the dominant version from the 1870s until after the First World War. In many ways his biological story, incorrect though it appears to be for plants and animals, provides a better metaphor for human affairs than does that of Darwin.

Darwin's idea of the 'survival of the fittest' was applied principally by Spencer to human affairs. In this unfeeling doctrine the weak were to go to the wall, while wealth was simply proof of superior fitness. Herbert Spencer in 'A General Theory of Population Deduced from the General Law of Animal Fertility' *The Westminster Review* (ns I (1852), 500–1), developed a theory of social evolution based on something very close to natural selection.

> From the beginning, pressure of population has been the proximate cause of progress . . . For those prematurely carried off must, in the average of cases, be those in whom the power of self preservation is the least, it unavoidably follows that those left behind to continue the race, are those in whom the power of self preservation is the greatest – are the select of their generation.

Sociobiologists, even if their intention was simply to apply the study of the social behaviour of animals to evolutionary theory, have become associated in the popular mind with an attempt to show that human behaviour is biologically, that is genetically, determined, that racial and sexual inequality was a result of a competitive struggle at the level of the gene.

Strangely the problem faced by the sociobiologists was not one of explaining competitive, but co-operative behaviour. A starting point was the well authenticated observation that animal populations, contrary to Malthus's speculation, rarely outran their food supplies. They would refrain from breeding rather than risk starvation. By self-regulation they would ensure that the group, if not the individual, at least could reproduce and survive.

'The fundamental unit of selection, and therefore of self-interest, is in the words of Richard Dawkins in his *Selfish Gene*, "not the species, nor the group, nor even strictly the individual. It is the gene, the unit of heredity".'

The essential biological point was that co-operation was most likely to occur between close genetic relatives, which gave rise to the idea that individual animals would co-operate to ensure that their genetic material was by some means transmitted down the generations.

This line of argument implied some kind of genetic determinism – that there was a direct link between genetic make-up and observed behaviour; something scientifically improbable and socially pessimistic, since, if true, it would imply that the world's problems were incurable and provide another route to Malthus's gloomy view of an 'evil so deeply seated that no human ingenuity can reach it'.

Let us, however, for a moment follow the sociobiologists' view. Altruism becomes something hard-wired into the genetic code, which acts to preserve and promote the species at the level of the gene; the mother dies that the child may live and so, through reproduction, transmit their genes into the future.

From this we can propose a view that reciprocity has a positive survival value. Members of a species, which have the capacity for mutual aid, will, in adverse circumstances, outperform, in terms of survival, those members whose behaviour is restricted to the selfish. The point of this brief look at sociobiology is to suggest that co-operation and altruism may be as much part of biological human nature as its competitive self-interest.

Richard Dawkins in *The Blind Watchmaker* suggests that evolution provides the best possible explanation for the living world around us.

KARL MARX

In place of the Malthusian society always on the edge of survival Marx observed that the capitalist system of production was capable of producing more than it could consume. The capitalists, who controlled the fruits of production, however, were doomed to a life of fierce competition, not for want of resources, but for fear of destruction by more successful (profitable) rivals. The workers, in contrast, in Marx's view, would develop ever more co-operative structures.

Marx, and his collaborator Frederick Engels, recognised the competitive marketplace had effectively eroded the old powers of Royal monopolies, feudal ties and Guild restrictive practices, which had been such features of Adam Smith's competitive landscape. In the *Communist Manifesto* they write:

> The bourgeoisie, during its rule of scarce one hundred years, has created more massive and more collossal productive forces than have all preceding generations together. Subjection of nature's forces to man: machinery, application of chemistry to industry and agriculture, steam navigation, railways, electric telegraphs, clearing of whole continents for cultivation, canalization of rivers, whole populations conjured out of the ground – what earlier century had even a presentiment that such productive forces slumbered in the lap of social labour.

Periodically, far from running into dearth and famine, overproduction would reach a point where capitalism in order to regain its momentum would destroy not only its products but its means of production; this destructive process being itself, paradoxically, driven by the competitive need to accumulate.

Competition, which Marx relies on at various stages in his argument to bring about alignments of prices, values and profits, is no abstraction, but is full-blooded and active. Owners of capital, given the internal laws of capitalism, have no choice, if they wish to remain capitalists, but to compete with all their might and will.

> No one capital can stand up against the competition if it is not brought to the highest pitch of activity. Nobody who enters the competitive struggle can endure it without the greatest exertion of his strength (*Outlines of a Critique of Political Economy*, 1844).

Competition had first an historic role for Marx. In his notebook drafts for *Capital*, we find, *Grundrisse* (Marx, 1973, p. 649), competition appears as the progressive solvent of feudal and mercantilist barriers and monopolies. These barriers, which had in the past been a means of facilitating feudal production, had become fetters as capital replaced labour as the dominant element in the production process.

Even as market relations spread through feudal society, goods, which were produced almost entirely by labour, exchanged more or less in the ratios of their labour content. Technical advances enabled the budding capitalists to hold their capital in the form of plant and machinery, rather than finished goods or other treasure. In order to make their capital work, they had to hire workers for their labour power.

Initially the move into capitalism is uneven, concentrating in textiles, mining and iron production, but soon accelerating throughout industry. With the spread of capital came institutions to facilitate its restless search for the highest returns.

> The restless never-ending process of profit making alone is what [the capitalist] aims at. This boundless greed after riches, this passionate chase after exchange value, is common to the capitalist and the miser; but while the miser is merely the capitalist gone mad, the capitalist is a rational miser.
>
> The never ending augmentation of exchange value, which the miser strives after, by seeking to save his money from circulation, is attained by the more acute capitalist, by constantly throwing it afresh into circulation (*Capital*, 1918, Vol.1: part II, Ch.IV, pp. 170–1).

The primary competitive struggle of capitalism is between one set of owners of capital, who wish to invade areas of high potential, and another, which wishes to protect positions of above average profit. Thus, in as far as the state is a reflection of the needs of the dominant capitalist class, we will expect to find contradictory policies as first one group then the other gains the upper hand.

Competition also enters into what for Marx was the basic contradiction of capitalism – the tendency of the rate of profit to fall. Over time capital equipment is accumulated as labour is displaced by machinery. In the short run this gives innovating firms an advantage, but as, under the pressure of competition, all firms in that industry adopt the new technology, the level of profit is driven down. The firms have more capital, or dead labour, to service with profit, and relatively less productive living labour to generate the necessary surplus.

Marx in *Capital* identifies various counteracting influences, but sees that inevitably capitalism will lurch from one destructive crisis to another – all because the individual capitals are driven by competition to struggle one with another for profits. In the end the system cannot work – individual capitalists are driven, on pain of extinction, to accumulate; in the process of accumulation living labour is shed to gain a competitive advantage, so over time reducing capital's capacity to generate surplus, which for Marx, can only be generated by work.

For a time the great concentrations of capital, which arise because 'one capitalist always kills many' (Marx, 1918 p. 837), may be able to resist the effects of declining profits by extracting monopoly rents through the erection of obstacles to entry and witnessing the physical destruction of rival capitals. They too, however, will be drawn into the general crisis, which, through revolution, will lead to socialism. Marx, while not underestimating the power of competition, appears to have underestimated capitalism's recuperative powers.

Free competition was not, however, simply the means of the destruction of the past, it was central to the nature of capitalism. It was not individuals who had been set free by competition, it was capital itself. The conclusions which Marx draws from competition are in stark contrast to the familiar ideas of neo-classical general equilibrium, as expounded by Leon Walras in the 1870s and Alfred Marshall in the Edwardian period.

'Competition', writes Marx, 'makes the immanent laws of capitalist production to be felt by each individual capitalist as external coercive laws' (Marx, 1918, Vol.I, p. 603).

> Capital comes more and more to the fore as a social power, whose agent is the capitalist. This social power no longer stands in any possible relation to that which the labour of a single individual can credit. It becomes an alienated, social power, which stands opposed to society as an object that is the capitalist's source of power (Marx, 1918, Vol.III, p. 259).

A rather different insight into competition is offered in a letter from Marx to Pavel Vassilyevich dated 1846 (*The Letters of Karl Marx*, ed. S. K. Padover, Prentice Hall, New Jersey, 1979, p. 5). Here there is a dialectical relationship between competition and its antithesis monopoly: competition produces monopoly – monopoly in turn produces competition.

Extending this analysis of the movement of competition, we can observe that in a fully competitive environment firms will naturally adopt defensive measures, which in time will lead to the increasing monopolisation of the market, until big firms' profits fall and openings occur for younger more aggressive capitals to break their way into the market, so reintroducing competition.

A PSYCHOLOGICAL MODEL

In this chapter thus far we have drawn on some of the ideas of the eighteenth century, as represented by Adam Smith, and of the nineteenth by Darwin and Marx. It is now the turn of the twentieth century to make a contribution to our understanding of competition, entering by way of the psychoanalysis of Freud, but rapidly embracing a wider reading of social psychology.

We face an initial problem in a psychological reading of competition, in that much that is relevant and useful to our exploration is categorised under the heading of 'aggression'. Freud wrote in *Civilisation and its Discontents* (1920, p. 102) that 'the tendency to aggression is an innate, independent, instinctual disposition'.

Freud, filled with pessimism after the First World War, postulated a death instinct, 'Thanatos', a compulsion to return to the original inorganic state; aggression, for him, is an expression of this death wish. The only hope for society lay in channelling this death wish into acceptable directions, such as sport and other safe competitive activities.

One can speculate, therefore, that a society driven by internal business competition would be less prone to aggression, violence and war, than one with a less sophisticated harnessing of Freud's dark forces. The evidence seems at best mixed and is further confused by the progressive mechanisation of violence. According to Freudian tradition, aggressive energy is being continuously generated and must seek expression. This energy can either be released in socially acceptable ways (sport, debate, business competition) or in unacceptable ways (fights, insults, self-destruction, suicide). Freud believed, in a modern version of Hobbes, that one of the main functions of organised society was to channel and check aggression.

A different view is taken by the ethologist Konrad Lorenz in *On Aggression* (1966). He described aggression as 'the fighting instinct in beast and man, which is directed against members of the same species'. The evolutionary purpose of the aggression instinct was two-fold – to ensure first that each creature had sufficient space for survival and second that only the best and strongest, in terms of aggressiveness, would continue the species through their breeding.

Sociobiology, as expressed by S. O. Wilson in *Sociobiology the New Synthesis* (1975), traces social behaviour back to its genetic roots. Put simply, behaviours which increase genetic fitness will be preserved. Aggressive behaviour is a useful trait from the perspective of genetic continuance, since it ensures differential access to the resources required for survival and successful reproduction.

The social psychologist, following Kurt Lewin in *Field theory in Social Science* (1951), proposes a model whereby human behaviour is a function of both the person and the environment. This simple model shifts emphasis away from the psychoanalytic concern with the interior mind and its unconscious drives and the behaviourist concern with external stimuli and observable responses.

We each have, in whatever form and for whatever reason, a capacity to compete and a capacity to co-operate; how these are expressed in personal and group behaviour will depend on the interaction between ourselves and our environment.

Social psychology's own history opens with an experiment in Indiana in 1897 by Norman Triplett, concerning the effects of competition on individual behaviour. Triplett, a keen cyclist, had noted that cyclists' times were faster, when racing against one another than when racing against the clock. That is competitive performance was superior to non-competitive (Triplett, 1897, 9, pp. 507-33).

Triplett extended his research to other tasks, such as winding kite string on to fishing reels, and found similar results. The subjects of the experiments were aware that their neighbours were engaged in similar tasks. They appeared to react by seeing the situation as a challenge, attempting to outperform their neighbours. This phenomenon has come to be known as, 'social facilitation' – its antithesis being 'social inhibition', where the presence of others, either as spectators or co-actors, worsens performance.

Competition appears to improve performance in the following way – through observation we can establish performance norms, against which we measure our own performance and to which we try to conform. We also appear able to learn from observation of our fellow co-actors, even when competing against them. Our co-actors also provide us with an audience.

The introduction of an audience greatly complicates the effects. Some people are stimulated by the mere presence of an audience, others inhibited; in general the better players perform better, the less accomplished worse. The presence of an audience appears to amplify feelings of success and failure. Interaction between player and audience seems to strengthen the effect and some players deliberately trade on this to improve their performance yet further.

Experiments suggest that competitive stimuli from the presence of co-actors seems to work best in raising performance levels where the tasks are relatively simple and well understood. On more complex less familiar tasks a co-operative approach appears better (Seta, 1982, pp. 281-91; Laughlin and Jacquard, 1975, 32, pp. 873-9).

Social-learning theorists, while admitting instinct as an explanation for aggressive competitive behaviour in animals, believe that in humans such behaviour is learnt. There are two main versions of this story: in one we learn to be competitive if competitive behaviour is rewarded (prizes, more status, more money); the other is we learn to compete by modelling our behaviur on that of others.

Pro-social behaviour – that is behaviour which benefits others – was for Adam Smith self-interested behaviour. Smith warns that deliberate attempts to help others may have quite unintended outcomes, which are far from generally beneficial. We do, however, observe selfless behaviour ranging from the high drama of the mountain rescue to the quietness of tea and sympathy, where the intention is, at personal cost to oneself, to help another.

Selfless altruism – that is the performance of an act at a cost to oneself with the benefit attaching wholly to another – seems to be at odds with the accepted view of selfishness as the norm for human behaviour.

Some observers even suggest that altruism is a special case of selfishness in terms of a calculation of rewards and benefits – rewards of improved self-perception and group esteem to be balanced against costs of time, effort and risk and even possible social embarrassment (Rosenham, 1978).

Alvin Gouldner (1960, pp. 161–78) believes the reciprocity norm is universal and essential to the maintenance of society. The only people exempt are the old, the sick and the very young. The existence of Gouldner's norm ensures that most people most of the time act pro-socially.

For such a norm to exist, we require that the group has an objective existence quite distinct from that of the individual. Simmel (Simmel, 1950) asks us to distinguish between the individual, the couple or dyad and the group of three or more people.

The essence of the group is that it continues to exist even if one of the members withdraws. Its members interact with each other, developing interdependent ties and group norms, which have an existence independent of the individual members, who voluntarily sacrifice part of their own freedom of action for the material and psychological benefits of belonging to a group.

Group cohesiveness means that the forces binding members together are strong enough to overcome external attractions and internal repulsions. The members of the group like each other, subscribe to the same norms and hold the same goals. A strong cohesive well motivated group will normally do better in both offensive and defensive plays than the lone player or ill-assorted group.

At the level of relatively complex physical tasks, such as sailing a ship, group work is more likely to pay off than individual efforts. However, when it comes to creative decision-making – shall we stay and fight or turn and run before the wind, surely the lone captain will serve better than the combined wisdom of the crew? Research findings are contradictory, but under certain conditions certain types of group, although more costly in time, produce more and better solutions to problems than do individuals.

Groups, like individuals, can interact with each other either competitively or co-operatively. They can compete to gain a goal for themselves, or they can co-operate for its joint achievement.

There are also situations where groups bargain with each other, discovering by give and take how well or badly they can live together. One familiar form of such bargaining is between unions and management. Here breakdown is frequently expressed by strike and lock-out action. Another example might be arms limitations talks, where much time is spent on pre-negotiation negotiations, because the costs of a full breakdown are too high.

There also exist situations where groups are in conflict, but where the issues cannot be isolated sufficiently for negotiations and where there are few formal relations between the groups. Examples of this can often be found in inter-racial relationships in many societies. Conflict may, however, be resolved in the presence of an over-arching goal that can only be achieved through co-operation, such as building a sea wall. Success, but not failure, powerfully reduces conflict.

The classic locus for this lies in the Robbers' Cave experiment conducted by Muzaphar Sherif, who took two groups of healthy middle-class American 12-year-olds and subjected them to a three-stage experiment. In the first stage the two groups, unbeknown to each other, developed their team spirit, one adopting the title the Rattlers, the other the Eagles.

In the second stage the two groups are introduced to each other and as might be predicted deep hostility breaks out between them. In the final stage the experimenters attempt to reduce hostility by various strategies – joint religious services, joint outings and a common enemy – without success, until the boys were required to complete a task – manhandling the broken-down food truck – requiring co-operation.

SUMMARY

In this chapter we have tried to show that at the root of much thinking about competition are a number of unresolved difficulties. Returning to the metaphor of the game introduced in the last chapter, the first question is when the players take to the field do they compete for prizes or do they collude and co-operate?

Hobbes would have us believe that ruthless competition would rule until the players were forced to invent a referee to bring some order to the game. Freud suggests that the players come to the game driven by the darkest of destructive anarchic subconscious forces and find that adherence to the rules of the game enables them to avoid self-destruction.

In Locke's game the players live amicably together and only start to quarrel and to play competitively once the refreshments run dry. At this stage the referee intervenes to prevent the play getting too rough. In Malthus's game there is no point in having a referee, as there can never be enough to go round – the stronger players simply eliminate the weaker.

Darwin, fascinated by the many possible forms the game can take, also has no referee, but watches to see what variations are capable of survival. Sociobiologists suggest that players have certain genetic controls to prevent the game getting too destructive.

Setting the metaphor aside, the most likely conclusion would be that individuals have a capacity both to compete and to co-operate. The observations of the social psychologists indicate that individuals have a strong need to belong and that they will voluntarily sacrifice some part of their own self-interest to that of the group as their admission price to the society that gives them psychic security.

Turning from analysis at the level of the individual to the level of the group, we find group development will be at the expense of individual transactions. Smith in his powerful use of the division of labour as the explanation of the amazing growth in the wealth of nations points implicitly to a reduction in the space left for market relations.

Marx makes the point with greater force, as he foresees the increasing centralisation of capital in fewer and fewer hands as individual capitalists are forced to accumulate to survive.

This points us in the direction of an analysis of competition between organised capitals rather than completion between individual entrepreneurs. In this world competition for customers becomes just one aspect of total competition for capital, which is as likely to be waged by the takeover cheque book as by the introduction of a better mousetrap.

3 Modern Models of Competition

NEO-CLASSICAL THEORY OF COMPETITION

Every undergraduate student of economics has been (painfully?) introduced to standard neo-classical microeconomics. Indeed students on many courses have probably been introduced to no other form of economics!

Neo-classical economics, developed by writers such as Jevons, Marshall, Walras, etc., differs in certain respects from the earlier classical theory, as set out by Smith, Malthus and Ricardo.

Ferguson (1969, p. 3) points out two differences between the theories. He states that:

> First, neo-classical theory is based upon the assumption that there are no fixed non-augmentable factors of production. This contrasts sharply with the classical assumption of a fixed supply of land. Second, in neo-classical theory the rate of growth of population or of the labour force is assumed to be determined exogenously. This too contrasts sharply with classical theory, in which population is very much an economic variable.

Neo-classical economics covers every area of microeconomic behaviour, from theories of consumer behaviour, to theories of production and distribution. In this section we are looking at how firms behave under different market structures in a neo-classical world and how neo-classical price theory has provided the underpinnings of industrial economics.

Neo-classical economics and market structure

The polar cases of monopoly and perfect competition tend to receive most coverage in the literature. Welfare economics suggests to us that competition is 'good' and monopoly is 'bad'. In particular we are told that perfect competition can result in an optimal distribution of resources in society. Let us consider the four different types of markets that firms can operate in.

Perfect competition

A perfectly competitive market can be viewed as some sort of theoretical construct that doesn't exist in the real world. However, the only sector of the economy that gets close to perfectly competitive markets is probably agriculture. Many farms are price takers and produce only a tiny fraction of the total supply of eggs, milk, etc., for which there are many buyers. The product sold in an agricultural market is often homogeneous in character and entry barriers are minimal. Also profit maximisation would seem to be a sensible, and probably necessary, objective if a small farm is to survive.

Ritson (1977, p. 121) has summarised the nature of a perfectly competitive market by giving the following set of five conditions required to attain it:

1. There are many buyers and sellers such that the action of no one individual buyer or seller can have a perceptible influence upon market price.
2. Producers and consumers have perfect knowledge of events in the market and act on this knowledge.
3. The product is homogeneous so that customers are indifferent between the produce of alternative suppliers.
4. Firms act independently of each other in such a way as to maximise their individual profits and each consumer acts similarly so as to maximise utility from consumption.
5. There are no barriers to the movement of goods or factors of production. Firms are therefore free to enter or leave the production of the product and are able to supply to the market whatever quantity they wish.

If all of the above, except condition 2, relating to perfect knowledge, are met then the term 'pure competition' as opposed to perfect competition is sometimes used.

The case for perfect competition as an ideal market structure for the entire economy, giving rise to the possibility of a Pareto optimal allocation of resources in society, is one of the fundamental theorems of welfare economics. Such an allocation is said to exist when it is impossible to make one person better off without making another worse off at the same time. (See Bator (1957) for the derivation of the conditions required for Pareto optimality to occur.)

Even though perfect competition satisfies these conditions it is neither necessary nor sufficient for an optimal allocation of resources. It is not necessary since a socialist economy with state officials controlling firms and operating where price equals marginal cost will also satisfy these conditions. Nor is perfect competition sufficient since the conditions are only first order and therefore must be supplemented by second order conditions to distinguish between maximum and minimum welfare positions. Even if both first and second order conditions are fulfilled an optimum may be local rather than global. Finally, there are an infinite number of Pareto optima and even if a perfectly competitive economy satisfies all the first and second order conditions it is unlikely that the resulting welfare distribution will be that which maximises some particular social welfare function, i.e. some particular value judgement as to the optimal distribution of welfare.

If public goods, such as defence, are provided at all in a free market economy they are likely to be provided at a suboptimal level. In addition to public goods, the existence of externalities are another reason why perfect competition may not achieve an optimal resource allocation. There is no guarantee that an optimal distribution of income will occur under perfect competition. Also diseconomies of scale must exist and indeed occur beyond a relatively small level of output. The efficient size of firm must be small enough for the industry to efficiently support a very large number of firms.

However, empirical evidence on this latter point suggests that the long-run average cost curve does not turn upwards over feasible output levels in most industries. This implies that small firms have an incentive to expand their size and reap the benefits of lower unit costs. Also, economies of scale imply that the marginal cost curve will be below the average cost curve and the profit maximising rule of setting price equal to marginal cost under perfect competition will result in financial losses for the firm.

These various problems associated with perfect competition resulted in the development of other theories of competitive behaviour, such as the theory of monopolistic competition which we will consider next.

Monopolistic competition

This theory was developed by Chamberlin (1933). It applies to market situations where a large number of firms are selling similar but differentiated products. Competition would not only apply to the price charged but also to the quality of the product, labelling, advertising and sales promotion. Hence non-price competition is important in such markets.

As in perfect competition the assumption of free entry into and exit from the market still applies. Unlike perfect competition each good is slightly different in composition or brand image. For instance, different brands of toothpaste or detergents are similar but not identical to one another. As a result each firm does not face a perfectly elastic demand curve for its product and hence is not a price taker. The firm's demand curve is downward sloping under conditions of monopolistic competition. One firm may charge a higher price than its rivals without losing all its customers due to brand loyalty for its product. Although supernormal profits are possible in the short run, because of the free entry assumption, only normal profits will be made in the long run. In other words, new firms would be attracted into the industry in the long run if short-run supernormal profits are being earned. The result of this new entry will be that each individual firm will be unable to operate at full capacity. Average costs of production will not be minimised and hence firms will be producing inefficiently. Figure 3.1 illustrates this result. P1 and Q1 are price and quantity in the long run for the firm. The minimum efficient size of firm would be at output Q2 on the figure where average cost is minimised at AC1. The distance P1 AC1 on the vertical axis is the gap between actual unit costs and minimum possible unit costs. Hence, the equilibrium size of firm is inefficiently small and only normal profits will be earned. Price is no longer equated at marginal cost as in perfect competition. Instead price is set higher than marginal cost at the long-run equilibrium output level, as seen from the figure.

There is also an incentive to spend money on advertising and sales promotion if demand is expanded sufficiently to increase short-run profits. There is no such incentive under perfect competition.

Although this theory is more relevant to modern industries than perfect competition and can also handle economies of scale over the feasible range of output, it has nevertheless been the centre of much controversy and criticism. Monopolistic competition is incapable of making predictions about how a firm would respond to a change in the demand or cost conditions facing it. The assumption of free entry and exit is most unlikely to be met in most industries. Also, it is difficult to define accurately the industry being used in this theory. Chamberlin refers to firms producing similar but not identical products. Clearly, one person's definition of 'similar' may differ from another. How high

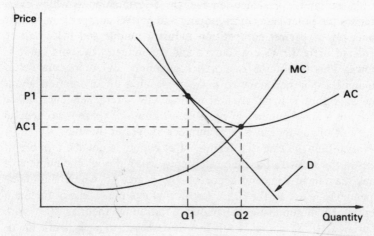

Figure 3.1 Long-run equilibrium for a firm operating under monopolistic competition

a cross elasticity of demand between two goods is required before they become 'similar' ?

Oligopoly

Probably most industries fit the definition of being oligopolistic in character. Oligopoly refers to a situation where there are a few producers. There is no longer complete freedom of entry into the industry. Instead entry barriers exist and help to explain why only a few firms are present in this market. Supernormal profits can exist in both the short and long run.

Do oligopolistic firms actively compete with one another to achieve their goal or goals? The question of how oligopolists respond to one another, and also to potential entrants hoping to enter their market, has been examined in various theories of oligopolistic behaviour which range from collusion to price warfare. Of course, the extent to which collusive tactics can be pursued will depend upon industrial legislation in the country concerned – see Chapter 5 for a full account of this.

Oligopoly is a market situation in which firms realise that their actions are interdependent, i.e. that a change in output by one firm will alter the profits of other firms, which will induce them to alter their outputs. This reaction alters the first firm's optimal output, which again causes the other firms to alter their behaviour and so on. This recognised interdependence removes the determinateness which characterises the polar cases of monopoly and perfect competition. Under monopoly or perfect competition industry output and price can be predicted if the firm's cost curves and the industry demand curve is known. This is not the case under oligopoly and to restore determinateness it is necessary to make some kind of assumption about how oligopolistic firms attempt to deal with interdependence. Since there are a large number of possible assumptions there is no general theory of oligopoly but a large number of special theories.

Notice that the essential feature of oligopoly is not the number of firms in the industry but their interdependence, though the number of firms may have some influence on the degree to which this interdependence is felt by the firms. Let us first examine some of the main theories of oligopolistic behaviour. Traditional theories start with Cournot's (1838) model. Each firm is assumed to seek profit maximisation taking its rivals' outputs as given. This provides us with an apparent inconsistency with the notion of oligopolistic interdependence. In situations of disequilibrium rivals will surely respond by changing their output levels which will nullify the Cournot assumption.

An early critique appeared in the work of Bertrand (1883) where he suggested that rivals' prices rather than outputs must be taken as given. This is consistent with later research into the theory of kinked demand curves and rigid pricing where rivals are assumed not to respond to price increases, although they do respond to cuts. Further variants of the Cournot solution were advanced by Edgeworth (1897) and von Stackelberg (1934).

Firms may react to interdependence by colluding, if public policy allows, and the most extreme form of collusion is joint profit maximisation in which total industry profits are maximised by the firms acting as a single monopolist. However, such a collusive solution is unlikely to be stable since each firm can increase its individual profits by cutting its price if the other firms abide by the collusive agreement. Industry price and output would be determined as for a multiple plant monopolist, with each firm producing where its marginal cost is equal to industry marginal revenue. But if an individual firm cuts its price and expands its output to a point where its marginal cost is equal to its own marginal revenue then its own profits will increase provided other firms adhere to the collusive agreement.

This will hold true for all firms in the cartel and so the cartel will not persist unless it can deter cheaters by detection and effective punishment. The theory 'asserts that the oligopolists wish to set a monopoly price, but they are limited by the difficulty of detecting secret competitive manoeuvres by individual firms' (Stigler, 1968, p. 31). Stigler goes on to point out that detection of such competitive price cutting is chiefly effected by 'watching the shares of each firm'.

Rather than attempting to maximise joint profits the members of a cartel may have the more limited aim of preventing entry into their industry to safeguard their existing profit levels. The basis of this theory is that a potential entrant will be deterred if he believes that the post-entry price will not cover his long-run average cost. If the potential entrant believes that the existing firms will maintain their current output levels after entry by a new firm and if existing firms actually behave in this passive manner (known as the Sylos Postulate), then the effective demand curve facing the entrant will be the segment of the market demand curve below the current price (see Figure 3.2). Entry is clearly profitable at the profit maximising price/quantity combination (P_1/Q_1) since the entrant can charge a price in excess of LRAC. However, entry is unprofitable at the limit price/quantity combination (P_2/Q_2) since LRAC > price at every possible output level.

Bain (1949) was the first to suggest that price is set below the profit maximising price in a number of highly concentrated industries to block the entry of potential competitors. The so-called Bain-Sylos model of limit pricing has been the subject of considerable criticism. For example, Stigler (1968, p. 21) believes that 'this theory [limit pricing] raises questions faster than it answers them'. Four are particularly troublesome:

1 Why should it be more profitable to exclude all entrants than merely to retard their rate of entry?
2 Why should a prospective entrant believe that after his entry a colluding group will not revise its policy so that all will earn returns above the competitive level?
3 If the industry's demand is growing over time, how is the prospective entrant to be pursuaded that he can have no share of the increments of demand?
4 Industry structure is irrelevant. The ability of the oligopolists to agree upon and police the limit price is apparently independent of the sizes and numbers of oligopolists.

Stigler (1968, p. 21) goes on to add that: 'No empirical evidence has been offered for the theory, which is not surprising' ! It should also be added that the response of a potential entrant may well depend upon the size and nature of the entrant. One would imagine that a large

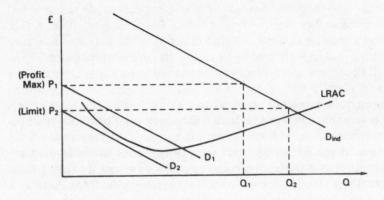

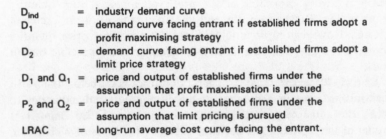

D_{ind}	=	industry demand curve
D_1	=	demand curve facing entrant if established firms adopt a profit maximising strategy
D_2	=	demand curve facing entrant if established firms adopt a limit price strategy
D_1 and Q_1	=	price and output of established firms under the assumption that profit maximisation is pursued
P_2 and Q_2	=	price and output of established firms under the assumption that limit pricing is pursued
LRAC	=	long-run average cost curve facing the entrant.

Figure 3.2 Profit maximising and entry forestalling price and output

diversifying firm would not be put off so easily from entering a market as a 'brand new' small business.

Certain types of oligopolistic markets may give rise to a dominant firm(s). The theory of price leadership applies to a market structure where one firm (or group of firms) sets (set) the industry price so as to maximise its (their) profits, with the other firms in the industry taking the price as given and adjusting their output to maximise their profits at the given price. In effect, the other firms in the industry act as if they were perfectly competitive price takers. This theory is capable of encompassing a market structure consisting of a few large powerful firms together with many small firms acting as price takers on the periphery of the industrial boundary.

The attributes of perfect competition have been recently applied to oligopolistic and monopolistic industries operating in 'perfectly contestable' markets by Baumol (1982). The crucial feature of such markets is their vulnerability to 'hit and run' entry. Because of free

Table 3.1 A pay-off matrix

		Duopolist B's output (000s)			
		40	60	80	100
Duopolist A's	60	8	13	11	5
Output (000s)	90	10	12	-10	-8

entry and exit, the monopolist or oligopolist may prevent entry only by behaving in a perfectly competitive manner or otherwise face 'hit and run' entry. When these markets are in a state of equilibrium, price is set equal to marginal cost. Only normal profits will be earned and maximum efficiency in production will be achieved. Here we have the notion of 'virtuous ogligopolists' and the phenomenon that high concentration and the absence of entry may be a sign of virtue and not vice.

Finally, an alternative approach to the analysis of the interdependence problem in oligopolistic decision-making is game theory. The underlying assumption in zero-sum games (where one's gain is another's loss) is that firms are actively competing against one another rather than engaging in some form of collusion. Game theory is concerned with preparing oneself against the optimal moves of one's competitors. Businesses are assumed to be capable of calculating the optimal moves of the opposition and of preparing their own defensive measures accordingly.

Game theory is a cautious approach to the problem since it is assumed that the worst will happen, namely that rivals will always use their best possible strategies against you. It is the so-called MAXIMIN approach, in the sense that it assumes that opponents will act in such a way as to reduce your market share or profits or whatever goal (or goals) is (are) being pursued to a MINIMUM and so you choose to minimise the damage by adopting the best (MAXI) strategy to counteract your opponents' moves.

As an illustration of a two-person zero-sum game consider a competitive struggle for market share by two duopolists (for example Unilever and Procter and Gamble in the detergents market). Here, every percentage point of the share of the market gained by one firm is necessarily lost by the other. This is in fact the only class of games where an unambiguous solution to the problem can be worked out. Suppose that duopolist A is considering two possible output strategies – either produce 60,000 or 90,000 units of output. Duopolist B is considering four possible output strategies – namely 40,000, 60,000, 80,000 or 100,000 units.

Corresponding to the various output combinations under consideration we assume that a pay-off matrix can be formed showing the gain (loss) in terms of percentage market share to dupolist A (B). Consider the example of a pay-off matrix in Table 3.1. If duopolist A produces 60,000 units and B produces 40,000 units, A gains 8 per cent of market share and B loses 8 per cent of market share. However, the situation would be reversed if A produces 90,000 units and B produces 100,000 units. In this situation A loses 8 per cent and B gains 8 per cent of market share.

The value of the game (V) is the final outcome of the game in terms of the gain to duopolist A and loss to duopolist B. The solution to a two-person zero-sum game provides us with the value of the game and the probabilities with which each firm employs each alternative open to it.

Under certain circumstances each firm will find that one strategy will always dominate the other(s) and we are led towards an equilibrium solution. An equilibrium pair of strategies will exist if the same element in the pay-off matrix is obtained by:

1 First minimise across the rows and then maximise, i.e. choose the largest of these minima, *and*
2 First maximise down the columns and then minimise, i.e. choose the smallest of these maxima.

1. corresponds to the business strategy adopted by duopolist A on the assumption that it adopts the cautious approach by assuming the worst (i.e. considers only the minimum gain in market share corresponding to each output strategy) and then chooses the least worst (i.e. the maximum of the minimum gains – MAXIMIN approach). This approach will only make sense if it is feasible to think of your fellow duopolist as an opponent or competitor ready and able to reduce your gain in market share to a minimum for any strategy you may adopt.

Likewise 2. corresponds to the business strategy adopted by duopolist B. Remember that the elements in the pay-off matrix are losses to B given the assumption of a zero-sum game. B adopts the cautious approach also by assuming the worst (i.e. considers only the maximum loss in market share corresponding to each output strategy) and then chooses the least worst (i.e. the minimum of these maximum losses – MINIMAX approach).

Does an equilibrium pair of optimal strategies exist for the two duopolists? Consider the optimal strategy for each of them in turn.

[5]
Duopolist A : Minimum =   [–10]
                   (rows)
      Maximin = 5
Duopolist B : Maximum =   [10 13 11 5]
                   (columns)
      Minimax = 5

The condition for an equilibrium solution exists since Maximin = Minimax. Duopolist A will employ his first strategy (i.e. produce 60,000 units of output) and duopolist B will employ his fourth strategy (i.e. product 100,000 units of output). These two strategies will be employed all of the time by A and B and the resulting value of the game will be 5. This means that A will gain 5 per cent of market share and B will lose 5 per cent of market share. This kind of equilibrium situation corresponds to static equilibrium in economics.

If the maximin strategy of A had resulted in a different solution to the minimax strategy of B then it will pay the duopolists to vary their output strategies over time. Mixed strategies should be employed which will mean that A will vary production between 60,000 and 90,000 units over time and similarly B will vary production between 40,000, 60,000, 80,000 and 100,000 units. To calculate the optimal combination of mixed strategies we would need to employ partial differentiation. (See, for example, Shubik (1982) for a full account of this and other aspects of game theory.) As a brief illustration, Shubik (1982, p. 225) considers the following example of a two-person zero-sum game where each player is faced with two possible strategies:

          Player B
          1   2
  Player 1 [10   –5]
    A   2 [–15   10]
   Minimum = [–5]   Maximin = –5
   (rows)   [–15]
   Maximum = [10 10]   Minimax = 10
   (columns)

The condition for an equilibrium pair of strategies is not met. Shubik shows that the optimal set of mixed strategies will be for Player A to adopt his first strategy 5/8th of the time and his second 3/8th of the time (or in a sequence of eight moves, the first strategy should be adopted five times and the second three times). In the case of Player 2 he should adopt his first strategy 3/8th of the time and his second 5/ 8th of the time (or in a sequence of eight moves, the first strategy should be adopted three times and the second five times).

However, game theory can also be used to illustrate how mutual co-operation can be used to advantage in non-zero-sum games. Indeed, the Prisoners' Dilemma example (see R. Luce and H. Raiffa (1957)) has been used to show how mutual co-operation can be a sensible strategy in oligopolistic markets. The translation into oligopoly situations illustrates how if firms co-operate they can all make a reasonable profit. However, if one firm is motivated by self-interest and makes a move to which other firms do not respond, it can earn even higher profits. But if its competitors retaliate strongly against the move, all the firms can end up being worse off than they would under co-operation. This is a classic example of a non-zero-sum game where the interests of the players are not directly opposed and co-operation may be mutually advantageous.

Sometimes vigorous reaction by competitors, in the form of, say, a price war, can achieve the long-term desired aim of eliminating an efficient firm from the market – so-called predatory pricing. Consumers may gain from the price war in the short run but will lose out in the long run with fewer competitors in the market.

Although industrial economics only considers predatory intent from the viewpoint of pricing policy, other forms of business behaviour may be predatory in nature. Consider the role of advertising. The literature is full of examples of advertising expenditure as a source of entry barrier (see, for example, Comanor and Wilson (1967)). Advertising can also be used in a predatory sense. Suppose a large multinational tobacco manufacturer has a virtual monopoly in the cigarette industry in a large South American country. Another multinational manufacturer makes its intentions known that it wishes to enter this market. The potential entrant is likely to be highly successful and uses the image of an American cowboy to sell its product.

The established firm decides to advertise a new very low quality line that it introduces, with the same image of a cowboy. Hence, South Americans are totally put off smoking cigarettes with a cowboy image. When the potential entrant enters into the market it discovers that its usually successful image fails to catch on and it quickly withdraws. The established firm retains its monopoly situation with the help of predatory advertising.

These theories of oligopoly are rather narrow in the sense of only considering rivalry amongst current competitors and potential entrants. A broader definition of competition has been made by Porter (1980). 'Extended rivalry' is introduced as a broad definition of competition. Porter sees firms as having to cope with five competitive forces, namely entry, the threat of substitution, bargaining power of buyers, bargaining power of suppliers and rivalry amongst current competitors. This is important in as much as it reminds us that the bargaining power of buyers and suppliers may be very important in a market. For example, it is hard to believe that the large supermarket chains don't wield considerable buying power over the wholesalers who supply them. It was Galbraith (1952) who introduced the notion of 'countervailing buying power' and he wrote (p. 118): 'The long trend toward concentration of industrial enterprise in the hands of relatively few firms has brought into existence not only strong sellers as economists have supposed, but also strong buyers as they have failed to see'. For a further discussion of retailing see the case study in Chapter 7.

In summary, we can conclude that there are many different theories relating to the goals and behaviour patterns of firms in oligopolistic industries. One would have to examine oligopolistic industries on a case by case approach to decide which theory is most relevant. However, we can say that there is likely to be a big incentive to collude to maximise joint industry profits if the firms can (1) get away with it and (2) effectively deter cheating. If this is not possible then competitive strategies could be either offensive (for example, limit pricing, predatory pricing or predatory advertising) or defensive (for example, the maximin approach of game theory).

Monopoly

At the other end of the spectrum from perfect competition, we have monopoly. Only one firm is producing in this market. Obviously entry barriers are extremely high, causing other firms to remain outside of the industry. There may be important scale economies, capital requirements, patent rights, etc., that make it extremely difficult for potential entrants actually to enter this market.

The standard neo-classical textbook treatment of the subject assumes that the monopolist wishes to maximise profits and hence chooses a level of output where marginal cost is equal to marginal revenue. Welfare economics teaches us that monopoly is 'bad' and will result in a misallocation of resources in society. Many attempts have been made in the literature to estimate welfare loss to society resulting from monopoly power, which is generally undertaken by estimating welfare loss triangles. See Chapter 5 for empirical work undertaken.

It is easy to show that monopoly will result in a higher price charged and lower output produced than under perfect competition, with the assumption that the cost curves and demand curve remain the same if a perfectly competitive market was suddenly transformed into a monopoly. Figure 3.3 illustrates the point. Since firms operating in a perfectly competitive industry equate price to marginal cost it follows that industry price and output must be given by P_c and Q_c, respectively, on the figure. The monopolist equates marginal cost to marginal revenue and produces Q_m units of output at a price of P_m. Hence with the same marginal cost curve (MC) the demand curve (D) the monopolist would restrict output and raise price if the perfectly competitive industry was duly transformed into a monopoly.

Also we have already noted that perfect competition satisfies a set of necessary conditions for a Pareto optimal allocation of resources in society. Monopoly fails to satisfy such a set of conditions. Indeed the appeal of competition over monopoly is much greater than this since competition is widely regarded as the economic equivalent of political democracy. It is seen as important in preserving democratic ideas by averting dangerous increases in the power of private enterprises and government agencies.

The analysis of monopoly can be extended into discriminating monopoly, where the monopolist sells the same product in two distinct markets, or into bilateral monopoly, where the monopolist sells to a single buyer (a monopsonist).

Neo-classical links with industrial economics

In the field of industrial economics the tools of standard neo-classical microeconomic analysis have been incorporated into the so-called 'structure-conduct-performance' approach first developed by Mason (1939) at Harvard University. The emphasis was placed on first studying market structure to be able to identify more general patterns of behaviour in markets. J. S. Bain is probably the best-known writer of the 'Harvard School' of industrial economics.

Historically, an important division developed between the 'Harvard School' and the 'Chicago School'. The former regards market power, resulting from a few large firms operating in a market, as harmful *per se* to society. It therefore believes that such power should be made illegal. This contrasts with the latter which instead emphasises the efficiency gains to society from large size. However, one thing that

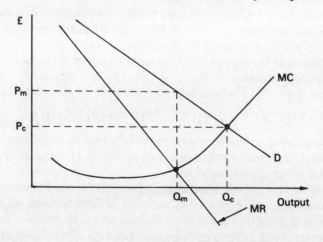

Figure 3.3 Perfectly competitive and monopolistic price and output

they have in common is that both views are derived from the neo-classical theory of perfect competition.

An area of conflict emerged between the Harvard and Chicago schools over public policy matters. The Chicago economists are often sceptical of arguments advanced by the Harvard School for policy interventions in private industry, frequently arguing that elements of conduct and structure offer no real case for government intervention. Divergent views about public policy clearly exist amongst industrial economists.

The Harvard School has recently evolved into the so-called Structuralist School – its modern offspring. It believes that large oligopolistic firms operating in highly concentrated markets can maintain prices well above the competitive level through the use of so-called exclusionary practices, the most important of these being the ability to erect high entry barriers. It was Bain (1956) who subdivided entry barriers into economies of scale, absolute cost advantages accruing to established firms and product differentiation. From a legal viewpoint we might add legal barriers to Bain's list, emanating from patent and design copyright laws. Indeed, the 'structuralists' have more recently added vertical restraints to the list, such as tie-in-sales, exclusive dealing and resale price maintenance. See Chapter 6 for a full account of these, and other anti-competitive practices.

The Chicago economists, on the other hand, do not view highly concentrated market power as necessarily evil. Rather, they stress the benefits of economies of scale and superior efficiency accruing to large firms. Whereas the 'Chicago School' point to competition as a means of achieving the sole objective of allocative efficiency, the Harvard School is also concerned with more liberal ideals such as income distribution and the reduction of concentrated power in the hands of a few large organisations.

'AUSTRIAN' ECONOMICS AND COMPETITION

Increasing attention has been paid recently to the 'Austrian' school of economists, whose interpretation of competition is far less mechanical than that of the neo-classicals.

Few of these economists live within a thousand miles of Vienna, but they take their inspiration from Austrian luminaries such as Carl Menger (1840–1921), Ludwig von Mises (1881–1973), Joseph Schumpeter (1883–1950) and Friedrich Hayek (b.1899). There are of course differences between the ideas of these individuals and their modern adherents, as there are between those of any economists. But their approaches are sufficiently similar – and sufficiently distinct from other groups of economists – to constitute a common tradition.

The elements of this common tradition include (i) a profound commitment to the principle of methodological individualism – the belief that society can only be understood in terms of the motives and attitudes of the (rational) individuals making it up; (ii) a strong emphasis on the inevitable incompleteness of knowledge and information in the real world; (iii) a distrust of collectivism and the implication that governments know better than the private sector and (iv) distaste for quantification, as they believe that there are no numerical constancies in economics.

In this perspective, the neo-classical model of competition is seen as of little relevance to the real world, and sometimes positively misleading in its implications. For instance take the neo-classical notion of equilibrium, which implies full information on the part of buyers and sellers – information about current and future prices, technology, the costs and availability of factors of production. 'Austrians' do not deny that there is a tendency towards such an equilibrium, but they prefer to think of an equilibrating *process*, a movement towards a goal which is forever shifting as new ideas, new discoveries and new information alter tastes, technologies and resource availabilities.

In this process, the individual – as consumer and producer – is paramount. Individuals are not, as the neo-classical approach models them, computer-like beings preprogrammed to maximise utility given constraints of income and prices. Rather they are creative and innovative. They change their minds. They think of new ways of doing things. Often these innovations are quite trivial: one Christmas everybody wants personal stereos; the next they want Filofaxes. Sometimes they are profound: advances in science or medicine. But in neither case are they well modelled by the neo-classical emphasis on static equilibrium where preferences and technologies are taken as given from outside the market.

For 'Austrians' the economy is continually and necessarily in flux. Opportunities and incentives for gain are thrown up all the time by well-functioning markets. As firms and individuals attempt to exploit these opportunities they change market conditions, closing off some options and opening up others. The system *never* settles down. As Schumpeter (1942) put it, competitive capitalist markets are subject to a 'perennial gale of creative destruction' whereby any tendency to equilibrium (and hence stagnation) is continually being defeated by market innovation.

Crucial to this dynamic view of competition is the need for *alertness* to market opportunities. And here the 'Austrians' place great emphasis on the role of the *entrepreneur*. This figure is totally absent from the orthodox neo-classical model of competition, where an ill-defined 'firm' simply chooses that output level which, given a market-determined price, maximises profits (indeed, it is even more peculiar than that, for in equilibrium, properly-defined profits don't exist!) *If* this was the real nature of business decision-making, we could indeed program a computer to simulate the behaviour of the firm. However, 'Austrians' assert, real decision-making is much more creative than this.

The 'Austrian' concept of entrepreneurship was first developed by Ludwig von Mises, but has more recently been elaborated by Israel Kirzner (1973). In Kirzner's view, alertness to new profitable opportunities previously ignored by others is the essence of entrepreneurship. Whereas in the neo-classical model of perfect competition complete information precludes the existence of such opportunities, in the 'Austrian' view the market is full of them.

The purest and simplest case of entrepreneurship is *arbitrage*, where price differentials between different parts of the market are exploited by individuals who buy cheap and sell dear. Financial markets are dominated by this type of activity, but at a lower level this is the objective of street traders and dealers. If old candlesticks can be bought in Brixton for £5 and sold in Portobello Road for £10, alert entrepreneurs can make a profit. What is often insufficiently understood is that *all* entrepreneurship is essentially of this kind, even where goods are produced. Entrepreneurs spot that they can purchase a bundle of inputs – labour, raw materials, capital equipment, etc. – for a particular price in factor markets, and resell them, suitably transformed into output, at a higher price in the market for goods and services. Or, with even more alertness and foresight, they may invent new products where no previous markets existed. They can see a potential for goods which consumers *cannot yet envisage*. (This is an everyday situation in the modern world, where new fads and fancies are offered to us all the time; but it is not adequately treated in neo-classical models with their emphasis on allocation of known resources to satisfy given tastes.)

The driving force behind all this creative activity is the profit motive. For the 'Austrians' profits play the vital role of stimulating alertness and innovation. Whereas neo-classical economists see 'supernormal' profits (i.e. those higher than the opportunity cost of capital, the return it could earn elsewhere) as an essentially functionless surplus, indicative of monopoly power and exploitation of the consumer, 'Austrians' see things very differently. Monopoly in the sense usually discussed in neo-classical economics is not seen as a problem.

Why? Suppose a firm, as a result of entrepreneurial alertness, captures a new market. It makes high profits. But its success will inevitably attract competitors. Orthodox theory tends to deny the likelihood of successful challenge to entrenched firms, stressing the significance of 'barriers to entry' such as the economies of large scale production, possession of patents, brand names, etc. However 'Austrians' argue that this misses the point. If we adopt the ideal held up by neo-classical economists, that of perfect competition, where large numbers of firms sell an *identical* product, then the prospects for new entry may look poor. But, 'Austrians' note, in reality new entrants will not want precisely to repeat the formula of the original firm. They will want to make their product appear new and exciting: to design it, package it and advertise it in such a way that the consumer will prefer it to the existing alternative. Such product differentiation, castigated by many orthodox economists as specious if not exploitative, is seen by 'Austrians' as being what competition is all about. If you see a firm dominating the potato crisp market, you search for new types of savoury snacks to tempt the nibbler, you don't just blindly copy. You make square-shaped crisps, or ones shaped like space monsters, or you give them stranger and stranger flavours. In this way consumer choice is widened.

This way of thinking leads 'Austrian' economists to take a very different view on both theoretical and policy matters from that of the neo-classicals. For instance, there is a long-established literature which attempts to measure the 'social costs' resulting from monopoly. Primarily these result from the 'prediction' (actually a tautology, given the way the terms are used) that a monopoly will produce less and charge a higher price than a perfectly competitive industry facing the same demand and cost conditions. In a celebrated article a leading British 'Austrian', Professor Steven Littlechild (1981), pointed out that this presupposes that the alternatives of perfect competition and monopoly exist, and that governments can control monopolies *without altering anything else*. In reality, without the possibility of temporary monopoly gains to act as an incentive to entrepreneurial alertness, many – perhaps most – products might never exist in the first place, for it would be in nobody's interest to invent them. Knowledge, taken for granted in neo-classical theory, has to be discovered by someone. This is central to 'Austrian' thinking.

What are the practical implications of this? Well, take the question of the regulation of monopolies, something very much in the news these days. A common practice in the past has been to put a limit on the rate of return monopolies can make on their investments. This has arguably had undesirable effects in leading to the choice of inappropriate technologies, and has discouraged firms from seeking diligently for cost-cutting methods. Far better, people like Littlechild argue, to control the rate of increase of charges (as with the regulation of British Telecom) but allow firms to make as high a rate of profit as they can – thus encouraging both greater efficiency by existing firms and new entry from firms attracted by the lure of high potential profits.

More radically, 'Austrian' economists argue against the need to regulate many apparent 'monopolies' at all. With their overriding faith in the virtues of the free market, they argue that very few firms which currently dominate particular markets can hope to do so indefinitely. New ideas and new entrepreneurs are continually threatening the dominance of existing producers. Where powerful monopolies exist for long periods, this will often be associated with protection they have received from the state – nationalised industries being an obvious case in point.

In other areas of industrial economics, too, 'Austrians' take a rather different position from that of neo-classical orthodoxy. In relation to mergers, for example; given that 'Austrians' are sceptical of the costs of monopoly, it follows that they are unworried by the fear that mergers will create monopolies. They therefore see no point in the current UK policy which gives the Monopolies and Mergers Commission powers to review the acceptability of potential mergers. Or take the question of patents, where they argue that patent law, by protecting the profits of innovators, increases the incentives for discovery and development, despite the costs in terms of higher prices to the consumer (a good example is the pharmaceuticals industry). Or advertising, where the common distinction between informative (good) and persuasive (bad) adverts is held to be meaningless. People don't just *know* things, in the 'Austrian' view – they have to be motivated to discover them. As with producers, so with consumers. You have to make it worthwhile for people to acquire the knowledge that your product exists, even if advertisers have to do this by associating it with apparently irrelevant images of wealth, power and beauty.

It's clear, then, that the 'Austrian' perspective on competition is a very different one from that of neo-classical economics. It points us to a number of features of real-world competition which other approaches don't stress, and its revival and development in the last decade or so has provoked a great deal of rethinking. However, it depends for its strong policy recommendations on an equally strong belief in the virtues of the market and faith in the drive and alertness of entrepreneurs. And when we say faith, we mean faith. 'Austrian' economists have always been reluctant to use quantitative empirical evidence to test their hypotheses, arguing that because individuals are unique and ever-changing there are no measurable regularities in economic behaviour. While this may be a defensible position, it leaves us with no way of testing propositions about the inevitability of competition and the temporary and precarious nature of supernormal profits. Those less ideologically committed to the virtues of the capitalist market economy may be forgiven a little scepticism about these ideas.

NEW THEORETICAL DEVELOPMENTS IN INDUSTRIAL ECONOMICS AND COMPETITION

Baumol *et al.* (1982), writing on the theory of perfectly contestable markets, have attempted to show that high market concentration and the absence of entry may actually be a real sign of virtue and not of vice. They argue that under certain specified market conditions it is actually possible for a monopolist or group of oligopolists to behave in a perfectly competitive manner.

This seemingly amazing phenomenon is explained via the concept of a perfectly contestable market situation. This occurs when there are conditions of free entry and exit in the market and the monopolist faces the real possibility of 'hit and run' entry. In other words, the monopolist faces the risk of a potential entrant entering the market and making a quick return on its investment before leaving. The only way this can be prevented from happening is if the monopolist behaves in a perfectly competitive manner and prices at marginal cost. Only normal profits will then be earned and no incentive for entry will exist.

All of this only makes sense if there exists complete ease of entry and exit for potential rivals, which seems highly unlikely under conditions of monopoly or oligopoly. Presumably there will be certain sunk costs involved in entering a market. The potential entrant must undercut the established firm's price for long enough to more than recover any sunk costs. Hence reaction speed must be slow and sunk costs must be low if the entrant is ever going to believe that a return on its investment is feasible. Furthermore the entrant must be capable of setting up production very quickly to engage in such 'hit and run' behaviour.

This seems most unlikely to occur in the real world. Such assumptions are also completely contrary to the popular ideas of game theory and strategic models where firms are constantly reacting to any change undertaken by a rival. In this sense, it might be more realistic to view the theory of perfectly contestable markets as counter-revolutionary rather than revolutionary. The chances of finding virtuous monopolists or oligopolists seems highly remote.

Recent privatisations in the UK certainly do not appear to have occurred in sectors even remotely resembling those of perfectly contestable markets. The Conservatives would be hard pushed to claim that their new private sector monopolies are behaving virtuously. Only certain service industries, such as fast foods or hairdressing, would appear close to matching the type of markets required for perfect contestability to prevail. But such markets are not highly concentrated. Hence it would appear that in the real world monopolists and oligopolists are unlikely to behave as virtuously as Baumol would have us believe.

In the neo-classical world the firm is simply viewed as a 'black box' operating in such a way as to equate marginal cost and marginal revenue to maximise profits. There is no underlying discussion or consideration of the characters and process involved in decision making. Recent theoretical work has attempted to remedy this omission. This is the basis of the principal-agent model developed by such writers as Spence and Zeckhauser (1971), Ross (1973), Jensen and Meckling (1976) and Arrow (1984).

Uncertainty is a key element in the principal-agent model which immediately sets it apart from the neo-classical world of perfect information. In particular it focuses on asymmetric information which recognises the fact that different individuals and groups within the organisation have access to different types of information. Managers can be regarded as agents of shareholders in large organisations. Shareholders are viewed as having limited information on the actions of managers who therefore have certain scope to pursue their own self-interests without the knowledge of the shareholders or principals. The possibility of such opportunistic behaviour by management highlights the possible cost of divorce of ownership from control to shareholders.

The principal-agent approach goes on to consider issues such as bonuses for managers based on performance and stock options to make managers share in the risks of the firm. It can also be applied to groups working at lower levels of the organisational pyramid. For example, the relationships between different levels of management and between management and the shop-floor workers can be analysed using the principal-agent approach. Clearly this is an exciting and long overdue area of development. For a fuller account of this see Strong and Waterson (1987) and Auerbach (1988).

Industrial economics has probably been handicapped by historically placing great reliance on standard neo-classical microeconomic theory. Gradually this is changing with more research into risk and uncertainty and relationships between different groups within an organisation.

LEGAL MODELS OF COMPETITION

Free competition in the sense only of the inalienable right to ply one's trade has its roots deeply set in the Old Testament and the proscription against repossession of a debtor's clothes or tools. Since the time of the Black Death, judges have refused to enforce a contract that unreasonably restrains a person from exercising his trade. (The courts reinforced that ethos in a number of cases during the 1970s, e.g. Schroeder v. Macawley 1974, and Ex Parte Island Records, 1978.) Because the courts would not enforce such agreements, methods of enforcement were devised that were not dependent on the courts: traders not abiding by the 'rules' might, for instance, be deprived of their supplies through a collective boycott. Hence, according to Valentine Korah (1982, pp. 5–6), the conspiracy laws were developed to permit traders to take legal action where they could show that they had been injured by several persons acting in concert. However, in Mogul S. S. v. McGregor Gow (1892), recovery was permitted only for acts intended to cause harm, rather than those deemed merely to be protecting 'legitimate trade interests' (Merkin and Williams, 1984, p. 10).

In this quasi-religious model, competition law does not have its roots in any specifically economic or sociological orthodoxy, but in a more ancient system of ethics and morality. The model accepts the right of free men to ply their trade without hindrance from other traders, the right of consumers to express their preferences without being 'held to ransom' by artificial restraints on trade, and the right of society to demand an optimum allocation of scarce resources. That is, the model perceives any form of vertical restraint, monopolistic competition, refusal to supply or horizontal collusion, as restraint of trade and contrary to the laws of morality.

It is important at this point to note a distinction which exists between individual rights to practise a trade – subject to the law and economics – and laws providing for the regulation of social and business behaviour.

The sociologists Emile Durkheim (1858–1917) and Max Weber (1864–1920) suggested that different kinds of society correlate with different kinds of law. Durkheim distinguished primitive from modern societies: primitive society had repressive laws which prescribed sanctions for violations of the collective conscience; modern society had restitutive law which provided for the restitution of the balance between society's components through civil remedy.

Weber provided more complex typologies and society/law correlations. He spoke of the social bond not in terms of solidarity but in terms of legitimate domination. In different historical settings, Weber found, people had accepted the right of others to control their lives for one of three reasons: the charismatic qualities of a leader, the traditional sanctity of an office, or the fact that imperative power was clothed with legal rationality. The rationalism of the bureaucrat and the expert made life more predictable and secure for the capitalist entrepreneur.

The legal paradigm presented by Friedrich Hayek (cited in Harris, 1980) distinguishes two types of social order and elucidates rules of just conduct – abstract, negative rules, restraining individuals from invading the free domain of others. Hayek sees a deplorable tendency for 'made social orders' and corresponding 'rules for the organisation of government' to replace the rules of just conduct, arising from the legal positivist heresy that all law is made law. Within the Hayekian paradigm, the likely outcome of such heresy is totalitarianism, and must apply equally to economic activity as well as to that of the individual.

Where Hayek offers two types of law, Unger (cited in Harris, 1980) offers three. This he does to account for a cultural phenomenon which he believes and which Hayek denies: an ineradicable sense of unjustified hierarchy, of illegitimate personal domination, as a pervasive attribute of the psychology of modern man. According to Unger, the legal order in the West arose because of the conjunction of two necessary conditions: political compromise between three interest groups – the nobles, the merchants and the princes and their bureaucratic staffs; and the belief in a higher law which made the articulation of the compromise take the form of the rule of law. Unger asserts that the legal order did not and could not produce a sense of legitimate domination because the reality of subjection by dominant groups forces itself on people's consciousness.

Whereas Hayek sees lawyer's law as the continuation of customary law, both being concerned with rules of just conduct, Unger regards feelings of unjustified hierarchy is the inevitable sequel to the loss of unreflective legitimacy which is characteristic of customary law. Law is not properly customary law if people have critical feelings about it. Under such circumstances it has little or no legitimacy and is open to continual challenge.

The conflict between Hayek and Unger is more apparent than real. In the last part of the twentieth-century, capitalists (merchants) proclaim themselves to be subjugated to the domination of organisational law. Feelings of unjustified hierarchy are acknowledged at all levels and indeed are, to a substantial extent, actively encouraged by the ruling hierarchy.

A most important point to note here is the peculiarity of the Anglo-Saxon legal system which relies not simply on statute or general principles, but upon individual decisions. Whilst it is legal precedent which has most force in forming the common law in Canada, the USA, UK, Australia and a number of other countries, it ought not be forgotten that the House of Lords, Supreme Court *et al.*, have the power to overturn decisions in the lower courts. To a great extent, therefore, it is lawyers and judges who determine what the laws shall be. In Sylvania 1977, the US Supreme Court 'seemed to go out of its way' to overrule one of its own earlier decisions, in order to reflect perceived change in economic thinking towards anti-trust (Posner, 1977, p. 2). In the House of Lords in 1981 (Lonrho v. Shell and British Petroleum) Lord Diplock took issue with an earlier decision by Lord Denning and declared himself 'unable to accept that this is the law'. But more worrying perhaps, is the court's ability to create new torts, or rediscover those which were thought to have fallen into disuse – the

1985 UK miners' strike saw the resurrection of an eighteenth-century tort successfully to challenge the legitimate rights of workers to take industrial action against their employers. And in determining cases involving intellectual property rights, the courts have given or taken away monopoly rights, depending upon their understanding of the mood within the country at the time. In Warnink v. Townsend, Lord Diplock stated this principle clearly:

> Where over a period of years there can be discerned a steady trend in legislation which reflects the view of successive parliaments as to what the public interest demands in a particular field of law, development of the common law in that part of the same field which has been left to it ought to proceed upon a parallel rather than a diverging course.

and at a later point in his judgement held:

> . . . the familiar argument that to extend the ambit of an actionable wrong beyond that to which effect has demonstrably been given in the previous cases would open the floodgates, or more ominously, a Pandora's box of litigation leaves me unmoved . . .

Challenging the legitimacy of anti-trust law in the United States, Richard Posner (Posner, 1976, p. 4) acknowledges the role of the law lords and perceives twentieth-century anti-trust legislation as a development of judicial interpretation. He asserts that the rules of law as they are articulated and as they are applied to alter behaviour are often two quite different things. The rules in practice, as distinct from the theory, are critically affected by sanctions, by procedures and by the policies and incentives of enforcers. Thus he finds the situation in anti-trust law fluid, uncertain and frequently in conflict with the legal theory.

> Economic theory provides a firm basis for the belief that monopoly pricing . . . is inefficient. Since efficiency is an important, although not the only, social value, this conclusion establishes a prima facie case for having an anti-trust policy. It also implies the limitations of that policy: to the extent that efficiency is the goal of anti-trust enforcement there is no justification for carrying enforcement into areas where competition is less efficient than monopoly because the costs of monopoly pricing are outweighed by the economies of centralising production in one or a very few firms. Nor is there justification for using the anti-trust laws to attain goals unrelated or

antithetical to efficiency, such as promoting a society of small tradespeople.

While it does not necessarily follow that the importance of efficiency as a social goal requires that it be the only goal of anti-trust law, Posner argues that it should be because:

the only competing goal suggested with any frequency or conviction – the protection of small businesses – whatever its intrinsic merit cannot be attained within the framework of anti-trust principles and procedures.

Cotterrell's discussion of the relationship between law and power (Cotterell, 1984, p. 132) – to which Posner's analysis alludes – suggests the need to reformulate the long debated question of how far law can effectively control corporate power. What is important is to analyse the kinds and sources of power acting upon and through law. In so far as large business corporations dominate Western economies, the state depends upon their welfare in a basic sense. As Ehrlich put it:

the state cannot destroy the economic conditions of its own existence. The state is conditioned upon the production of economic goods within society in sufficient quantities to supply it with nourishment to furnish the resources to finance state activity (cited in Cotterrell, 1984).

Thus in the late 1980s we arrive at a situation where the dialectic counterposing increased degrees of regulation with administrative pronouncements on the necessity to relieve entrepreneurs from the constraints arising from all forms of market intervention becomes understandable.

On the one hand, the Weberian paradigm explains the entrepreneur's acceptance of increased regulation: charismatic leaders within Japan, the US and UK, together with the need for security during a period of worldwide recession, have encouraged an acknowledgement of the need for constraints upon corporate activity and muffled demands for increased trade liberalisation. (The continued existence of the General Agreement on Tariffs and Trades, and numerous other trade agreements – not least the Rome Treaty itself – is testimony to the corporate *qua* national desire for security and stability but not necessarily free trade.)

On the other hand, Hayek, Unger and the 'Chicago School' have provided administrators within the UK and USA with a philosophical imperative encompassed within the notion that the only barriers to new companies effecting market entry (competition and economic efficiency) are those created by government regulation. Allow free markets to function without interference and they will function in the most efficient *qua* competitive manner possible.

The legal profession's pronouncements on US, UK and EEC competition policy underlines the existence of conflicting legal/economic philosophies which have created an atmosphere of inconsistency and confusion. In the UK, the four various forms of control covered by three statutes (described in Chapter 5) have led to the creation of a 'haphazard' system whose antecedents rest amongst the debris of the post-war Labour government's desire to nationalise major industries and cure unemployment. In the United States, the present attempt to free vertical restraints from anti-trust legislation and apply the 'rule of reason' test, arises from an acknowledgement that the post-war necessity to guard against monopolies, and emasculate industry to appease the farmers, no longer exists. Equally, however, nowhere is the extreme Chicago view more prevalent than within the United States.

While many would date the current UK legal framework with its attendant necessity for English lawyers to consider the economic ramifications of legal judgements from 1948, it is more realistic to suggest that it dates from more recent times: UK membership of the EEC. Before 1972, the impact of US, European and Japanese direct investment on the UK had been minimal (certainly by comparison with the late 1970s–80s) and UK direct investment had centred on expansion within the Commonwealth. Exposure to European unfair competition laws and the notion of anti-competitive conduct came with the UK's membership of the EEC.

It was thus inevitable that the economic framework taken up and favoured by lawyers suddenly forced to consider the economic ramifications of their work within the context of EEC competition laws would be those theories fashionable amongst economists in the early 1970s: accessible, readily digestible, Chicago School *laissez-faire* monetarism – theory which had an immediate appeal to the traditional conservatism of the legal profession.

As a consequence there has developed a substantial body of eminent legal opinion which seeks to suggest that many of the cases decided by the European Commission, Restrictive Trade Practices Court, Office of Fair Trading and Monopolies and Mergers Commission, are misguided either because they are 'inconsistent with allocative efficiency' as lawyers understand that term, or, because the case-by-case approach leads to apparently contradictory decisions and no precedent.

Most often cited criticism of the European Commission, is its determination of markets. For example, in AEG Telefunken, the Commission found 5 per cent of the relevant market sufficient to warrant investigation and a subsequent finding that the company's selective distribution system infringed Article 85(1). In Michelin, the Commission found that new replacement tyres for lorries and buses was a valid single-product market. In United Brands, the Commission held that the market for bananas was a separate product market within the market for fruit. In its investigation of the Ford Motor Company (unpublished), it found that in the market for Ford car spare parts, Ford held a dominant position.

Equally, the Commission's effective prohibition of vertical agreements causes lawyers (who most frequently defend the company accused of infringement), to denounce the 'free rider' who circumvents companies' attempts to isolate markets and undercuts the distributor with whom an exclusive distribution agreement exists. Thus they criticise the AEG Telefunken decision, Consten and Grundig, Distillers and many more. While only few legal practices specialise in competition law and even fewer employ economists, cases such as E.C.S./AKZO will continue to baffle lawyers who accept the Chicago view of predatory pricing as fictitious (see Chapter 6).

The view most often propagated within the profession requires that the observer should: 'never accuse a monopolist of bad practice. Dominant firms must be allowed to compete on their merits'. It emanates from the inevitable truth that the majority of lawyers specialising in competition or its concomitant, intellectual property law, gain their experience acting on behalf of large companies. Only large companies can afford to employ either teams of in-house lawyers or seek advice from highly paid specialist counsel. Thus the sentiment arises from lawyers identifying with their clients. In doing so, they at once claim that excessive government intervention increases barriers to entry and that insufficient government regulation fails to protect their clients' legitimate interests.

Lawyers untrained in anything more than rudimentary economics are understandably unable to reconcile defence of intellectual property rights with their defence of the free market. The dichotomy exemplifies the late twentieth-century role of law as the defender of those contemporary groups who previously took the form of nobles, merchants, princes and their bureaucratic staffs. Lawyers have accepted the position as agents of the ruling hierarchy. As a consequence they require legal precedent to guide them and provide simple, ready-made answers to highly complex, political and economic issues. It is this necessity to find accord with the mono-dimensional views of the client group, which determines the legal form which competition is permitted to take, and the nature and role of competition law within developed Western economies.

> The law, as many lawyers view it, is little more than a series of rules which must be taken into account when advising clients as to the extent of their rights, duties and liberties, but the law, as enacted by Parliament, is an organism of the greatest complexity. The desirability of monopolies and the degree of control which may be exercised over them is a subject which falls within the specialist knowledge of the economist; the likely effect of market incentives and stimuli is properly the subject of the industrial psychologist; the ideological acceptability of rules which promote private privilege falls to be gauged by the political scientist; the likely shop-floor consequences are noted by the industrial sociologist . . . By the time a measure such as a Patents Act has obtained the Queen's signature, it is likely that every one of these disciplines will have registered its opinion as to the appropriateness (or otherwise) of the measure, and the end product will represent a compromise between their frequently conflicting demands. It is the lawyer who is the author of this compromise. He is, at the last resort, little other than a hired hand, and it is only through the exercise of his unique skills that economic, social and industrial policy, not to mention morality, are metamorphosed into law (Phillips, 1986, p. 89).

POLITICAL MODELS

There is a particular significance in moving directly from legal to political models of competition. Not least because, certainly within the UK, US and EEC, the political process is dominated by the legal profession. Members of the professional classes in general dominate Congress, the Senate, the European Parliament and Westminster, but it is the legal profession which has particular dominance through its numbers and the deferential approach to law taken by members of the professional classes.

Where you have elected authorities, citizens with financial assets and the ability to maintain their links with their previous employment – in case of future election failure – must almost inevitably be those most likely to accept nomination. The legal profession meets both requirements. Unfortunately for the democratic process, in the many years of study undertaken before a lawyer qualifies, there is little or no time spent learning political science, sociology, philosophy or economics. What law students do learn is respect for private property, respect for individual rights and respect for the law (the importance of maintaining the *status quo*). The form and content of commercial relations are important only in so far as they accord with commercial and contract law; and any suggested change in the structure of society and market operations can be considered only within a strict legal framework.

Within this paradigm it is axiomatic that traditional Conservative politicians at least – either lawyers themselves or professionals from equivalent wealthy groups – will constantly encounter political contradictions which rarely, if ever, will they perceive as such. In general they regard their political activity as exercising their power in favour of individual need and general improvements in social welfare, resulting from policies theoretically aimed at stimulating economic growth.

Until the rise of the 'new pragmatism' in 1986 (which occurred at the same time as suggestions of an early general election), Margaret Thatcher hailed Hayek as her philosophical mentor and attributed to him the view that government intervention of any kind in the marketplace is unhelpful. Her administration has advocated the 'hard discipline of the market' as the best route to the achievement of increasing levels of economic growth. Or as suggested by Sarah Benton:

> The 'new' right had in essence one message and part of its success lies in the simplicity of that message. Drawing on the works of Friedrich Hayek and Austrian and American economists such as Ludwig von Mises and Milton Friedman, it is this: there are immutable laws of the market which no society can thwart and survive; obedience to the laws of the market is the best guarantee of our freedom precisely because the laws are natural and immutable and human intervention, through the state, monopolies or trade unions creates economic disaster – and the need for more state intervention. State intervention is itself a denial of freedom.
>
> To move towards this utopia, this absolute rule of the market, it is essential to reduce, if not eliminate, the powers of the state and of trade unions; they must be ousted first in the economic sphere but also in the welfare and social spheres because there they can thwart market laws . . . by holding back the vigorous though spurious notions of equality and social justice . . . It is on the vigour of the

few that the wealth of the nation depends . . . the gutless, the moaning minnies, the spongers – have no place in that nation (Benton, 1987, p. 20).

Yet, according to Roger Scruton, the Conservative Party has moved away from the view that economic affairs are self-regulating, towards that of the posture of state as all-important. Without the state's surveillance, he avers, destitution and unemployment could result at any time. 'The triumph of Conservatism . . . [is] due in part to its economic sense, to its recognition that, after all, the free movements of labour, and the concentration of capital, are matters for discipline, and that the "crises" to which they are subject are by no means accidental, but a chronic liability of industrial power' (Scruton, 1980, p. 113).

Despite the substantial contribution to Conservative thinking made by Scruton and other self-styled philosophers of the new right, if Scruton is here referring to the need for competition policy, it is questionable as to whether he can genuinely be said to be representing the philosophy of the Conservative Party in government. Certainly his views are not wholly comparable with those represented by the Institute of Directors – whose 'business leaders manifesto' pressed the aim of 'rolling back the encroachment of the state on the country's commercial and industrial life'. In 1983, Mrs Thatcher claimed that the aims of the Institute were the aims of the government. Within that statement there is a strong negation of a need for anti-trust enforcement.

From policy statements made by the UK Conservative government during its 1979–87 administration, Conservative thought on the question of anti-trust appears contradictory. On the one hand, it appears to regard competition as defender of the small businessman and the consumer, and as a prerequisite for the efficient allocation of scarce resources. The Business Start-Up and Business Expansion Schemes, introduced by the Finance Act, 1983, enabled individuals to obtain substantial tax relief when investing in new or small, expanding businesses. The New Enterprise Allowance, introduced some two years later, was aimed at encouraging individuals to don the role of entrepreneur. Thus government policy appeared geared to the promotion and indeed protection of small businesses.

Yet at the same time, policy statements encouraged observers to believe that the government perceived anti-trust regulation as: encouraging waste through unnecessary litigation, a constraint upon the benefits available through the free play of market forces, and responsible for placing the needs of the inefficient above those of the efficient in the interests of some misplaced notion of 'fairness'. Indeed, during this period, a Conservative minister for Trade and Industry declared that mergers should only be investigated on competition grounds – that consideration of factors such as employment, regional development and the public interest, were inadmissible. An example of that approach is exemplified by the BTR bid for Pilkington, January 1987 (*Financial Times*), which whilst representing the potential take-over of a large independent firm by a major conglomerate, was not referred to the Monopolies and Mergers Commission on the grounds that it offered no potential detriment to completion.

A possible conclusion to be drawn from such contradictory evidence is that Conservative economic philosophy precludes intervention, particularly in the area of anti-trust. Statements supporting small businesses arise from the exigencies of the electoral system and are essentially a cynical response to calls for help from the small shop-keeper and the middle-classes whose less intelligent sons and daughters fear they might become unemployed. If Arthur Seldon is to be believed, such cynical interventions will not be required for long, for representative democracy is to be replaced by subservience to the free market:

> However suitable it may have been until the inter-war years, representative democracy is no longer equipped to interpret, represent and respond to public wishes, public opinion or public preferences. The British – social democrats, liberal democrats or Christian democrats – will have to accept that the Age of Representative Democracy is over (Seldon, 1986, quoted in Benton, 1987, p. 19).

Billed as a philosophy which supports the rights of the individual, traditional Conservatism must involve the pursuit of contradictory goals. Protecting the right of big business to be big and small business to be small, requires careful intellectual juggling. Such problems as beset governments before 1980 were problems arising from an absence of any political philosophy other than that frequently gained through attendance at selective (often fee-paying) schools and universities – the metaphorical playing fields of Eton.

Legislators of the new right today are epitomised by their less clear descendance from the old aristocratic order, a 'new brutalism' and a crusading zeal against socialism. Together these characteristics represent a substantial concurrence with the politics and economics of America and represent a rising emphasis upon the right of the private individual to increasing levels of personal gain. The emphasis upon the rights of the individual simultaneously requires the propagation of the denial of any necessity for the state to involve itself in reducing levels of social deprivation. If we regard reductions in social welfare as a 'bad' which competition is designed to correct, then there are parallels with the notion of seeking to reduce poverty. If such a parallel is appropriate, anti-trust becomes part of the 'nannying' with which the Conservative state should not involve itself.

In the immediate post-war period until the 1970s, it may have been reasonable to ask whether the interests of politicians on the left differed very much from those on the right. Certainly, as expressed by Roy Hattersley, Stuart Holland and others during the last Labour administration, the left perceived competition within the economy as an aspect which needed to be envigorated and strengthened. In this they superficially agreed with the right. However, for the left, the aim of such envigorated competition was to attack the perceived increasing trend toward over-concentration, monopoly and the unfettered power of the multinationals. This, they considered, had created a *mezo-economic* system between that of the micro and macro economies and created 'a new domination over the mode of production, distribution and exchange in the heartland of the British economy' (Holland, 1975).

Thus politicians on the left (as represented by mainstream Labour party thinking) understood, and indeed continue to this day to understand, competition within a Keynesian framework: markets composed of many small firms, with low capital costs and easy entry to new markets such that prices are kept down and consumer choice is sovereign. More importantly however:

. . . socialism is not only a narrowly pragmatic political enterprise, it is also based on certain fundamental principles about how society should be organised and how people are to be treated in it. Socialists favour co-operation and mutual assistance over competition, the greatest measure of equality of condition attainable between individuals, economic autonomy rather than the subordination to management or owner of the worker, the highest amount of democratic self-government and freedom of expression attainable. These principles rather than any specific institutional arrangements – like central planning or state welfare – are what is at the heart of the socialist enterprise (Hirst, 1987, p. 8).

Others on the left express the same sentiment somewhat more trenchantly:

Rampant capitalism is unattractive because it exploits labour through its monopoly of employment and because it exploits consumers through monopolising goods markets. Traditional socialism expropriates capital and subordinates the interests of consumers to the interests of the workers. Liberalism puts peoples' livelihoods and their savings at the mercy of consumer taste and fashion.

What is needed is a model of society where power is more evenly distributed between these groups: where the interests of owners of capital, of workers and of consumers are all taken into account with none taking automatic priority (Legrand, 1987, p. 16).

However, a major difficulty for the more extreme left is the problem of competition *per se*. In terms of education and personal development, competition is a bad thing. People should not be encouraged to 'beat' their contemporaries, 'winning' is an anti-social activity, and indeed in some Labour-controlled London schools, non-competitive sports are the only type regarded as acceptable. Yet British management is constantly berated for its inability to 'beat' its foreign rivals and protect British workers, and the current Conservative administration is blamed for having made UK industry less competitive. Thus while claiming to hate competition, the left requires more of it so that small companies can beat off big ones.

Were the Labour Party 'Marxist' as the Conservatives claim it to be, it would be immune to such arguments. In theory, the rising trend towards the increasing concentration of capital in fewer and fewer hands via the growth of giant transnational corporations, presages the 'inevitable' crisis of capitalism and the eventual overthrow of the capitalist system. Marxists could be expected to welcome such a result rather than subject such conduct to increasing levels of regulation.

But the British Labour Party makes no pretence at a Marxist analysis of competition. The central plank of its current industrial policy requires an increased role for the competition authorities; a requirement that predator companies in take-over battles show improvements in competition resulting from any proposed merger; and increased supervision of financial markets – but that is with a view to reducing the possibility of fraud and insider dealing, rather than specifically seeking to increase competition.

If a Labour government were to replace the current Conservative administration at the next election, current policy proposals suggest a restoration of the role of those government departments responsible for protecting and sponsoring free enterprise with a concomitant restoration of culture, conservation and competition to the policital agenda.

Perhaps of greater significance than these various pronouncements is the failure of each of the political parties to address themselves to a clear, direct analysis of the purpose of competition policy. The notion of allocative efficiency suggests that efficiency is an empirically verifiable sum. Yet in reality decisions about optimal allocations of resources are value laden and thus political. The left are expected to seek to increase competition in the interests of a more equitable distribution of income and power over resources; the right to seek that allocation of resources which will achieve optimal levels of economic growth. Social Democrats within Europe and Democrats within the US, seek to achieve some compromise between both extremes.

Yet the constraints arising from the necessity of ensuring continued election victory, which depends heavily upon donations from business, labour organisations and the party faithful (i.e. one's peers), has created a political model of anti-trust which is unworkable. Whether left, right or centre, politicians must simultaneously combine four contradictory goals if they are to guarantee their ability to form the next government and thus introduce the policies contained within their manifestos. They must:

1 Seek to protect major domestic industries from cheap imports or face the wrath of major party fund donors, and labour organisations whose workers will become unemployed as a result of any contraction in demand for domestically produced goods. (The Multi-Fibre Agreement is an international example of such protection.)

2 Seek to protect small and medium-sized business from predation by the majors, for in rural and provincial areas such businesses provide an important social function as well as local employment.

3 Sponsor and encourage domestic industries in the interests of economic growth. This may occasionally require politicians and bureaucrats to turn a blind eye to anti-competitive activities by companies considered to be major national income earners. (In the UK, the problem is exacerbated where monopsonistic public purchasing agencies are also the government departments responsible for sponsoring those industries with whom they are required to negotiate.)

4 Attack industries within small markets to encourage the notion that the defence of the consumer is the primary goal of anti-trust. (See for example, the Competition Act investigations of Brighton Taxis; and The British Airports Authority Arrange-

ments for the Provision of Chauffeur-Driven Hire Car Services
at Gatwick Airport.)

In seeking to reconcile such irreconcilable targets, it is inevitable that
only rarely are major transnational corporations investigated under
domestic anti-trust laws. This is not because the bureaucrats are blind
to abuse of the law or incapable of judging the economic impact of
such abuse, but because their political masters seek substantial
evidence, most commonly of the type presented in a trial brief, before
they will formally permit an investigation to be launched.

And this essentially arises because nine out of ten politicians never
actually think about competition. It is a form of intellectual baggage
they find themselves gratefully able to leave behind on any journey
into the political hinterland. Only on those very rare occasions when
they are required to apply naive views to constituency problems, will
they form any response and such response will depend upon the
formulation of a knee-jerk reaction to calls to protect the interests of
their constituents. Thus the political model of competition cannot be
sustained because it is a chimera – an irrelevance to the voters who are
of greatest relevance to the politicians.

It is hardly surprising under these circumstances that the Big Bang
of 1986 which opened the UK's capital markets to close inspection and
permitted information sharing between the US Securities and
Exchange Commission and the UK Stock Exchange, rocked the City
with insider dealing scandals. In the absence of clear policy, there is no
block to individual actors taking advantage of the opportunities for
personal gain.

On these grounds at least, it would seem that the time has come for
politicians on both sides of the Atlantic and across Europe, to
politicise and prioritise the goals of anti-trust. Industrial and commercial activity mirrors the ruthlessness and mud-slinging of American football, rather than the courteousness and civility of English
cricket. Until politicians grasp the relevance of anti-trust to any
proposals aimed at improving national economic growth, the rhetoric
of liberty and freedom will continue to permit the free market
mechanism to subject outsiders to the detrimental impact of inevitable
market failure.

4 Competition in Business Strategy

THE STRUCTURE OF MARKETS IN WHICH BUSINESS STRATEGY IS FORMULATED

Empirical evidence on the structure of industry in Western industrial economies points to the growing importance of the large firm, especially in manufacturing industries. The size distribution of firms is highly skewed and power has become increasingly placed in the hands of a few large firms during the post-Second World War era. The concentration of power has become the major phenomenon of the development of the business environment.

The previous chapters have outlined various approaches to competition. In this chapter we are going to examine the links between competition and business strategy. An important distinction between competition and the objectives of businessmen was made by Stigler (1968, p. 5): 'In economic life competition is not a goal: it is a means of organising economic activity to achieve a goal. The economic role of competition is to discipline the various participants in economic life to provide their goods and services skilfully and cheaply.'

Galbraith (1969) pointed out to us that the small, competitive firm was no longer at the heart of the modern industrial economy. Instead it had been replaced by the giant corporation, a dominant feature of his 'new industrial state', which was seen to be technically progressive and massively capitalised.

Baran and Sweezy (1967) looking at the rise of the giant corporation from a Marxist viewpoint, characterised the stage of capitalism in the mid-1960s as that of monopoly capitalism. A distinction is made between two stages of capitalist development. The earlier stage of competitive capitalism began to change towards the formation of monopolies at the end of the nineteenth century. This process continued throughout the twentieth century, resulting in the replacement of competitive by monopoly capitalism.

A distinction can be made between unstructured and structured competition. Unstructured competition is akin to perfect competition in neo-classical economics, where the firms have no or little choice. In essence, they must obey the law of the market or exit from the market. Only one basic form of behaviour is compatible with survival in the market. Efficiency is a necessary condition for survival. On the other hand, structured competition is found in the vast majority of markets where a strictly limited number of firms are able to determine the extent and form of competition, thus being able to exercise a substantial measure of choice over how they behave. Business strategy is, therefore, generally formulated under conditions of structured competition where a few firms exercise considerable power in the market.

Economists generally analyse changes in the number, size, and distribution of firms within an industry over time to see how the underlying structure of the industry is changing. Measures of concentration are used for this purpose and concentration ratios are the most frequently used of these measures. They inform us of the percentage of industry output produced (or employment generated) by a certain number (generally four, five or eight) of the largest firms in that industry. It should be noted, however, that concentration is not a perfect indicator of monopoly power in an industry. For a useful discussion of this see, for example, Evely and Little (1960, pp. 41–9).

What changes have been occurring in the structure of UK industries during the twentieth century? The Galbraith view of the 'new industrial state' would suggest a rise in concentration over time as the giant corporation has grown in power and importance. This is exactly what empirical evidence reveals, at least until the early 1970s. For example, Aaronavitch and Sawyer (1975, p. 117) show that for aggregate concentration the share of the largest 100 firms in all UK output rose from 16 per cent in 1909, to 24 per cent in 1935, to 32.3 per cent in 1958, to 42 per cent in 1968 and 46 per cent (estimated figure) in 1970. Similar results were found for relative concentration (sectors/industries within the UK economy) and also similar results were found in most Western countries. Locksley and Ward (1979, p. 96) produced comparable figures for the EEC: 'Whereas the largest 50 companies controlled 15% of manufacturing output in the EEC in 1965, this had increased to 20% by 1970 and to almost 25% by 1976.'

However, the 1970s and early 1980s have not witnessed the sharp increases in aggregate concentration discovered in the earlier post-war period. Hughes and Kumar (1984) concluded that during the early

1970s aggregate concentration across the whole economy increased, but then started to decline in the latter half of the decade. Obtaining comparable data for the 1980s is difficult due to a definitional change in the Standard Industrial Classification (SIC). The results that are available show a fairly stable pattern up to 1984.

The Department of Trade and Industry (DTI) (1988, Annex D) produced figures for the percentage share of the largest 100 private sector enterprises in manufacturing net output between 1970–84 in the UK, as follows:

Year	1970	1972	1974	1976	1978	1980	1982	1984
CR100	39.3	41.0	42.1	41.8	41.1	40.5	41.1	38.7

Although these figures show relative stability over the 14-year period covered up to 1984, it is not possible to see the effects of the recent merger boom on industrial concentration.

Aaronavitch and Sawyer (1975) attribute their observed rise in industrial concentration in large part to a pro-merger policy pursued by UK governments. This view has not gone unchallenged. For instance, Walshe (1975) found that mergers had promoted high concentration in only one-third of the cases investigated. (See Chapter 5 for a fuller account of UK merger policy.) Also, in spite of the rapid rise in concentration levels in the 1950s and 1960s, we have seen that evidence points to a slowdown in the rate of increase in the UK particularly after 1974. Sawyer (1979) associates this change with a slower growth rate and reduction in merger activity.

Having noted the apparent rise in relative and aggregate concentration in the UK during the 1950s and 1960s in particular, let us consider inter-industry differences in concentration, or differential concentration. DTI (1988, Annex D) produced the table (Figure 4.1) showing the gross output-weighted mean CR5 (Gross Output) for a sample of 199 industries by UK manufacturing sector for each of the years 1979, 1981 and 1984 and also the change that occurred over this period.

The gross output-weighted mean CR5 for this entire sample of 199 comparable industries changed from 54.2 per cent in 1979, to 54.9 per cent in 1981 and to 52.6 per cent in 1984. Hence the largest five firms in an industry covered within this sample produced on average more than half of gross output. Even though there was a slight reduction in this figure, namely 1.6 per cent, over the period 1979–84, it still suggests a highly concentrated oligopolistic market structure in UK manufacturing. Also note the important point made earlier that these figures do not show the effects of the recent mergers boom.

Figure 4.1: Industry concentration by UK manufacturing sector. Constant (1979) weighted mean % CR5 (Gross Output)

Description of Sector SIC Class (2-digit)	No. of Industries	1979	1981	1984	Change 1979–84
Fuels, minerals & nuclear	4	76.0	81.5	72.4	–3.6
Extraction, metal manufacture	8	64.0	61.9	61.4	–2.6
Non-metallic mineral products	12	54.2	53.5	54.4	0.2
Chemicals	21	64.8	64.0	63.5	–1.3
Metal goods	14	31.6	31.1	30.0	–1.6
Mechanical Engineering	28	43.9	42.3	42.0	–1.9
Elec./Electronic engineering	15	60.7	61.0	54.4	–6.3
Vehicles, transport, equipment	9	73.8	74.9	70.5	–3.3
Instrument engineering	6	42.4	42.3	41.4	–1.0
Food, drink, tobacco	19	64.0	63.4	60.9	–3.1
Textiles	15	39.6	40.3	36.8	–2.8
Leather, footwear, clothing	16	27.9	29.8	29.0	1.1
Timber, wooden furniture	9	19.1	18.2	20.4	1.3
Paper, printing	11	36.6	34.3	31.6	–5.0
Other	12	30.6	30.6	26.7	–3.9
Total no. of industries	199				

It should be apparent from Figure 4.1 that some major differences do exist in concentration levels among manufacturing sectors in the UK. For example, this Figure shows us that in 1981 the highest CR5 figure was 81.5 per cent (fuels, mineral and nuclear) and the lowest 18.2 per cent (timber, wooden furniture).

Various theories have been put forward to explain differential concentration. Ornstein, Weston, Intriligator and Shrieves (1973) provide a good summary of the various theories together with empirical results obtained. They list four main theories explaining concentration.

1. Concentration is determined by scale economies. The optimal number of firms in an industry is the total market divided by the optimal firm size. Hence few firms should have large economies of scale relative to market size.

2. Concentration is explained by barriers to entry. Entry barriers are traditionally defined by the size of capital requirements, product differentiation, economies of scale, and the comparative levels of cost functions. High barriers lead to high concentration and vice versa.

3. Concentration is caused by cumulative stochastic processes. Gibrat's 'Law of Proportionate Effect' (Gibrat, 1931) can be used to analyse the process of random growth amongst firms. The level of concentration in an industry at any point in time is deemed to be the product of a series of random growth paths in the history of the market.

4. Mergers are a major source of concentration. The merger movements have been widely held to be a major cause of concentration in the United States. Much attention has been given to mergers and government policy towards mergers and absolute firm size as important influences on concentration levels.

This last theory accords with Aaronovitch and Sawyer's (1975) findings for the UK. Although they are sceptical of the contribution of scale economies to the concentration process, they see mergers and acquisitions as having played an important role. The period 1955–73 is identified as the most intensive period of merger activity in UK history. UK mergers are predominantly of the horizontal and vertical type in contrast to the USA where a dramatic growth in conglomerate merger activity occurred. This can be explained, at least in part, by the lenient attitude, taken by US anti-trust laws towards conglomerate *vis-à-vis* other forms of merger. (See Chapter 5 for a fuller discussion of international differences in industrial policy.)

We have earlier noted that in the typical manufacturing industry the size distribution of firms is highly skewed with a few large firms controlling a large proportion of industry output. In the middle range of the distribution we may have rather more medium-sized firms and a large tail of small firms at the other end of the distribution. The idea that a small number of large firms at one end of the distribution is counterbalanced by a very large number of small and weak firms at the other end has been put forward by writers such as Williamson (1972). He states that '. . . even allowing for significant leadership by the large firm core . . . it is presumptuous to suggest that an analysis which focuses on these large firms is addressed to most of what is relevant in the American economy.'

This raises the question of how small firms are able to survive alongside their large opponents. Clearly they must possess some positive features to counterbalance against the benefits of economies of scale and technological advantages that are usually ascribed to large corporations.

Curran and Stanworth (1984) offer the following answer to this question: 'Small firms more generally are being seen as opportunity-seeking, risk-taking, innovative and flexible. Large firms, in contrast, are frequently castigated for displaying the opposite qualities and, because they are so capital intensive, for being negative contributors to employment'. Indeed, Curran and Stanworth (1984) go on to add that 'The current economic environment [in the UK] can be viewed as being highly favourable for the small enterprise. Changes in industrial relations laws, the decline in trade union power and the increasing flexibility of the labour market have helped in removing hurdles to small businesses . . . The Loan Guarantee Scheme (1981) and other new sources of finance have emerged to fill the investment vacuum previously faced by small firms . . .'.

Curran and Stanworth (1984) maintain that not only is the current environment favourable to the small firm but that in addition small firms are fashionable and may give British industry the growth impetus it needs. 'The fashion for small, flexible, decentralised organisational units which many behaviourable scientists argue are most suited to innovation and rapid economic change, is said to be epitomised by the small firm. Many of Britain's larger firms are struggling to adopt similar structures'. See Curran, Stanworth and Watkins (1986) for a full discussion of these issues.

Clearly there is a strong case to be made for identifying a central role for the small firm in British industry, as many politicians are advocating. This may not only help to rejuvenate British industry but also to break down the power of the large firm as illustrated in the trends in aggregate concentration. However, at present the small firm occupies a passive role on the periphery of the industrial boundary.

Government help and high levels of unemployment have encouraged large numbers of British people to start up their own small businesses. However, although thousands of small businesses start up each year, very few survive to become significant employers. In an article in the *Economist* entitled 'Little acorns fail to sprout' (13 December 1986) a rather gloomy picture of the impact small business starts can have on unemployment in depressed areas is painted. 'In the county of Cleveland in north-east England, it took 15 years for 2,000 jobs to be created by small manufacturing businesses in the 1960s and 1970s; then on one day in 1980, British Steel closed a factory employing 3,000 people. Small firms will need a good deal of jollying along if they are to replace traditional sources of employment'.

Economists generally have little to say about the strategies adopted by small businesses. Most theories of the firm relate to the large corporation operating in a situation of oligopoly. A study by Storey *et al.* (1987) concentrates on small manufacturing businesses in north-east England over a 16-year period. It looks at how they work and why they fail. It also looks at the characteristics of a two-year-old firm that will survive and grow to be a winner, which are:

1 The firm is generally three times as large, both in assets and employment, as its average contemporary.
2 It is operating on lower gross profit margins than its rivals but retaining more of its profits.
3 It is likely to be owned by experienced directors, rather than being run as a family firm or by skilled workers starting up a firm in their trade.
4 It has started relatively large and is managed professionally.
5 In the next few years, its asset growth will not be exceptionally high, though its workforce will continue to grow quickly.

A go-ahead firm, as defined by 1–5 above, needs government help according to Storey *et al.* (1987). Government assistance is required to give the firm access to overseas markets, to capital and to skilled labour. Commercial banks are usually too cautious in lending money and too concerned about possible business failure to fully aid the small business in this respect.

The main conclusion of this section is that UK industries are essentially oligopolistic in structure with, on average, approximately half of industry net output controlled by the largest five firms – the position in 1975. Hence decision-making and business strategy are formulated under such conditions of oligopoly. In the following section we consider what theories of the firm can tell us about decision-making and the goals of firms in oligopolistic markets.

BUSINESS STRATEGY AND THEORIES OF THE FIRM

Traditionally, economists from Adam Smith to John Maynard Keynes viewed business decision-making as uni-dimensional with the single goal of profit maximisation. The underlying reason for this was a belief in the notion of material self-interest which, for businessmen, translated into the desire to maximise profits. The 'economic theory of the firm' subscribed to by the classical and neo-classical economists of the nineteenth and early twentieth centuries was that of profit maximisation and the firm was treated as having a utility function to maximise where utility depends only on profits (shown diagrammatically in Figure 4.2).

This so-called neo-classical theory of the firm assumes that demand

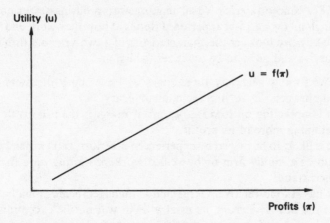

Figure 4.2 Utility depends solely on profits

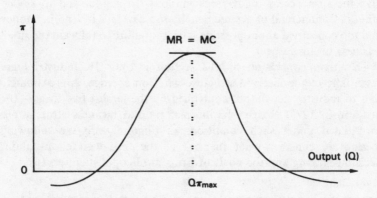

Figure 4.3 Selection of profit maximising level of output

conditions are known perfectly and that cost functions can be derived given the prices of inputs and the production function facing the firm. The firm then selects output to maximise profits where MR = MC (Figure 4.3).

The main criticism of this theory is the assumption that $u = f(\pi)$. It appears most plausible in the case of owner-controlled firms since the owner will be maximising his or her income in this case. A pioneering study by Berle and Means (1932) investigated the extent to which large firms were owner as opposed to manager controlled. Using data on the largest 200 non-financial firms in 1929, they discovered that 88 were clearly manager controlled in the sense that no well-defined group held more than 10 per cent of the shares of the company.

Hence in the large organisations there was evidence in the late 1920s to suggest that divorce of ownership from control existed in the sense that shareholders own the firm but the management team run the firm. In this situation the interests of the shareholders were seen as presenting only a constraint on the running of the firm. The utility function that the firm is trying to maximise is the management utility function and not the shareholders. In an updated version of the Berle and Means (1932) study, Larner (1966) discovered that by 1963 nearly 85 per cent of the largest 200 US non-financial corporations were under management control.

The important question to consider is whether or not the interests of managers and shareholders are likely to differ in any way. If they are then the divorce of ownership from control permits management to pursue its own interests rather than those of shareholders. Several theories have been advanced to suggest that variables other than profits enter the managerial utility function in oligopolistic markets. For instance, Baumol (1959) suggested a revenue maximising firm operating subject to a profit constraint; Williamson (1964) developed an expense preference theory of the firm; Marris (1964) suggested a growth maximising firm operating subject to security constraints; and Cyert and March (1963) rejected the orthodox theory of utility maximisation subject to constraints. For a fuller account of these see, for example, Sawyer (1979b).

These theories are based upon the notion that in large firms operating in oligopolistic market structures managers have the ability to pursue their own interests, subject only to constraints imposed by the interests of the owners. It is suggested that managers derive satisfaction from variables such as salary, perks, status, prestige, power, etc. The main problem facing a theory of the firm based on the divorce of ownership from control is to connect the economic decision variables of the firm, namely outputs, inputs, investment and advertising with variables that give satisfaction to management.

Scitovsky (1943) pointed out that in an owner-controlled firm, because there is a trade-off for the owner between profits earned and leisure time spent on the golf course, etc., he will generally not strive for maximum attainable profits, as defined by economists. In fact it will only be under the very special circumstance that the money value placed on his marginal unit of effort is independent of his income that will lead him rationally to maximise profits. This appears to be highly implausible since it implies that the psychology of the profit maximiser must be such that he does not place a higher value on his spare time, at the margin, as he becomes wealthier.

Adam Smith was probably the first economist to comment on the question of separation of corporate ownership from managerial control. In his view, 'Negligence and profusion, therefore, must always prevail, more or less, in the management of such a [manager-controlled] company'. The reason for his pessimistic outlook can be summed up with his words: 'The directors of such companies, however, being the managers rather of other people's money than their own, it cannot well be expected that they should watch over it with the same anxious vigilance with which the partners of a private copartnery frequently watch over their own' (Smith, 1937, p. 700).

In an article by Bothwell (1980) two hypotheses about the separation of ownership from control are jointly tested. The first is that the executives of manager-controlled firms are less likely to engage in strict profit maximising behaviour than are the executives of owner-controlled firms. The second is that the executives of manager-controlled firms exhibit more risk-averse behaviour due to asymmetries in managerial reward structures. This implies that such firms would constitute less risky investments for equity holders. Using the Capital Asset Pricing Model (CAPM), he attempts to allow for the simultaneous impact of the separation of ownership from control on both risk and profit.

Bothwell (1980) used data from two different samples. One presented estimates of the market shares of 231 large US industrial corporations taken from the 1967 *Fortune Directory*. The other provided a classification of firms appearing in the 1965 *Fortune Directory* by the type of control – a firm was deemed as having either strong owner control, weak owner control or management control according to whether the largest identifiable shareholding party owns an amount of the outstanding common stock equal to 30 per cent or more, between 10 and 29.9 per cent, or less than 10 per cent, respectively. The firms were also classified into high, substantial or moderate entry barrier categories.

Bothwell (1980) discovered that in every entry barrier category, the average profit margins of both weak and strong owner-controlled firms were greater than the average for manager-controlled firms. These profit margins have been adjusted to allow for difference in risk by use of the CAPM. These results provide additional support for the proposition that professional managers may deviate from profit maximising behaviour when the constraints imposed by a competitive market and effective owner control are both weak. Bothwell (1980) illustrates the importance of adjusting profits for inter-firm differences in risk by demonstrating that unadjusted profits would lead one to arrive at the opposite conclusion, namely that there is no support for the view that profits are significantly higher for owner-controlled firms.

Previous studies provided mixed results in this field. For example, Stano (1976) discovered that the executives of management-controlled firms had not acted in the best interests of the shareholders which accords with the views of Adam Smith. Stano (1976) analysed the rate of return that shareholders received on their investment in the stock of the firm (stock return). He argues that this is more important to shareholders than the usual measures employed in the literature of the rate of return on shareholder's equity (profit rate).

This measure of stock return was in fact employed in an earlier study of Sorenson (1974) who discovered that stock return for owner-controlled firms was greater than for manager-controlled firms in seven out of eleven industries examined. However, these differences were not found to be statistically significant at the 5 per cent level.

Stano (1976) developed a model to explain a firm's stock return in terms of the growth rate of earnings, the growth rate of sales and risk. Using data on 354 firms over the period 1963–72, he discovered that:

1 Owner-controlled firms had a significantly higher estimated growth rate of earnings per share; and
2 Executives of owner-controlled firms were more risk averse as indicated by a significantly higher equity-asset ratio.

Stano (1976) agrees with Adam Smith that the executives of manager-controlled firms have not acted in the best interests of their shareholders. There does appear to be strong evidence that goals other than profit maximisation are pursued in manager-controlled organisations. Also it may be quite rational for an owner-controlled firm to deviate from strict profit maximisation as Scitovsky (1943) has illustrated.

Further support for the abandonment of profit maximisation as the only objective of the firm comes from studies into how firms set their price. The most famous of these is the study by Hall and Hitch (1939) using data collected on 38 UK firms. They discovered that no attempt was made to set MC = MR when determining price. Instead the majority (27 firms) adhered to full-cost pricing, which basically consists of placing a mark-up on to AC.

Similar results were obtained from more recent studies. For example, Hague (1971), in a study of 13 UK manufacturing companies, found that pricing policy depended upon a variety of factors, including the nature of the products, the extent of competition, the economic climate and the attitudes and personalities of decision-makers within the firms. He found that six of the firms in his sample adhered to full-cost pricing, three made some attempt at estimating MC and then applied some sophisticated formula to arrive at price (basically MC plus mark-up), and the remaining four adhered to a fairly complete MC and competitive pricing policy.

Nevertheless, attempts to defend the profit maximising goal have been made, most notable by Friedman (1953) and Machlup (1967). Friedman makes the point that the presence of false assumptions does not necessarily produce any significant handicap to the ability of a theory to produce reliable predictions. The only true and significant test of a theory is a comparison of its predictions with reality. The fact that businessmen do not understand economists' jargon does not mean that they are not striving for maximum profits. Hence, although the typical reaction by businessmen or women to the propositions of marginalism may be an amused disbelief that anyone would want to think of the pricing problem in this way (i.e. set MC = MR), they may still be striving for maximum profits according to Friedman.

It can be shown that Baumol's sales revenue maximisation theory is akin to a form of full-cost pricing as discovered by Hall and Hitch, Hague, etc. In Baumol's model the firm operates under a minimum profit constraint (π°) that is required to keep shareholders happy. Hence the sales revenue maximiser has to meet the following constraint,

$$\text{T.R.} \geq \text{T.C.} + \pi^\circ$$

Dividing throughout by output (Q) gives

$$\text{A.R.} \geq \text{AC} + (\pi^\circ/Q), \text{ or } P \geq \text{AC} + (\pi^\circ/Q)$$

(π°/Q) can be considered as an overhead cost to the firm since price must be sufficient to cover both AC and this profit constraint per unit of output.

But the sales revenue maximiser will use up any surplus profits above π° to increase advertising expenditure which will in turn increase its sales revenue. Therefore in equilibrium, with the profit constraint binding on the firm,

$$P = \text{AC} + (\pi^\circ/Q)$$

Note the analogy to full-cost pricing since price is determined via the formula

$$P = AC + (\text{mark up})$$

where the sales revenue maximiser sets his mark-up according to the size of the profit constraint (π°) and the level of output produced (Q).

Any theory of the firm should be capable of making predictions about how a firm will respond to a changing environment. The comparative static properties of different theories can be compared to see how they differ. Figure 4.4 illustrates the comparative static properties of the profit and sales revenue maximisation theories. The qualitative effects of an increase in lump sum tax and profits tax are different in the two theories. The profit maximising firm does not respond as the same level of output still meets the MC = MR criteria. However, the Baumol-type firm is forced to cut back on output and increase price in order to meet the profit constraint imposed by shareholders. Its output moves closer to the profit maximising level.

This type of analysis enables us to consider the plausibility of the two theories. It seems rather improbable that a rise in corporation tax would yield no response from firms, as implied by the profit maximising theory. Short-run sales maximisation may, of course, be viewed as a route to long-run profit maximisation. See, for example, Peston (1959).

To view business decision-making in terms of one goal to maximise profits or sales or growth subject to constraints may be rather unrealistic. Instead, the firm may be viewed as attempting to achieve satisfactory levels of several key variables such as profits, growth, sales, market share and inventory. This is the basis of the behavioural theory of the firm. It rejects the notion of maximising a utility function subject to constraints in favour of 'satisficing', i.e. achieving satisfactory results. This is the only theory to reject the classical framework of optimisation under conditions of perfect information and complete certainty.

Uncertainty and incomplete information result in the abandonment of maximisation in favour of achieving a satisfactory result. The behavioural theory, as developed by Cyert and March (1963), views the firm as an organisation – that is, a coalition or group of individuals – where the coalition members hold different goals or objectives which may arise from the different departments within the organisation itself. A continuous process of bargaining between the various members of the coalition is envisaged by Cyert and March. Unlike the alternative theories considered, the behavioural theory attempts to analyse and deal with the internal organisational structure within a firm.

Figure 4.4 Comparative static properties of profit and sales revenue maximisation theories

	Increase in demand	Increase in lump sum tax	Increase in specific tax	Increase in proportional profits tax
Response of profit maximising firm in respect of				
Q	+	0	−	0
P	+	0	+	0
Response of sales revenue maximising firm in respect of				
Q	+	−	−	−
P	+	+	+	+

Cyert and March reject the classical maximisation approach on the grounds that entrepreneurs do not have the information to generate demand and cost curves to make the necessary calculations. Information is subject to distortions and is costly to gather. Instead, entrepreneurs engage in a process of sequential decision-making as they try to gather information by undertaking research. This is the basis of 'satisficing' as originally developed by Simon (1959).

In Simon's view the decision-maker has an aspiration level – a concept of what constitutes a satisfactory outcome or target level – and he or she then undertakes a search procedure to obtain a general idea of what is happening. In a world of imperfect information the decision-maker does not generate the whole cost or demand curve as search is localised around present output levels. The aspiration level in fact becomes endogenous to the research procedure in the sense that if it is easily achieved the aspiration level is raised but if it proves extremely difficult to achieve it will be lowered. Hence, rational choice in Simon's world is seen as finding satisfactory outcomes rather than maximising.

The relevant question is under what conditions might Simon's dynamic process converge on a profit maximising position. Certainly if we think of information as having a cost and yield attached to it, then this approach could be viewed as equivalent to finding a local maximum level of profits, where revenue and cost are properly defined to include information gathering. However, although 'satisficing' might result in the attainment of a local maximum it may fall short of finding a global maximum.

Until now we have only considered decision-making internal to the firm without taking full account of the external environment in which the firm operates. This will be dealt with in the next section. In concluding this section it should be noted that the theories developed within the classical framework of maximisation are capable of generating predictions about how firms will respond to a changing environment – comparative static properties. In contrast, the behavioural theory has few powers of prediction but it does take account of the internal organisational structure and decision-making processes of firms.

However, if we view Baumol's theory as akin to long-run profit maximisation and the behavioural theory as akin to local profit maximisation with the return and cost of information gathering included (the organisation would also be striving for local maxima for its other four goals), then the various theories may have more in common with one another than first appreciated.

A BUSINESS MODEL OF COMPETITION

Introduction

In this section we look at competition from the point of view of the firm. A business has to find a safe route through the competitive environment to secure profits. This route is vulnerable to spoiling tactics by the other players and to whistle blowing by the owners of capital.

The discussion highlights the importance of size to success and the related survival issues of barriers to entry and exit. An analytical model is introduced which is dynamised by the introduction of a product life-cycle story and questions of varying intensity of inter-firm rivalry.

The section concludes with a sketch of the main competitive choices open to a business, focusing on the critical distinction between cost leadership and product differentiation strategies.

A fuller discussion of these topics is to be found in Michael Porter, *Competitive Strategy; Techniques for Analysing Industries and Companies* (1980) and Gerry Johnson and Kevan Scholes *Exploring Corporate Strategy* (1984).

An interactive game

The business manager looks out at the world outside and makes what may, for the firm, be life or death decisions. He or she makes these decisions on a calculus of risks and rewards. The riskiest plan is to confront the other players head on and challenge them for a part of a particularly lucrative market – that is to compete for business in the full sense of the word.

A safer plan would be to search for some part of the market that offered maximum rewards with minimum risks of tangling with other players. A slightly less safe game plan would be to enter into collusive agreements with the other players. The danger here comes from the ever present temptation for one player to break ranks and scoop the pool, while the others are looking elsewhere.

Firms compete for customers, and against rival suppliers and substitutes, both domestic and foreign. Firms also compete against rivals for inputs – materials, labour, technology and finance – and for distribution.

Sometimes powerful customers, such as governments with fat defence contracts or major supermarket chains with million-case orders, can dictate the form that competition takes. Sometimes, as in UK brewing, control of distribution shapes events. Sometimes control over the supply of inputs, as with diamonds, is critical. Sometimes external influences are dominant, as when government grants a monopoly, as in much UK privatisation, or lays down conditions for licensing practitioners, as is commonly found in medicine.

But if we look inside a market, the two central issues are the likely behaviour and reactions of existing competitors and the probability of new entrants coming into the market. The reactions of firms will be partly determined by the objective conditions of the business environment, but also by the firms' own cultures, the resources available for a fight back and the costs to the firm of losing the battle.

A market leader analyses its environment, identifies its own interest and then decides whether to put the interest of the whole industry first (see Tragedy of the Commons) or to gain advantage for itself (Prisoners' Dilemma). For a description of these two games see Chapter 1. The judgement depends on the assessment of the likely strength and direction of responses by the other players.

Firms planning to take a co-operative route will pay a lot of attention to signalling their intentions to the rest of the players. Co-operation depends crucially on mutual trust – a commonly held belief that the players will do as they say – on a substantial convergence of expectations and on a fairly narrow definition of areas available for competition. The narrower the area of competitive struggle, the fewer the unknowns.

Firms taking an offensive route will, however, give themselves as much lead time as possible so as to prepare their defences. This implies the use of stealth, diversionary tactics and unexpected competitive actions.

In making strategic and other decisions, the manager looks to see where the firm stands relative to the other existing and potential players, considers the rules of the game and assesses likely direction of changes in the overall business environment. This next section follows through a stylised version of his analysis, indicating relationships with the likely form and the intensity of the ruling competitive processes.

We can list the main questions to be answered:

1 Who are the principal players?
2 What are the trends within the industry? How many players are there? What is the pattern of recent entries and exits? What are the current rules of the game?
3 Who are the rule-makers?

4 What are the strengths of the players relative to their suppliers and customers?
5 What players are waiting on the touchline?
6 What substitutes are active? What is happening in their markets?
7 What is the nature and height of any barriers to entry and exit? What is the type and intensity of competition in the market?
8 What are the regulatory controls on competition?
9 What are the political and social pressures to conform?
10 What are the economic trends? How do these relate to trends in consumer behaviour?
11 What, in recent history, has been the industry attitude to diversification and integration? To change?
12 What are the current technological trends? Is the industry basically high tec or low tec? Is its development potential exhausted?

Managers and the competition for capital

The capital market is an easy place for a firm to live or to die. Lenders of money make their own assessment of risks in lending money to firms. In general, the small new firm finds it harder to borrow than the long established large blue chip company. These different assessments of risk are likely to be reflected in the interest rates facing the borrower, the small firm often finding itself facing the need to pay out cripplingly high fixed debt service charges irrespective of point levels.

The obvious alternative to debt is the issue of shares. This too poses dangers for the firm. Managers of small to medium-sized quoted companies are under a continuous pressure to produce adequate returns. The owners of capital have freedom to shift their involvement from one firm to another, in a way that neither management nor labour can. Money can be moved almost instantaneously from one business to another, in the process leaping from country to country and from one financial asset to another. The City of London and similar financial centres exist in order to facilitate this movement of capital.

Larger organisations are substantially, at least in the short run, sheltered from these immediate profit pressures as they have the ability to raise their own capital internally. Also the size of their capital base relative to the resources of their stockholders, shields them from the worst effects of short-run changes in share prices.

The imperative that drives the restless investor is a fear that the value of their asset is falling in one place, while they are missing out on higher returns in another. The decision by an investor to hold or move depends basically on two factors – on relative current returns on money invested and on future expectations.

If the financial markets work well, the current price of the asset will reflect all publicly known information. Price changes will only result from new information entering the market, which causes shifts in the supply and demand schedules for the assets concerned. Owners of capital make windfall gains by anticipating the arrival of new information, either as a result of luck or of superior intelligence – whether lawfully or unlawfully obtained.

Firms wishing to maintain investor confidence have to convince the market that their current profits are reasonable, given the prospects for future profits. Failure to maintain short-term confidence results in investors shifting their capital – sellers outnumber buyers, resulting in rapid asset price falls, until the market value of the firm approaches or passes its asset book value. At this point the firm is likely to be absorbed by a predator looking for low-cost growth through acquisition of an under-performing firm.

Success can also bring its own dangers. A firm may, despite reasonable profits and solid future expectations, be subjected to a hostile take-over by another firm wishing either to reduce competition in, or buy its way into, a profitable market. Successful owner-managers may in the event welcome such bids as a way of converting paper wealth locked up in their firm into more mobile liquid assets.

New entrants will be drawn to markets where they see above average returns or weak existing firms, which would be unlikely to withstand any additional competition. New entrants, with good access to capital, bring additional, often technologically more advanced, capacity, thus having a direct impact on prices, costs and profits and on the technically efficient sizes of firms. Potential new entrants, and the owners of their capital, will weigh up likely reactions from existing producers and the probable costs of failure before committing themselves.

The mobility of capital, and the restlessness of its owners, puts a specific pressure on managers to produce short-term profits and to avoid unnecessary risks. Capital investment, particularly for labour and other cost saving equipment, is relatively easy for a profitable firm to obtain and can be written off over a number of years. What is much harder is to raise new money for the longer term development of a business, possibly through investment in research and development.

The costs of innovation stretch far beyond the initial expenditure on

R&D through to staff training, bringing the product successfully on-stream and introducing it to the market. Often the only way to finance development is by building current share prices, through quick profits, and then raising capital via a new issue. This new money, which itself will require servicing, may or may not enable a firm to shift its time horizon from the short to the long run.

The competition between capitals for short-run profits operates with different intensities in different parts of the world. The Japanese firms tend to have very long-time horizons and through complex linkages of joint ownership with the larger banks and massive investment institutions, such as Nomura Securities, have access to low-cost long-term capital. Germany and Italy for historic reasons have underdeveloped stock exchanges and their firms rely more on banks for their capital requirements. US and even more UK firms rely on the short-term market for finance.

The competition between owners of capital for higher returns imposes on managers a financial discipline, which produces a bias towards short-run profits and safety positions. This produces a dilemma for the manager – growth can mean safety, but requires the sacrifice of immediate profits. Low profits will, however, fail to satisfy the owners of capital who will take their wealth elsewhere so leaving the firm vulnerable to acquisition and liquidation.

A question of size

The exigencies of the capital market tend to favour the larger units in terms of access to capital and long-run support. Smaller firms are forced to shorten their time horizons. We have observed in the first section that most markets show a drift towards concentration – i.e. fewer and fewer firms come to dominate more and more of a particular market. But apart from any built-in bias in the capital market there are other even more powerful technical and economic reasons why we should expect concentration to increase.

We can usefully identify three size benchmarks:

1. MFS – the minimum feasible size, below which it would be impossible for the firm to function.
2. MES – the minimum efficient size; firms have over a plausible range of output an L-shaped long-run average or unit cost curve, i.e. at low levels of output, unit costs fall as production rises, until a point is reached where cost savings bottom out and unit costs become approximately constant.

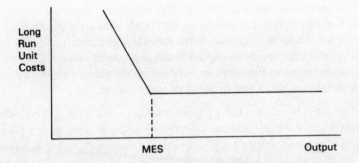

Figure 4.5 Minimum efficient size of a firm

3. LMS – limit of market size, which is determined by total possible sales. A firm which gets a 'good start' in life will race its rivals down the unit cost curve, seeking the lower unit costs which come with increased output until it finally runs out of market.

A typical market structure will consist of a small number of oligopolists, all at or beyond MES and a larger number of small firms closer to the MFS. An ideal type version of such a market might have 50 per cent of output produced by five firms, all above MES, with a larger number of smaller firms whose sizes lie between MFS and MES providing the other 50 per cent of output. Few markets will precisely match this ideal type, although this is approximately the average figure found by Sawyer (1979a) using 1975 UK Census of Production data.

The distinctive variations will lie in the number of surviving large firms and the size, or even existence at all, of the tail of small firms. A pure monopoly is a special case with only one large firm and a tail with zero occupants.

The few large firms in the market will determine the precise nature of the competitive process; the smaller firms will survive either by finding niches and doing things larger firms cannot do (serving small high-value market segments) or by working around the edges of the large firms and riding in on opportunities created by them (offering low-price no frills products to markets sustained by heavy branding).

The benefits to the firm stemming from size, fall under two broad headings – those related to the ability to cut costs and/or improve quality and those related to the power to transfer surplus from suppliers and customers to the firm.

The main sources of scale economies are:

1 Technical economies of scale in production.
2 Use of discrete sub-processes each with their own MESs.
3 Finer division of labour, both manual and mental.
4 Lower cost access to capital because of lower risks.
5 Economies in distribution – including advertising efficiency.
6 Better access to and analysis of information.

The main benefits resulting from market power lie in getting better terms from suppliers due an asymmetry of bargaining power (lower input costs) and charging higher prices to consumers, either as a result of an asymmetry of information or through the exercise of monopoly power.

We should also note the possibility of diseconomies of scale, due to loss of control, distance from the customer, sluggishness in response and scale effects of wrong decisions. Diseconomies of scale appear to relate mainly to the use of inappropriate management techniques and could presumably be overcome in a well-run corporation.

Barriers to entry

One obvious strategy open to a firm wishing to reduce the effects of the full blast of competition is to shelter behind suitable barriers to entry. A commonly employed strategy to this end is via product differentiation by means of new product development and strong branding.

The aim is to create differences between the product or service and its rivals so reducing price cross-elasticities by building consumer loyalty. The effect of successful differentiation is to reduce the forces of competition, thus enabling the firm, in relative safety, to raise prices and expand sales.

Barriers to entry can be categorised as follows:

1. Product differentiation – leading to consumer loyalty and associated psychic, human and physical costs of switching to another product or service. Differentiation is basically achieved through design, marketing and location activities.

2. Economies of scale – these can be found in almost every aspect of business. They result not only from increased output, but also from sharing common facilities provided by a parent company and from joint output (by-products, sales force carrying more than one line).

3. Capital requirements. This is not only a question of the lumpiness of the capital required to finance a plant capable of

taking advantages of economies of scale but also of the lender's assessment of the risks involved in the loan.

4. A good reputation – a company name, backed by several years of marketing and public relations activity, which has achieved a reasonable degree of salience in the public mind, provides an effective umbrella for a range of activities.

5. Access to distribution channels – control of or influence over, all or part of the channel of distribution which stretches from producer to end consumer, can effectively shut out a new entrant.

6. Cost advantages independent of scale:

(a) Experience – an early lead on the learning curve may enable a firm to stay ahead of its rivals; it may also give low-cost opportunities for diversification into related fields.

Economies of scale and experience often appear to coincide, but are in reality quite distinct categories. Cost savings from the scale of production are built into the process and can only be lost through managerial loss of control or through increased risk due to lack of portfolio spread or be frittered away in product line proliferation.

Experience, however, is more portable and can be gained by hiring staff or through intelligent imitation. Experience can lead to an over-reliance on the past and to a 'me too' stance. This reduces a firm's openness to new ideas and to innovation and effectively prevents them deciding to 'leapfrog' into the next generation of products.

(b) Patents and licence – legal protection normally a reward to encourage innovation.

(c) Favourable access to supplies, through ownership, special relationships, legal contracts and location.

(d) Location in terms of access to markets.

(e) Government subsidies and other preferential forms of support.

7. Government policy, towards monopolies, licences, regulations, safety laws, pollution control, etc. These government interventions may simply be aimed at increasing public welfare, or they may favour specific regions or industries or may be directed at excluding new entrants, especially from overseas.

Government policy may be consciously used to change the rules of the competitive game, or, as is more common, an act aimed at one target produces unexpected outcomes in other parts of the competitive environment.

	ENTRY BARRIERS	EXIT BARRIERS	
		Low	High
Profits		LOW	LOW
Riskiness	Low	NEUTRAL	HIGH, UNSTABLE
Prices		LOW	LOW + PRICE WARS
Competition		UNSTRUCTURED	UNSTRUCTURED
Mature capacity		AT CAPACITY	OVERCAPACITY
Profits		HIGH	HIGH, BUT RISKY
Riskiness	High	LOW	UNSTABLE
Prices		HIGH	HIGH + PRICE WARS
Competition		STRUCTURED	STRUCTURED
Mature capacity		UNDERCAPACITY	OVERCAPACITY

Figure 4.6 Barriers and business behaviour

Barriers to exit

Firms may find themselves locked into a market, that is they have acquired resources for which there is little or no resale value or profitable alternative use.

The existence of exit barriers has two main effects – it deters new entrants almost as effectively as entry barriers and powerfully modifies the competitive behaviour of existing firms. Their existence effectively rules out the 'hit-and-run' player.

One good area, for example, is in the provision of the infrastructure. For example, one toll bridge may provide monopoly profits for one owner, while two can lead to a dead loss for both players, since there are no ready alternative uses for surplus toll bridges.

The fear of exit barriers is likely to lead to a chronic failure by private industry to provide an adequate infrastructure. In almost every case roads and rail are state provided. A current example might be the initial problems which faced the Anglo-French channel tunnel consortium in raising private finance. This would not be true of air travel, where routes can, in principle, be switched and redundant planes resold.

In more commercial spheres the existence of barriers to exit is likely to deter firms from entering the market, unless they are very confident that they can completely oust an existing firm.

Examples of barriers to exit are:

1 Ownership of a specialised asset with no alternative uses.
2 Labour agreements with redundancy clauses.
3 Contracts to supply spare parts or after-sales services.
4 Emotional and cultural attachments.
5 Government pressures to stay in.
6 Lack of opportunities to move elsewhere.

Effects of entry and exit barriers on firms' behaviour

Firms within a market like high barriers to entry, and, if possible, low barriers to exit. In contrast firms considering entering a market like low entry and exit barriers. High exit barriers imply over-capacity building up over time as the market matures and firms all increase capacity in pursuit of economies of scale until there is too much capacity chasing too few customers.

We can display the impact of entry and exit barriers by means of a 2 × 2 matrix (Figure 4.5). Profits and prices will tend to be high where there are entry barriers to deter new, more competitive entrants. The riskiness attached to investing capital rises with exit barriers, due to anticipated difficulties in realising assets should the venture fail. The presence of exit barriers is also likely to result in overcapacity, since marginal firms are unable to leave the market in response to changing circumstances.

Competition and the life-cycle

One useful metaphor, or dynamic model, for the study of competitive markets is that of the life-cycle where products are seen, like trees or other plants, to follow a predictable sequence. There is an initial phase when the product may or may not take, followed by a period of more or less unchallenged growth. After a time the producer runs into others competing for the same space. After a period of struggle, the survivors reach an exhausted accommodation, which is a prelude to a rapid collapse of the market as replacement products come on stream.

We can develop the model as follows:

1 Phase zero: There is a potential market that has yet to be entered, although some entrepreneurs have engaged in search activities, including R&D.
Competitive process: Firms in secret prepare to enter market.

2 Exploratory Stage: One or two firms enter the market.

Competitive process: Firms, which are likely to be at or around the MFS, although large diversified firms may attempt to enter directly at the MES level, test out the market. There is little direct competition to fear. The main worry is that someone else may try to follow them in before they are established. Profits are miniscule.

3 Growth phase: Firms either discover that they have tapped a growth market, in which case the race to MES and beyond is on, or that the market is strictly limited, in which case they either exit, with minimum losses, or decide to stay small.

Competitive process: Profits are relatively easy to make. Pricing is not a problem, providing they are kept low enough to open up enough of the market to gain economies of scale. The main marketing activity is aimed at rapid market penetration.

4 Competitive phase: Other firms are attracted into the market. Inter-firm competition, in both price and non-price terms, becomes the norm.

Competitive process: Firms consolidate any advantages, defend any barriers to competition, reinforce product differentiation, and engage in occasional price wars. This is a period of rising costs, due to additional marketing expenditure, and tighter prices, thus putting pressure on profits. Competition is highly structured.

5 Collusive phase: Weaker firms either exit from the market or are taken over by their larger and more successful rivals. The market is characterised by a tendency to rising profits and, especially in the presence of barriers to exit, overcapacity.

Competitive process: Strategy is highly stylised, and takes the form of widespread use of anti-competitive practices, collusion and formation of cartels to raise profits. The co-operative process will be disturbed from time to time by damaging price wars.

6 Post-maturity: The profit potential of the market is exhausted; products increasingly fail to match consumer needs; replacement products are entering their growth phases.

Competitive process: Firms either exit, diversify, or face extinction. This is a period of toppling giants, of once household names being turned into 'cash cows'.

The intensity of competition at any given stage depends on the profit or loss potential facing firms within the market and on the existence of any potential entrants. In general, the lower the profit returned the more intense the competition since in an open competitive market profit will be driven down to the minimum necessary for survival, a level known to economists as 'normal profit'.

Intensity of rivalry

The intensity of rivalry between firms in a market will depend in part on the relationship between total producer capacities and overall market size and in part on the actions of the lead player, who may or not turn out to be the strongest player.

There are a number of special features which can trigger off particular competitive situations. First we consider the arrival of the maverick, who is driven to break the pattern. The conditions which favour the arrival of a maverick are:

1 Where there are many small firms and little dominance, individuals will, from time to time, be tempted to break away from the pack and go for leadership.
2 Overseas firms with different home rules try to enter the market without adjusting to the existing competitive conditions – or, having covered their fixed costs in the home market, wish to dump produce at low prices, which barely cover marginal costs.
3 In a period of slow growth one firm with a backlog of debts is forced to go for rapid volume sales through price cuts.
4 A firm trapped in a market with high fixed costs, which may simply be the result of capital accumulated over time, will try to unload spare capacity through dumping.

Another cause of instability is where firms have diverse objectives, so there is little agreement over 'the rules of the game'. This could arise because firms have different origins or different time horizons – one looking for a cash cow, another for a long-term growth investment, another with a powerful corporate need for rapid penetration of a market.

The constraint of the need to make at least normal profits may be relaxed in some circumstances leading to non-standard behaviour. Examples might be small enterprises, which are run by their owners, who may be willing to accept subnormal profits simply to stay in business, the 'peasant' producer/shopkeeper, or mega-corporations with long purses which may accept losses in order to buy their way into a market.

It is not clear from the consumers' point of view whether or not competition along these dimensions will lead to a better quality of life.

There is a fear, based on experience, that 'cut-throat' competition leads to a lowering of standards and a waste of resources in purely rivalrous activities, whether in the form of predatory price cuts or combative advertising. There is also some experience which suggests that while collusive agreements of the 'gentlemanly' kind may avoid the grosser forms of competition, they can all too easily turn into a cosy conspiracy against the consumer.

Competitive choices

The competitive choices open to a firm's managers depend on the structure of the market. In an open unstructured market, there is only one form of viable competitive behaviour – cost minimisation and production at the level where marginal cost equals marginal revenue. Prices will be given by the market and products will be broadly homogeneous.

In more structured markets, firms are faced with a choice of strategies, whose appropriateness depends on:

1 The evolutionary state of the market – place in life-cycle.
2 The number of relative sizes of the other players.
3 The state of the business environment.
4 The operating rules of the game.
5 The aims and objectives of the firm.

For any strategy to succeed it has to be
realistic:

 – taking cognisance of the resources, strengths and weaknesses of the firm over the likely life of the game plan relative to other players.
 – capable of implementation, given the firm's value system and its managerial capabilities.
consistent:
 –using operational goals which are mutually achievable, or at the very least capable of trade-off resolution in line with the overall strategy.
 – using policy instruments which are mutually reinforcing and goal directed.
opportune:
 –taking account of changes in the business environment in terms of consumer and competitor behaviour; technological changes and opportunities; anticipating and responding to broad societal developments in the economic, political and social spheres.

–working within the rules of the game as operating at that time and being alert for likely changes.

committed:

–having decided on a course of action, a firm must commit itself to action, so that there is no turning back, no half-hearted advance.

–ensuring cohesion and follow through, drawing together the various parts of the firm and uniting them in a common purpose.

– communicating back into the firm and to other players, that the firm means what it says, that it has the necessary assets (we have the guns, we have the men, we have the money too), that it has a history of getting what it wanted.

Rivalry between firms occcurs either because one firm sees an opportunity to improve its position in terms of either market share or profitability or because it fears loss of position, due to actions of other firms or changes in the overall business environment. Competitive actions based on misunderstanding are quite likely to prove disastrous for the moving player.

The central point is that in most situations firms are mutually dependent. At every stage of the game managers are looking over their shoulders at what consumers will accept, at what government will permit, at what newcomers are warming-up on the touchline to do and at what competitors are likely to do next.

The main tactical weapons open to a firm are:

1 Price – undercut competitors. This strategy is easy to imitate, undermines own profitability, and, especially if price elasticities are low, can ruin the whole industry serving that market.

2 Advertising and promotion (including sales and distribution) – differentiates product away from competitors, thus isolating the product from immediate competitive pressures. Over time advertising forms a formidable barrier to entry, because of in-depth consumer loyalty. Advertising enables a firm to hold (or raise) prices and also to build consumer demand. Given a favourable conjunction of circumstances, advertising, by increasing sales, could lead to lower prices through economies of scale.

3 Product or service innovation – innovation offers a firm a chance to cut costs and/or to add value to the product. It may also lead the firm into a totally new market.

The strategic options open have defensive and offensive aspects. We can see this clearly with decisions as to where to *position* a firm –

whether the aim is one of getting there first, taking the initiative to ride down the learning curve ahead of the others, of using existing strengths to go where the hostile forces are weakest.

This duality can be extended to a firm's *acquisition* policy, whether vertical or horizontal. Firms may acquire firms in order to:

1 Reduce competition by buying direct rivals (horizontal).
2 Gain economies of scale (vertical and/or horizontal).
3 Improve R&D (vertical and/or horizontal).
4 Reduce transaction costs between component supplies and immediate customers (vertical).
5 Improve co-ordination and planning (vertical).
6 Raise barriers to entry (vertical and/or horizontal).

Diversification also offers a firm a defensive/offensive choice – a defensive move away from a mature industry in order to build a better balanced portfolio or an aggressive move into new high growth areas. Diversification may follow some industrial logic so that a firm's expertise in one area can be spread into another or it may involve true diversification into unrelated areas where the risks and rewards are quite different.

To compete or not to compete

Managers decide either to go for market share by cutting costs and increasing volume sales, or for higher profits by charging consumers more by offering something different.

Pay less, make more

In a typical cost-driven company the emphasis will be on achieving scale economies coupled with a cost minimisation approach. Cost control dominates managerial activity. Overheads are pared to a minimum. A small headquarters staff controls the company, principally through financial reporting. Products are designed for low-cost volume production. Expenditure on marketing, training, R&D and customer services is kept to a minimum. Payments to suppliers are tightly controlled.

The basic strategy is to design a product that is simple to make and which is offered as part of a carefully rationalised, probably modular, product range. This lowest cost strategy probably implies substantial start-up costs in buying state-of-the-art production equipment, sufficient to take the firm past minimum efficient size, and aggressive initial pricing and promotion to gain the market share needed to realise the wider economies of scale in production.

Having the lowest unit costs in the industry gives a firm a strong price and profit position, especially in the presence of barriers to entry. The firm uses its price advantage to build market share, which through scale economies, automatically increases its cost advantages. The broad strategy is one of low-price volume production, with broad market cover, concentrating on the higher volume segments. An undisciplined search for volume can lead to proliferation of lines with consequent loss of the cost-cutting edge.

Unless rival firms adopt effective defensive strategies, the low-cost producer will see each highest cost producer eliminated in turn. The net result of this successful competitive strategy is to reduce the number of firms supplying a market, so increasing the industry's concentration.

The low-cost strategy is always vulnerable to exogenous cost inflation, to imitation and to loss of flexibility in adapting to bigger changes in the total business environment. This lack of flexibility is likely to be reinforced by the probable reliance on a management hierarchical structure for tight cost controls.

Be different, earn more

Instead of chasing cost leadership, a firm may prefer the route to product differentiation, added value, consumer loyalty, higher prices and resultant higher margins. Differentiation almost certainly will involve the firm in higher research and design, sales and marketing costs. The pressure for cost minimisation in production and overheads is likely to be weak relative to that experienced in a cost-driven firm.

Differentiation may, but not necessarily, imply exclusivity and satisfaction with a relatively low market share. The risk facing the company is that consumers may not continue to be willing to pay a premium price for the differentiated product.

The differentiation strategy requires a management with strong marketing abilities and a company culture that values style and creativity. The appropriate organisational structure is likely to be some version of a matrix which co-ordinates diverse functions behind tasks, in the process allowing space for flexibility.

Within the two broad strategic approaches of cost leadership and product differentiation, firms can also choose between a broad approach, serving all or most of the market, or a tightly focused approach, targeting in on one particular segment. A tight focus may allow the company to cut its costs right down, or it may open the way for a highly specialised product or service capable of commanding a premium price.

The focus approach requires a well defined market that can be reached and which has specific needs. The sub-market might be defined geographically, or by type of consumer (professional chefs, as opposed to hobby cooks, or homemakers).

Extension versus diversification

Apart from the cost leadership/differentiation and broad spectrum/ tight focus choices, a firm may decide either to extend their cover of current activities, or to diversify into new markets. Broad coverage of an extensive market leaves a firm vulnerable to raids by more focused opponents and in time will give rise to conflicting goals within the organisation.

Diversification spreads the risks and enables firms to balance their portfolios of activities between potential high-growth activities, steady generators of resources and old mature businesses which can be for a short period milked for cash. This balanced approach provides for long-run stability. The portfolio approach also enables firms to position businesses to block off potential entrants, thus securing barriers to entry.

Conclusion

In this section we have seen how a business player analyses the game and selects the most advantageous strategy for that firm. At the end of most rounds of play there is likely to be less competition in the market as winners displace losers; as winners block off new entrants.

Competition, in the economist's sense, is only re-established by the arrival of powerful new entrants or replacement products, or by the actions of some external agency changing the rules of the game.

SUMMARY OF IDEAS

In the first section we observed that industries, especially in the UK, have become increasingly oligopolistic in structure with increasing levels of industrial concentration and highly skewed distributions of firm size. In the second section we noted that one result of this is that goals other than profit maximisation will be pursued by manager-controlled, large corporations, which may not be in the best interests of shareholders. Finally in the third section we have seen that this can result in anti-competitive business behaviour such as collusion.

In the next chapter government policy towards anti-competitive behaviour will be considered from an international viewpoint. Anti-competitive practices (ACPs) will be covered in much greater depth in Chapter 6. The important message from this chapter is that we require a much tighter control over mergers in the UK and a concerted effort by government to break down entry barriers to give greater encouragement for small business starts if the trend towards less competition in business strategy is to be halted and indeed reversed. It is vitally important that we have strong and effective competition policy on the statute books.

5 The Rules of the Game: UK, EEC, USA, Japan

Industrial legislation relating to restrictive practices and monopoly power exists in all the major Western industrialised economies. How should governments attempt to regulate industry? From an economic viewpoint there would appear to be a case for attempting to achieve both efficiency and equity through the legislative framework. However, firms claim they can only achieve their minimum efficient size (MES – see Chapter 4) if they are allowed a substantial share of the market which would conflict with equity considerations. Equity requires competition amongst many firms making only normal profits. This poses a problem for regulators as to whether to go for efficiency or equity.

In practice, it is often very difficult to identify accurately the MES of firm or plant in an industry. Indeed, if LRAC curves slope downwards over the entire range of feasible output levels then MES is indeterminate as no minimum value turning point exists.

> Our main conclusion is that in many basic industries, such as petroleum refining, primary metals, and electric power, economies of scale are found up to very large plant sizes (often the largest built or contemplated) (Haldi and Whitcomb, 1967, p. 373).

There is no single, universally accepted method for finding the shape of the LRAC curve. Instead, several methods have been employed, including statistical cost analysis, engineering estimates method, the survivor technique and the growth rate approach. For a fuller discussion of these approaches see, for example, Hay and Morris (1979, pp. 37–82). The optimal plant size can sometimes only be expressed within a range of numbers. For example, Stigler (1958), in an early study using the survivor method and applying it to the US steel industry, discovered that the range of optimum plant size was between 0.75 and 10 per cent of the industry's total capacity. This suggests that the number of efficient plants within the US steel industry is somewhere between 10 and 133 (to the nearest integer)!

Clearly, an important aim of industrial policy must be to ensure that the nation's firms are operating at efficient levels of production close to the MES level in their industry.

A key issue in all anti-trust policy is the matter of economies of scale or the extent to which a nation's industrial firms have reached the minimum optimum size of operation. In order to maximise the economic welfare of its citizens, a country's industrial structure needs to satisfy at least two major criteria. First, each of the productive establishments (plants, stores and so forth) in its individual industries must be sufficiently large that they are individually able to exhaust all available economies of scale, i.e. to produce and sell at the lowest possible per-unit costs, given the existing state of world technology. Secondly each of those industries must be composed of a sufficiently large number of competing firms to assure [*sic*] that the fruits of this productive efficiency are passed on to the society's constituent citizens at large rather than being retained as inflated profits or wages for the narrow group of individuals that make up the managers, shareholders and workers of a relatively small cluster of monopolised industries (Winthrop, 1976).

Winthrop, a Washington attorney, goes on to point out that 'these two criteria are not simultaneously attainable in all countries of the world, particularly the smaller and poorer ones'. The need for a large market area to support a reasonably large number of firms operating at efficient levels of production within industries was, of course, an important argument in favour of Britain's membership of the EEC. The principle is that a group of countries can join together in a multinational trading bloc to expand the free-trading area of each over the geographic expanse of the group as a whole and thus create a large integrated market.

Hence Winthrop has developed these two criteria that, in his opinion, are necessary for public policy to achieve if economic welfare is to be maximised. We could, perhaps, think of these criteria as efficiency and equity. We require efficient production close to MES level of operation and we simultaneously require that there is active and intense competition in industries. Winthrop goes on to point out that, to the best of his knowledge, such an aggressive competition-maximising policy is not pursued by any country. Unfortunately, the United Nations (or any known collector of international information) does not provide us with up-to-date information on the state of industrial competition and the preferences of policy-makers towards efficiency and equity considerations in each nation of the world.

It seems sensible to regard industrial policy-makers as being faced with a trade-off between efficiency from few large-sized firms benefiting from economies of scale and equity from competition amongst many smaller firms making only normal profits in an industry.

A rather different view has been recently developed by Baumol (1982) who argues that in an ideal contestable market situation, a monopoly or oligopoly may be forced to behave like firms operating under perfect competition and set price equal to marginal cost. This, of course, only holds true if there is ease of entry and exit for potential rivals, which seems extremely unlikely under monopoly or oligopoly.

However, it would be very dangerous to conclude that large-sized firms are efficient in the sense of minimising unit costs. Leibenstein (1966) categorised the gap between actually attained production costs and the minimum theoretically available as X-inefficiency. He suggested that in non-competitive markets actual production costs tend to be higher than the minimum attainable level under efficient production. Only in competitive markets will this gap be removed and firms will be operating on the lowest possible cost curves. Both management and shop floor workers are regarded as capable of non-co-operation which leads to inefficiency in non-competitive markets. X-inefficiency can be rooted out, either by internal policing procedures (an additional element of cost to the firm) or by competition.

It would also be dangerous to assume that very many small firms operating in perfectly competitive markets will create an equitable society in the welfare economic sense of creating a Pareto optimal allocation of resources. It is, of course, true that perfect competition satisfies a set of first-order conditions for the attainment of Pareto optimality (see Chapter 3, first section).

A study by Bain (1966) discovered some rather alarming deficiencies in both efficiency and equity when comparing the US economy with the economies of India, Japan, UK, Italy, France, Canada and Sweden. He concluded that:

1 The more modern industrial sectors of his other seven countries were at least as concentrated – and often more so – as their US counterparts.
2 The prevailing level of concentration in those other countries, like the prevailing structure in the USA, tended to be some three or four times greater than would be required by the requirements of scale economies in production.

3 Plant sizes tended to be inefficiently small in those other seven countries. (Note that because a single company can own several plants, concentration can be, and often is, higher at the firm level than at the plant level.)

4 Much of this small-plant inefficiency was probably due, at least in substantial part, to the greater tolerance of cartels in those other nations than in the United States.

Bain discovered that, on average, US plants were three times as large as their foreign counterparts. Taking the median plant size of the 20 largest plants in selected industries, expressed as a percentage of US plants, Bain found that the figures ranged from 78 per cent for the UK to 13 per cent for Sweden.

How can we explain higher levels of concentration than can be justified on scale economy grounds and inefficient plant sizes given the existence of a complex system of competition legislation in Western countries? The obvious answer would appear to be that the legislation is failing to work properly at the level of individual countries in safeguarding the public interest. Let us look at the form of legislation that exists in the UK, EEC, USA and Japan and consider possible reasons for the ineffectiveness of some of the legislation.

UK LEGISLATION

The original legislation relating to abuse of monopoly power occurred in 1948 with the Monopolies and Restrictive Practices (Inquiry and Control) Act. It was concerned with both the supply of goods, including imports, in the UK and the supply of exports. A monopoly situation was defined in terms of a firm or cartel controlling one-third or more of industrial supply. The Board of Trade could refer cases to the Monopolies and Restrictive Practices Commission for investigation.

The Act specified a case-by-case approach. There was general condemnation of monopolies as being undesirable. Each case would be judged on its merits. The notion of 'public interest' was vaguely introduced in the sense that the Board of Trade could require the Monopolies Commission to consider whether the firm or firms were operating against the public interest. A report was to be drawn up and sent to the Board of Trade, which in turn would present the report to Parliament.

There have been many criticisms over the years about the vagueness of the 'public interest' criteria and the reluctance of the government to act against monopoly situations in spite of rapidly increasing levels of industrial concentration in the UK.

Hartley (1975, pp. 52–4) points out that such criticisms can be understood by applying the Downs model (Downs, 1957) of vote-maximising governments to explain monopoly legislation in the UK:

> The Downs model suggests that democratic governments will favour producers more than consumers. The model predicts that any pro-competition or vigorous anti-monopoly policy is unlikely to be introduced and enforced simply because of the opposition from producer interest groups. In addition, in formulating anti-monopoly policy, vote-maximising governments find it difficult to access the preferences of the median voter, who is likely to be undecided between the benefits of large firms and the 'unacceptable face of capitalism'. A possible outcome is that a vote-maximising government which wishes to avoid risks will introduce inconsistent legislation; this occurs where a government accepts a recommendation of the Monopolies Commission and then fails to implement it. A further example occurred in the late 1960s when the government simultaneously pursued policies for controlling monopolies and mergers (1965 Act) and policies for promoting mergers in the economy (Industrial Reorganisation Corporation, 1966).

UK policy-makers have been prepared to justify a monopoly situation on the grounds of benefits from scale economies or technical progressiveness through research and development if they are thought to exceed welfare losses due to reduced competition. The latter are extremely difficult to access and the literature is full of contradictory results ranging from Harberger's (1954) study where the welfare losses attributable to monopoly were claimed to be very small (of the order of 0.1 per cent of GNP in the USA during the 1920s), to Cowling and Mueller's (1978) study where welfare losses representing some 13 per cent of Gross Corporate Product for the US over the period 1963–6 were claimed to be found. Littlechild (1981) was critical of previous attempts to estimate welfare loss from monopoly power, especially the Cowling and Mueller study. He argues (pp. 348–9):

> (a) That even within the framework of their own model, Cowling and Mueller have overestimated the costs of monopoly power in four major respects; (b) that the very framework of long-run equilibrium, used by all writers from Harberger onwards, precludes the recognition of profits due to uncertainty and innovation and wrongly interprets them as due to monopoly; (c) that in con-

sequence all these studies are completely misleading as to the location, extent, duration and costs of monopoly power; and (d) that such studies are therefore quite inappropriate as a basis for public policy.

The implication is that any attempt at inputting exact numbers into a cost-benefit analysis relating to a situation of a monopoly power will be extremely difficult and hazardous.

The next major piece of industrial legislation, following on from the 1948 Act, occurred in 1956 with the Restrictive Trade Practices Act. The Restrictive Trade Practices Court was set up to deal with collusive agreements between firms and took this element of the law away from the Monopolies Commission. The 1956 Act began by requiring that the terms of a wide variety of trade association agreements be made public – 'registered' with a Registrar of Restrictive Practices. All agreements between two or more firms or organisations were covered relating to restrictions on the prices of goods supplied, terms or conditions of sale, quotations produced, processes of manufacture employed, or classes of persons to whom goods are supplied. The Registrar functioned as a prosecutor and could refer registrable agreements to the Restrictive Practices Board for evaluation.

A series of 'special' circumstances or 'gateways' were introduced whereby parties to a challenged agreement may preserve it in law. The seven 'gateways' covered areas such as protection of the public against injury, countervailing power, unemployment issues, exports, etc. There was a widespread feeling that these 'gateways' provided convenient loopholes in the piece of legislation and were analytically unsound and imprecise. (See, for example, Hunter (1966) and Stevens and Yamey (1965).)

However, producers had, in addition to passing through one or more of the 'gateways', to convince the court that the specific advantages of the agreement outweighed any detriment to the public (the 'tailpiece'). The agreement has to be proved to be in the public interest.

Until 1956 no restrictions were imposed on the stipulation of resale prices by manufacturers in the UK. Resale price maintenance (RPM) led to uniformity in the selling prices of many branded goods. Three methods of enforcement were open to manufacturers:

1 The manufacturer could withhold supplies of all his goods to a retailer who was not adhering to his resale terms.
2 Legal action could be taken against a retailer who had entered into an agreement with a manufacturer for the maintenance of

resale prices. Courts could restrain price cutting by an offending retailer and/or award damages to the manufacturer for breach of contract.

3 Associations existed in some trades which applied collective sanctions against price-cutting retailers. All manufacturers in the group agreed to jointly withhold supplies of their price maintained goods from any retailer who was found to be cutting the prices of any one, or more, of their brands. Financial penalties could also be levied on a price-cutter who wished to be reinstated as a regular customer and promised to adhere to RPM in future.

Methods 1 and 2 above were known as 'individual RPM' since each manufacturer could act on his own. Method 3 was known as 'collective RPM'. 'Collective RPM' was strictly prohibited under Part II of the 1956 Restrictive Practices Act. However, 'individual RPM' was actually made more effective by giving the manufacturer the assistance of the courts in enforcing resale prices and conditions. The 1956 Act failed to bring about any major reduction in RPM in the UK.

In 1964 the Resale Prices Act created a general presumption in law that RPM was contrary to the public interest. RPM was dealt with in a very similar way to restrictive trade practices under the 1956 Act. A general prohibition existed subject to specific exceptions under a series of escape clauses (or 'gateways'). RPM ceased to be a common practice in the UK. A typical reaction was for a manufacturer to substitute, and advertise, recommended prices instead.

The 1965 Monopolies and Mergers Act added to the powers of the Monopolies Commission to require publication of price lists by firms, to regulate prices and to order the dissolution of monopolies. Most importantly the Monopolies Commission became the Monopolies and Mergers Commission and the Board of Trade could refer prospective or actual mergers to the Monopolies and Mergers Commission provided that:

1 the merger would create or increase a situation of monopoly in the supply of goods or services in the UK.
or
2 the value of assets either taken over or to be taken over exceeded £5 million. Subsequently, the combined assets threshold was raised first to £15 million (April 1980), and then to £30 million (July 1984).

A merger may be referred to the Monopolies and Mergers Commission any time up to six months after it has taken place.

No pre-supposition is built into UK legislation that monopoly is necessarily bad, and the onus is on the Monopolies and Mergers Commission (MMC) to show whether or not a monopoly which has been referred for investigation operates against the public interest.

UK merger policy takes the same cost-benefit approach as monopoly policy, each merger which is referred being examined on its individual merits, with performance criteria being used to determine whether it should be allowed to proceed. The underlying attitude is that most mergers are beneficial but that a small number may operate against the public interest and therefore need to be investigated (George, 1985, p. 1).

Although UK policy appears to recognise that mergers and single firm monopolies involve not only costs in the form of welfare losses due to reduced competition, but also possible benefits in the form of economies of scale and increased research and development, there has been a general reluctance to act against monopoly situations and to investigate more than a small number of proposed mergers. UK merger policy, in particular, has been heavily criticised for its vagueness and inconsistency. For example, *The Economist* (5.2.83), in an article entitled 'Muddling with Mergers', started with the general comment that:

Britain's fondness for fudge and compromise produces many bad decisions and unworkable policies: nowhere more unworkable than in its supervision of company mergers. Confusion and controversy have been the hallmarks of the most recent government rulings on mergers, suggesting a need for clearer guidelines for judging mergers, and clearer division of responsibility between those parts of the government involved in merger policy.

In particular, economists of the so-called 'structuralist school' have advocated a more vigorous merger policy.

The power of veto conferred on government ministers over MMC recommendations has come in for special criticism. In 1983, Peter Rees, the trade minister, acted against the advice of the MMC with respect to the proposed Charter Consolidated – Anderson Strathclyde merger. This led The Economist to recommend (among other things) that: 'Decisions by the Monopolies Commission on the grounds of competition policy alone should be binding on ministers.'

Further tightening up of the restrictive practices legislation occurred in 1968 with The Restrictive Practices Act which made information agreements among firms relating to prices, terms, quantities supplied, processes applied, persons and areas supplied and costs registrable. In 1973 The Fair Trading Act established a Director General of Fair Trading with responsibilities for the control of monopolies, mergers and restrictive practices. A new emphasis on consumer protection was introduced and The Price Commission came into being under the 1973 Counter-Inflation Act. Also the statutory definition of a monopoly was reduced from a third to a quarter of the relevant market.

A new attempt was made to clarify the 'public interest' under the 1973 Act. It was stated that

> In determining . . . whether any particular matter operates, or may be expected to operate, against the public interest the Commission shall take into account all matters which appear to them in the particular circumstances to be relevant.

This vague definition allows for individual interpretation by the politicians and civil servants of the day. The Act goes on to define such matters that affect the public interest as promotion of competition, interests of consumers, efficiency in industry, regional distribution of industry and employment and exports. The regional dimension was important in the Chartered Consolidated – Anderson Strathclyde proposed merger. The majority view of the MMC was that the merger would result in significant damage to Scotland. George (1985) makes the following recommendation.

> As far as the MMC is concerned, and so long as the existing legislation remains intact, one possibility would be to treat those mergers in which the major issues relate to regional or balance of payments problems as special cases outside the main stream of merger references.

At present the burden of proof lies with the MMC to find and specify particular effects and not on the firm(s) to demonstrate benefits. George (1985) believes that

> On the question of where the burden of proof should lie there are good reasons for reversing the present position. One argument in favour of such a change is that a bidding company should be better informed than anyone else about the pros and cons of an acquisition because it will have given careful thought to the various key issues before launching a bid. It should be expected therefore to use its superior knowledge to demonstrate benefit.

A point of view now advocated by Sir Gordon Borrie – Director General of Fair Trading. (Proposed changes to EEC merger law affecting all Member States is discussed in the section on 'EEC legislation' below.)

The 1974–78 Labour administration felt that a review of competition Policy was necessary because of:

1 increasing levels of concentration of ownership of British industry;
2 increasing degree of import penetration;
3 the rise of the conglomerate – their centralised decision making processes, their power and lack of accountability and their location within the South East of England;
4 the rise of EEC competition policy and the problem of sovereignty;
5 pressure from industry to protect it from EEC procedures.

In 1975, the Labour Government developed their Long Term Industrial Strategy, a strategy aimed at the problem of poor performance within the manufacturing sector of the British economy. Four major reasons were identified as possible causes for the decline in UK industry and within the second broad category were listed 'restrictive practices'.

Roy Hattersley, Secretary of State for Prices and Consumer Protection at the time, clarified the point further when he stated in the House:

The review (of competition policy) will reflect the fact that competition policy and the industrial strategy are complementary in that they share the same basic objective of increasing the efficiency of British industry.

In 1976 the Restrictive Trade Practices Act was revised to include restrictive agreements relating to services which now had to be registered. The Restrictive Trade Practices Court has been most successful in dealing with traditional cartels and resale price maintenance. However, it has been suggested that the success of the Court has led firms to consider merger activity as a replacement for the traditional cartel and a wave of mergers has resulted. In addition, other forms of agreement or tacit agreement have replaced the cartel. UK industry has an inherent tendency towards co-operation rather than competition.

In 1977 an interdepartmental committee was established under Liesner (Chief Economic Adviser at the Department of Trade). The first Review of Monopolies and Mergers Policy (May 1978) was intended to form the basis of a revised monopolies and mergers policy and to provide guidelines to industry on what would and what would not be investigated by the MMC.

The Review of Restrictive Trade Practices Policy (published March 1979) took much the same form as its forerunner and was charged with tightening existing legislation – legislation which companies were finding it possible to circumvent.

Both reviews (Green Papers) were to form the basis of a tighter, more vigorous competition policy which would in some measure deal with the problems outlined in points 1 to 5. The Labour administration conceived this policy as a means by which to deal with perceived excesses perpetrated within the 'commanding heights' of the economy.

When the Labour Government was replaced by a Conservative administration in 1979, the proposals contained within the two Green Papers officially died. But the Conservatives were returned with a commitment to abolish the Price Commission and they needed a peg on which to hang that legislation. Hattersley's Reviews were very convenient – specifically those sections dealing with anti-competitive practices. Labour's long-term industrial strategy was now replaced by the Conservative's Anti-Inflation Strategy and anti-competitive practice legislation was applicable to both, specifically when measures to increase competition were claimed to be much more effective in reducing prices and raising standards than the Price Commission.

Annex B of the Review of Monopolies and Mergers policy provided just the peg that the Tories needed. Entitled 'Monopolistic Behaviour and Performance' it is Annex B which deals specifically with those practices that the MMC had consistently found to be against the public interest.

The 1980 Competition Act fulfils the ideological requirements of the Tory administration. Section 1 deals with the abolition of the Price Commission – a wasteful interference in the free play of market forces. Sections 2–10 of the Act define anti-competitive practices, determine how they should be investigated and outline how the policy should be operated. Sections 11–13 provide for the inclusion of nationalised industries – previously exempt from competition legislation – as a precursor to privatisation.

The politics of the anti-competitive practice legislation are thus particularly interesting. Introduced as Conservative legislation, it is based on two Green Papers prepared and published by a Labour Government. Both Labour and Conservative were agreed that while in certain circumstances a practice might be considered to be anti-competitive, in others, the same practice might increase competition.

They therefore agreed that the very wide definition, ostensibly intended as a catch-all, should stand:

> a person engages in an anti-competitive practice if, in the course of business, that person pursues a course of conduct which, of itself or when taken together with a course of conduct pursued by persons associated with him, has or is intended to have, or is likely to have the effect of restricting, distorting or preventing competition in connection with the production, supply or acquisition of goods in the United Kingdom or any part of it or the supply or securing of services in the United Kingdom or any part of it (Section 2 of the 1980 Competition Act).

In the committee debates, numerous practices were described as those which 'might be capable of investigation'. The vast majority of these fall under the general heading of vertical restraints such as: exclusive dealing arrangements, refusal to supply, tie-in sales, full-line forcing.

Sections 2–10 provide for the Director-General of the Office of Fair Trading to investigate a complaint received either from the Secretary of State or a member of the public. The complaint is then investigated and, if the company is found to be following an undesirable 'course of conduct' they are expected and encouraged to give it up. Failure to do so results in reference to the Monopolies and Mergers Commission which must then investigate the complaint all over again to determine whether or not the conduct is 'against the public interest'. It had been expected that companies would not wish to be referred to the MMC.

Indeed, in 1980, much was expected that has not been fulfilled. It was suggested that the 1980 Act was a draconian piece of legislation with far-reaching implications for the British economy. There is, after all, no requirement that this course of conduct be consistently applied, no requirement that the company holds either a monopoly or dominant position, no requirement that the effect on competition be substantial.

The Act has developed in a way almost completely unexpected by the officials responsible. The reality is that the Office of Fair Trading has to deal with numerous insignificant complaints. Section 2 of the 1980 Act has been described as a gold mine for people wishing to complain about vertical restraints.

The White Paper ('Opening Markets: New Policy on Restrictive Trade Practices', HMSO Cmnd. 727, July 1989) sets out the Government's intentions for legislation to update policy towards restrictive trade practices. In addition to providing 'a more effective way of rooting out anti-competitive agreements which raise costs and prices', the proposed reform is aiming to produce greater harmony with EEC Competition legislation, as established under Article 85.

There will be, according to the aims set out in this White Paper, an 'illustrative list of practices falling within the prohibition, including price-fixing (including resale price maintenance – rpm), collusive tendering, market-sharing and collective boycotts'. The DGFT (Director General of Fair Trading – Sir Gordon Borrie) will be responsible for initiating investigations and will issue guidance to indicate the kinds of agreement which are not regarded as anti-competitive.

In addition, the Government aims to appoint 'up to ten extra part-time members to the MMC to constitute a restrictive trade practices tribunal. They will sit in panels of three to reach final decisions when the published conclusions of the DGFT are disputed and to impose penalties in appropriate cases'.

This is an attempt to move in the direction of EEC legislation. Guilty parties will be liable to 'civil penalties of up to 10% of their total UK turnover or £250,000, whichever is the higher. Penalties will be imposed by the tribunal (not the DGFT) up to a maximum of £1 million; application will be made to the High Court for penalties above this level within the 10% maximum. The Court will also be able to impose penalties of up to £100,000 on company directors and managers who negotiate or operate prohibitive agreements'.

This is, potentially, a substantial change. However, we must wait and see just how substantial this in fact turns out to be.

EEC LEGISLATION

A principal objective of the European Commission is to establish a Common Market between member states and secure the benefits of economic integration. Thus Articles 85–94 of the Rome Treaty establishing the EEC are designed to ensure that the behaviour of undertakings within the EEC does not thwart the establishment of a Common Market through the maintenance of non-tariff barriers to trade. Article 3 of the Treaty lays down the prime objectives of the EEC and includes among these a call for the 'institution of a system ensuring that competition in the Common Market is not distorted'. It is to this prime aim that Articles 85–94 apply, with Articles 85 and 86 providing the substantive law as it relates to the behaviour of undertakings. Article 87 clearly dictates that while UK companies are still fully subject to national law in all respects, they are, in addition, subject to EEC law and, in the final analysis, EEC law takes precedence. Thus, for example, an agreement initially upheld by the Restrictive Practices Court may, nevertheless, be declared null and void if it cannot be held to fall within the block exemption afforded under Article 85 (3) of the Treaty or obtain 'negative clearance' from the Commission.

Extract from the Rome Treaty establishing the EEC

Article 85

1. The following shall be deemed to be incompatible with the Common Market and shall hereby be prohibited: any agreement between enterprises, any decisions by associations of enterprises and any concerted practices which are likely to affect trade between Member States and which have as their object or result the prevention, restriction or distortion of competition within the Common Market, in particular those resulting in: (a) The direct or indirect fixing of purchase or selling price or any other trading conditions; (b) the limitation or control of production, marketing, technical development or investment; (c) market sharing or the sharing of sources of supply; (d) the application to parties to transactions of unequal terms in respect of equivalent supplies, thereby placing them at a competitive disadvantage; or (e) the subjecting of the conclusion of a contract to the acceptance by a party of additional supplies which, either by their nature or according to commercial usage, have no connection with the subject of such contract.

2. Any agreement or decisions prohibited pursuant to this article shall be null and void.

3. Nevertheless, the provisions of paragraph I may be declared inapplicable in the case of:
– any agreements or classes of agreement between enterprises;
– any decisions or classes of decisions by associations of enterprises, and
– any concerted practices or classes of concerted practice which contribute to the improvement of the production or distribution of goods or to the promotion of technical or economic progress while reserving to users an equitable share in the profit resulting therefrom and which:
(a) neither impose on the enterprises concerned any restrictions not indispensable to the attainment of the above objectives;

(b) nor enable such enterprises to eliminate competition of a substantial proportion of the goods concerned.

Article 86

To the extent to which trade between any Member States may be affected thereby, action by one or more enterprises to take improper advantage of a dominant position within the Common Market or within a substantial part of it shall be deemed to be incompatible with the Common Market and shall hereby be prohibited.

Such improper practices may in particular result in:

(a) the direct or indirect imposition of any inequitable purchase or selling prices or of any other inequitable trading conditions;

(b) the limitation of production, markets or technical development to the prejudice of consumers;

(c) the application to parties to transactions of unequal terms in respect of equivalent supplies, thereby placing them at a competitive disadvantage; or

(d) the subjecting of the conclusion of a contract to the acceptance by a party of additional supplies which, either by their nature or according to commercial usage, have no connection with the subject of such a contract.

UK and EEC competition laws are often said to be in harmony with one another. While the question of *per se* legality of a practice might be comparable, the operation and conception differ vastly.

(a) EEC legislation must be written in such a way as to be readily translated into nine languages without changing the meaning. It must therefore be clear and concise leaving considerable room for interpretation.

(b) It is the practice, rather than what the practice does, which infringes Articles 85 and 86. Thus companies must apply for negative clearance or exemption. In either case, the Competition Directorate, Directorate IV (DGIV) will have to carry out a full investigation and, if the company receives neither, fines can be imposed retrospectively. The OFT remains interested in what the practice does, and (officially) investigates only where it has received a complaint.

(c) DGIV is required to investigate every complaint that it receives. The OFT has, and exercises, considerable discretion.

(d) DGIV is not required to inform the company under investigation of the source of the complaint, or the nature of the investigation, nor is it required to show the company all the documents it has relating to the investigation. Companies may not necessarily know, therefore, whether they are being investigated for abuse of a dominant position (Article 86) or for entering an agreement prohibited under Article 85. The OFT, on the other hand, must give companies a clear and full account of the investigations.

(e) DGIV requires information from companies and they must reply within a relatively short period of time or face a fine. The OFT requests information from undertakings and has to hope that they will co-operate.

(f) Where DGIV suspects that a company might destroy incriminating documents if made aware of any investigation, it has the power to enter company premises (not by force), and copy all documents it thinks might be of interest to it. Equally, therefore DGIV has the power to go on 'fishing expeditions' just to see what it might uncover; and, if in the course of any investigation it requires an oral response to a question, that response must be given on the spot. There is no provision for the presence of a lawyer during these swoops and no provision that the investigators wait for a lawyer to arrive before questions are asked and filing cabinets opened. Although this type of behaviour is not unknown in the UK (the Inland Revenue is permitted to effect a forced entry, for example) it would not be acceptable if carried out by the OFT.

(g) Sanctions resulting from an investigation differ too. DGIV has the power to impose prohibition and heavy fines: up to 10 per cent of annual turnover. It also publishes a good deal of sensitive information in its case reports. The OFT, on the other hand, can request a company to cease a course of conduct. If such a request is ignored or refused, the whole issue is referred to the MMC where it is investigated again. The MMC has the power to request a company to enter into an undertaking, and to monitor any undertaking given; it has the power to criticise and to recommend. In the absence of an undertaking, the Secretary of State may make an order prohibiting the practice and remedying any adverse effects.

(h) DGIV is an investigator, prosecutor and judge. It is accountable to the Member States in only a very limited way through an Advisory Committee whose deliberations and findings are confidential. Cases are referred to the European Court only on appeal and appeal can be based only on the level of fine or on a point of law. Thus DGIV undoubtedly has considerable power and is considered capable of political acts. The combined powers of the

OFT and MMC are puny by comparison, particularly as the activities of both are subject to veto by the Secretary of State.

These eight major areas of divergence in the operation of competition policy explain why the majority of cases go straight to Brussels and indeed why, even though remedy is available under Articles 85 and 86 through the British courts, there is no record of a complainant having gone the distance. A complaint to DGIV which will ensure a full, if protracted investigation, costs only the price of a stamp.

The polarity exemplified by the efficiency versus equity dichotomy expressed at the beginning of this chapter, is no less apparent within European administration of competition policy than elsewhere. Yet, rooted in immediate post-war German anti-cartel legislation and informed by USA anti-trust laws, EEC competition law differs substantially from that of the UK.

As a consequence of competition's place within the section establishing the goals of the European Economic Community, there are many commentators (predominantly lawyers) who consider that the practice of competition policy is motivated more by the desire to create and protect the free movement of goods, services, labour and capital, as required for the creation of a common market, than simply by the need to institute a system protecting competition.

If this is so, it suggests that the EEC is operating from a fairly traditional theoretical base. The attainment of Pareto optimality *qua* perfectly competitive markets requires equilibrium within the labour and capital, goods and services, distribution and exchange markets for an omega point to be attained. While discussion of the advisability of seeking to attain such a single optimum solution has been dealt with elsewhere, we refer to it here purely for the purpose of suggesting that the most frequent criticism of the European Commission may be considered by some as unjustified.

The policy outlined within Article 3(f) is codified within Articles 85–90, with Articles 85 and 86 clearly delineating prohibitions upon perceived anti-competitive firm behaviour. Of equal importance, but often overlooked, are Article 5, paragraph 2, and Article 30. Article 5 (2) requires that: '[Member States] shall abstain from any measure which could jeopardise the attainment of the objectives of this Treaty' and Article 30 states that: 'Quantitative restrictions on imports and all measures having equivalent effect shall . . . be prohibited between Member States.'

With the deepening recession across Europe, the necessity to optimise the trade-off between protection of national economies and commitment to the European ideal, has found all member states, at one time or another, in contravention of Article 30. The Cassis de Dijon case arose out of West Germany's insistence that all liqueurs contain a minimum 25 per cent alcohol content. Thus this liqueur's 20 per cent alcohol content barred it from being described or sold as a liqueur within West Germany. The European Court held that national laws could infringe Article 30 by discriminating against imports and that goods which have met one set of requirements laid down by national regulation, should not be required to meet a separate second set laid down in another member state. West Germany's attempt to protect its alcohol beverage market from European imports had been breached. Equally infamous is the French turkeys, or Bourgoine case, where the UK's Ministry of Agriculture, Fisheries and Food banned imports of French turkeys on rather transparently discriminatory grounds. At the time of writing, the House of Lords was in the process of deciding whether or not French turkey producers could claim damages against the British government. Other examples include Greek protection of its general insurance market, French resale price maintenance on books (Centres Leclerc), etc. The existence of the Common Market would be a farce if it were not possible for the Commission to investigate and prohibit such behaviour. Yet the readiness of national governments to submit to the Commission's prohibitions is a rather eloquent proof that in times of recession, even the most isolationist member prefers membership of the Common Market to isolationism. Presumably because, within highly developed market economies, the twin goals of equity and efficiency are achieved only when international trade is supervised by a supra-national authority – an independent referee.

Article 85(1) prohibits all vertical and horizontal agreements between undertakings, decisions by trade associations, and concerted practices which may affect trade between member states, 'and which have as their object or effect the prevention, restriction or distortion of competition within the Common Market . . .'.

While 85 (1) may appear to parallel aspects of the UK's Restrictive Trade Practices Act, it is distinguished by its prohibition upon vertical as well as horizontal agreements, and by its extra-territoriality. Equally, exemption from 85(1) under Article 85(3) is dependent upon parties to any agreement being able to show either that the agreement contributes to improvements in the production or distribution of goods, or to promoting technical or economic progress,

while allowing consumers a fair share of the resulting benefits, and which does not:
(a) impose on the undertakings concerned restrictions which are not indispensable to the attainment of these objectives;
(b) afford such undertakings the possibility of eliminating competition in respect of a substantial part of the products in question.

The exemption suggests that the architects of the Treaty required a solution to the equity/efficiency dilemma. Companies forming agreements must show that they increase either allocative or technical efficiency, and that equitable shares of resultant benefits are distributed to the consumer. While the Hoffman La Roche case is probably one of the most obvious examples of this thesis being put into practice, the more recent turn-around permitting Distillers a network of distribution agreements is considerably less so. Such (presumably) politically inspired decisions aside, however, the Commission's commitment to the wording of the Rome Treaty, and the underlying thesis as exemplified by 85(3), is well established through such decisions as AEG Telefunken, United Brands, etc.

Articles 85(1) and 86 (but not 85(3)) have 'direct effect'. That is, actions for infringement of Articles 85 and 86 can be heard in national courts, but not applications for exemption. Thus it is perfectly possible for an agreement to pass through the RTPA legislative framework, yet be caught under Articles 85 or 86. Indeed Garden Cottage Foods obtained an interlocutory injunction against the Milk Marketing Board under Article 86 within the UK courts – an option unavailable under UK law.

Article 86 legislates against abuse of a dominant position. That is it applies the equivalent prohibition against price fixing, sales quotas, selective distribution systems and tie-in sales as found within Article 85, but to individual companies dominant within separate markets.

It is for its decisions under Article 86 that the Commission has probably been most heavily criticised, most notably for its precise definition of markets providing support for its determination of dominance, which the European Court defined in United Brands as:

. . . a position of economic strength enjoyed by an undertaking which enables it to prevent effective competition being maintained in the relevant market by giving it the power to behave to an appreciable extent independently of its competitors, customers and ultimately of its consumers.

This has meant, however, that 10 per cent (BP) and indeed as little as 5 per cent (AEG Telefunken) market share have been regarded as sufficient for market dominance.

Almost as frequently criticised is the Commission's interpretation of the terms 'within the Common Market' and 'trade between member states'. Certainly, while Michelin's agreement with its distributors in the Netherlands was found to be within the Common Market, not even the Commission suggested that it affected trade between member states – only that by dint of covering the whole of that country, it had the potentiality to do so. As the European Court found in Dutch Cement Dealers: an agreement operating throughout a member state 'by its very nature may affect trade between member states'. Or, as the court made clear in Consten and Grundig versus the Commission:

. . . what is important is whether the agreement is capable of constituting a threat, whether direct or indirect, actual or potential, to freedom of trade between Member States, in a manner which might harm the attainment of the objectives of a single market between States.

(It is this sort of remark which has encouraged non-economists to believe there is a contradiction between the pursuit of competition and the creation of a common market.)

Unlike the UK, however, where a company found to be engaging in a course of conduct amounting to an anti-competitive practice must wait another six months to see whether the Monopolies and Mergers Commission will deem it to be against the public interest, companies found to be abusing their dominant position within the EEC, face *per se* prohibition. Any basis for appeal to the European Court emanates solely from discussion of legal points and the scale of penalty to be applied. For example, AKZO, found to have abused its dominant position by the European Commission, appealed to the European Court against the allegedly punitive nature of the fine.

The most important difference between EEC and UK legislation is often considered to be between form and effect. The Restrictive Trade Practices Act attends to the form of agreements, thus allowing well-drafted restrictive agreements to exist (e.g. Ceramic Tiles, and Windows) and striking down poorly-drafted agreements which have no business being considered (e.g. Topliss showers). This may also have a good deal to do with the fact that economists have no representation within the Restrictive Trade Practices Court, and because those who are involved have a lawyer's view of the true meaning of the term efficiency (as discussed in Chapter 3).

The EEC's emphasis upon effects, does rather more to ensure that agreements which seek either to isolate markets within the community (e.g. Hasselblad) or to force distributors to charge unreasonably high prices (e.g. AEG Telefunken) are prohibited, however well drafted they may be. The problem for economists then, is the problem of determining whether the attainment of the Community's objectives has hindered the attainment of efficiency. For example, by denying AEG the right to establish a selective distribution system, has the Commission denied AEG the right to distribute its products in the most efficient manner possible? While the protection of competition and the creation of a common market are not mutually exclusive, they are not mutually inclusive either. The history of UK competition policy suggests the most highly supervised and effective laws always exist beside a highly developed and sophisticated legal profession, access to which is determined by a corporation's power and ability to pay.

Development of the European Community's competition policy does not entirely mirror that evolution, particularly in so far as it has given rise to a belief in some quarters that the Commission is 'out to get the multinationals'. While this may or may not be so, the necessity for companies to notify the DGIV of agreements, the Directorate's draconian powers of search and seizure, and its role as judge, jury and prosecutor over companies charged with infringing Article 85 or 86, make it a most important regulatory authority.

An attempt to regulate mergers throughout the EEC, in the light of 1992, has been set out in Council Regulation (EEC) No. 4064/89 (December 1989). This Regulation will be directly applicable to all Member States and will become law in September 1990. A cross-border EEC merger boom in the 1990s looks extremely likely. Indeed, there is evidence of such a merger bandwagon already rolling. In 1989 cross-border acquisitions in Western Europe were at a record level of some 50 billion ECUs. The movement towards, and the desire to form, European megamerged-conglomerates is clearly apparent. The need to protect EEC consumers from highly concentrated market structures is of the upmost importance.

Under this new EEC Regulation a merger may be investigated under the following criteria:

1 It involves an aggregate worldwide turnover of all undertakings concerned of more than 5000 million ECUs, and

2 It has an aggregate Community-wide turnover of each of at least two of the undertakings concerned of more than 250 million ECUs.

In appraising such mergers account will be taken of many economic factors, including:

1 the need to preserve and develop effective competition within the EEC, and
2 the market position of the undertakings concerned and their economic and financial power.

Power will be granted to suspend mergers and to impose fines on firms or individuals who fail to comply with EEC law. The Commission may impose fines not exceeding 10 per cent of the aggregate turnover of the undertakings concerned. It may also impose period penalty payments where unnecessary delays are deemed to have occurred.

USA LEGISLATION

Legislation to control the centralisation of power in the hands of an industrial oligarchy of big businessmen was introduced towards the end of the last century in the United States of America. There was a feeling of great hostility towards the concentration of enormous power in private hands. It was felt that only a government directly elected by the people should possess such power.

> It is possible, because of its indirect social or moral effect, to prefer a system of small producers, each dependent upon his own skill and character, to one in which the great mass of those engaged must accept the direction of a few . . . We have been speaking only of the economic reasons which forbid monopoly; but, as we have already implied, there are others, based on the belief that great industrial consolidations are inherently undesirable, regardless of their economic results. In the debates in Congress, Senator Sherman himself . . . showed that among the purposes of Congress in 1890 was a desire to put an end to great aggregations of capital because of the helplessness of the individual before them . . . Throughout the history of these statutes it has been constantly assumed that one of their purposes was to perpetuate and preserve, for its own sake and in spite of possible cost, an organisation of industry in small units which can effectively compete with each other (Judge Learned Hand in the anti-trust case against the Aluminium Company of America (1945, pp. 427–9)).

US anti-trust laws predate UK legislation by 60 years. Senator John Sherman (Republican from Ohio) introduced a series of anti-trust bills during the period 1888–90. His 1890 bill was the most successful piece of legislation during this period and is known as the Sherman Act. However, it was not until Theodore Roosevelt became president in 1901 that legislation began to be effectively enforced in the USA. Legislation designed to streamline judicial procedures for civil anti-trust cases and to create a special anti-trust enforcement division in the Department of Justice was passed during Roosevelt's period in office.

The 1890 Sherman Act has two major provisions:

Section 1. Every contract, combination in the form of a trust or otherwise, or conspiracy, in restraint of trade or commerce among the several States, or with foreign nations, is hereby declared to be illegal . . .

Section 2. Every person who shall monopolise, or attempt to monopolise, or combine or conspire with any other person or persons to monopolise any part of the trade or commerce among the several States, or with foreign nations, shall be guilty of a mis-demeanour . . .

Two further important pieces of US anti-trust legislation can be attributed to President Woodrow Wilson. The Federal Trade Commission Act was passed in 1914 and set up the Federal Trade Commission to strengthen the anti-trust legislation. The Clayton Act was also passed in 1914 and this forbids certain kinds of price discrimination, exclusive dealing, acquisition of corporate stock and interlocking directorates. The Federal Trade Commission Act forbids unfair competitive practices and includes not only a variety of offences characterised by misrepresentation and similar breaches of commercial ethics, but also conspiracies to fix prices, efforts to intimidate or destroy competitors and similar anti-competitive schemes.

The Commission's jurisdiction was extended under the 1938 Wheeler-Lea Act to include cases where the general public, and not just fellow competitors, were injured by unfair competitive practices. In 1952 the McGuire Act was passed to permit the enforcement of resale price maintenance by manufacturers upon non-signing sellers where state laws permit. However, horizontal price fixing agreements were still strictly illegal.

Section 2 of the Clayton Act, which covers price discrimination, was amended in 1936 by the Robinson-Patman Act which provides added restrictions on the freedom of suppliers to discriminate. Also, Section 7 of the Clayton Act, which covers acquisition of corporate stock, was amended by the Celler-Kefauver Act in 1950 to cover mergers accomplished through asset purchases as well as share purchases.

In spite of anti-trust legislation dating back to the late 1880s, the USA has witnessed a fairly rapid increase in both relative and aggregate levels of concentration, especially in the post-Second World War era. For example, Blair (1972) has shown that the top 200 firms in the US in 1968 controlled the same fraction of assets as the top 1,000 firms in 1941. However, Hannah and Kay (1977) have shown that the growth rate of the share of the largest 100 firms in manufacturing net output has been slower in the US over the period 1907–73 than in the UK.

It seems that economic society in the United States, as well as in other Western industrialised nations, has become increasingly dominated by a small number of very large and powerful industrial units, at least in the manufacturing sector of the economy. These large multi-product corporations appear to have successfully evaded anti-trust legislation as originally set out by Senator Sherman in his 1890 Act.

The main criticisms made by the Structuralist School of UK merger policy appeared to have been overcome in the USA by the 1968 merger guidelines. The emphasis was placed on the preservation and promotion of competitive market structures. This was seen as a model of the Structural approach to merger policy. In the case of horizontal mergers, prime importance was given to the market share of the acquiring and the acquired firms. Also it was made apparent that economies of scale would be accepted as a justification for a merger only in exceptional circumstances.

However, a pronounced shift in US merger policy occurred in the 1980s, coinciding with a different economic strategy under the Reagan administration. In 1982 the guidelines of mergers aimed to widen the market and increase the number of firms considered to be competitors. This had the effect of reducing the number of mergers under investigation. The 1984 guidelines were concerned with protecting US industries from intense foreign competition (e.g. the automobile industry faced intense competition from Japanese and German manufacturers). Foreign imports were included into the relevant US market which again increased the size of the market and reduced the likelihood of a merger between two or more domestic firms being challenged. The 1982 and 1984 guidelines emphasised that most mergers do *not* threaten competition. Hence the divergence between UK and US merger policy in the post-1968 era was effectively removed in the 1980s.

Finally consider the case of vertical restraints under US law. These constitute conditions imposed by a manufacturer on its distributors or retail outlets. Examples include resale price maintenance, territorial allocation and exclusive dealing. The judicial attitude towards such restraints was, up until 1977, a fairly hostile one. Basically, vertical restraints were viewed in much the same way as horizontal agreements amongst firms and were considered as likely to be against the public interest.

The argument that horizontal and vertical agreements have similar economic consequences and that similar legal treatment would be required in both cases, was seriously challenged by writers such as Bork (1954). The economic literature of Bork *et al.* eventually began to influence policy in the USA. In the Sylvania decision in 1977, the Supreme Court abandoned the notion of *per se* illegality for all vertical restraints in favour of a more lenient attitude. Vertical price restraints continued to be unlawful *per se*, but non-price restraints would be subject to rule of reason analysis. There is a fundamental problem of how exactly courts should distinguish between price and non-price vertical restraints. Obviously plaintiffs have an incentive to characterise every restrain as a price restraint. Also, the Sylvania court gave no indication as to how a rule of reason analysis should be conducted for non-price restrictions. The US Justice Department has published its 'Vertical Restraint Guidelines' which are intended to state the enforcement intentions of the Justice Department in the post-Sylvania era. George Hay (1985) has made an interesting comparison between the US and EEC law with respect to vertical restraints:

> Hence, while the [US] Guidelines provide a safe harbour for a small manufacturer (10 per cent or less market share), or a manufacturer in a relatively unconcentrated industry to impose airtight territorial allocations on its dealers, such behaviour would run foul of Article 85(1) and would almost certainly not be exempted under 85(3), nor would it come under the block exemption for exclusive distribution since the latter cannot be used to prevent or discourage parallel imports. In addition, to the extent that the Justice Department's 'hidden agenda' is to have similar rules apply to resale price maintenance, the policy is likely to be unacceptable in the EEC.

With regard to the UK, Hay goes on to argue that

> the UK has already gone well beyond the [US] Guidelines in immunising non-price vertical restraints. Properly drafted agreements awarding exclusive distributorships or assigning exclusive geographic territories are not registrable under the Restrictive Trade Practices Act. In addition, while vertical practices may be picked up under the Fair Trading Act or the more recent Competition Act,

this should happen only for dominant firms, almost certainly requiring more than the 10 per cent safe harbour allowed under the Guidelines.

Hay does, however, go on to point out that the US market definition, as set out under the 1984 Merger Guidelines, is much broader than in the UK and that dominance has been defined to include market shares as low as 30 per cent.

JAPANESE LEGISLATION

Japanese industrial policy comprises general measures to enhance the environment of industry rather than selective interventions on the contemporary European model. Japan's post-war economic development began with extensive government protection. By adopting protective trade policies and limiting direct foreign investments, Japan was able to protect its infant industries. Behind the tariff walls there was fierce, if constrained, competition.

> Japan has indeed given the impression of being a nation reluctant to open its markets. Still under import control or subject to high import duties are many products, including oranges, beef, leather, bananas, chocolates, whiskies, cognacs and marine products – all of which are of prime concern to North American, European and south-east Asian countries (Tsurata, 1985).

Perhaps it is more relevant to consider Japanese policy from a dynamic rather than a static viewpoint. Japan has gradually removed its government protection and controls over industry. 'Decontrol' is the key word and any protective policies still in operation are the remains of the post-war economic system.

Tsurata (1985) has identified three separate stages in the development of Japan's industrial policy.

> The first phase in the 1950s was one of industrial recovery and reconstruction. Two types of policy were implemented to attain that goal. One was the protection of infant industry through import curbs in the form of quotas and restrictions on direct investments . . . Industrialisation was also promoted through fiscal, tax and monetary policies . . .
> The second phase of industrial policy came in the 1960s. The policy goal during this period was internationalisation of the

Japanese economy through the liberalisation of trade and inward direct investments, in order to adapt it to the international economy order . . . The Japanese government's cautious attitude toward trade liberalisation can be illustrated by the fact that trade decontrol was carried out step by step and that the government agreed to open the market not willingly but only under pressure from foreign countries . . .

The third stage of industrial policy occurred in the 1970s, when the Japanese economy was hit by the 'Nixon Shock' (the upward revaluation of the yen in 1971), the oil crisis and high inflation during 1972–74. The conditions that had permitted rapid post-war economic growth changed dramatically. As a result the growth rate of the Japanese economy slowed considerably. The necessary industrial adjustments strained trade relations with foreign countries . . . In the 1970s industrial policy sought to establish restrictive policies based on new rules, such as tougher anti-monopoly law, and laid greater emphasis on environmental protection.

Hence each new decade has seen a shift in Japan's industrial policy from early protectionism, to intermediate internationalisation, and then to environmentalism and competition policy. Tsurata (1985, p. 169) makes the point that Japan's industrial policy has 'evolved in an impromptu fashion in order to cope, hastily, with individual issues'.

During the 1960s in particular, the policy of promoting oligopoly was pursued in Japan by facilitating mergers in the belief that economies of scale were important and that greater technological development would result from larger sized firms. It was hoped that this would help Japanese industry to compete more effectively in an international environment.

Some writers, such as Baba (1976), have been alarmed by the rapid rise in industrial concentration in Japan during the 1960s and 1970s and have observed a change from competitive behaviour to collusive behaviour. Dore (1986) also observes that Japanese markets, with the exception of consumer goods industries, are far less competitive than most people imagine them to be. He attributes Japanese industrial success in the 1970s mainly to non-economic factors. The legacy of Confucianism rules OK!

The merger movement in the 1960s in Western European countries undoubtedly had an important impact on the Japanese government. Larger business units, with the advantages of economies of scale, etc., were required in order to compete successfully with the giant corporations in America and Europe. A very similar philosophy existed in the UK at this time with the setting up of the Industrial Re-organisation Corporation (1966) in order to prompt mergers. Both countries pursued an active policy designed to promote oligopolistic business units. One crucial difference, however, was that in Japan the government encouraged merger activity and the creation of oligopolistic corporations in certain basic industries producing key raw materials, such as the steel industry. The merger between Yawata and Fuji steel mills into the Nippon Steel Corporation was supported by the government in spite of a lengthy period of time required to achieve the merger and to get around anti-monopoly laws – some one-and-a-half years after the initial announcement of the merger proposal. The processing industries in Japan remain highly competitive, which probably explains the domestic and international success of, for example, the Japanese automobile industry. No other industrial country has as many as nine car manufacturers, as Japan has today.

The Japanese economic miracle has been officially supervised by the Ministry of International Trade and Industry (MITI), a government department with strong interventionist bureaucrats and light political controls. MITI not only guides investment and research but also regulates competition within an industry.

Japanese industrial policy is based upon two kinds of government intervention – administrative guidance and legally endorsed intervention. Japan's anti-trust legislation started just before the UK's in 1947. Certainly, anti-trust policy in Japan is not as ingrained as in the USA. There was growing support amongst the public for tougher anti-trust legislation in Japan in the 1960s. Mergers such as the Yawata and Fuji steel companies led to a demand for tighter legislation from economists, consumer groups, etc.

The result was a strengthening of the anti-monopoly law in the 1970s which was prompted by a series of illegal cartel arrangements operating in industry. Between 1975 and 1977 legislation was passed which enabled the government to impose surcharges, sell part of the organisation, and impose firmer control on corporate stock holdings.

In 1980 the anti-monopoly laws were extended to cover distribution as well as manufacturing. Also, criminal penalties were levied for the first time in 1980 on an unauthorised cartel in the oil industry. In one sense, at least, Japan's anti-monopoly legislation has gone further than the UK's!

A key role of government in Japan has been the promotion of an environment conducive to research and development, resulting in technical progress. Technical progress has been particularly impressive in the processing industries near to the final market product.

It is probable that the post-war [Japanese] government's chief contribution to economic progress was its provision of a congenial environment for innovators. (Allen, 1978, p. 30).

The Japanese encourage innovation from an early age. Junior Inventors Clubs are formed for schoolchildren. Companies parade lists of patents as demonstrations of technological capability. Employee suggestions for innovation are taken seriously and patented wherever possible, even if the chances of commercialisation are remote, in order not to dampen enthusiasm (A report into 'Intellectual Property Rights and Innovation' (HMSO, December 1983, section 3.7)).

Japan now suffers from an unbalanced development between its processing and basic raw material industries. The former are far more competitive internationally and have exhibited a much faster rate of growth in the last decade.

Many writers look to Japan with envy and have proposed a Japanese-style industrial policy for the UK. For example, Burton (1983, p. 67) writes that:

The economy of Japan is highly competitive and its public sector is very small in terms of employment and as a proportion of GNP compared with other industrialised countries. A policy stance of enhancing the environment of industry by general measures (such as constraining the size of the non-market sector) must be adopted if Western countries are to match the widely-admired economic success of Japan in recent decades.

By 1985 Japan was responsible for approximately one-fifth of total world trade. Notable export successes include motorcycles, consumer electronics, shipbuilding, cars and machine tools. The key to success has probably been Japanese skills in production and marketing. They specialise in the production of good quality standard items. These are produced in large numbers at relatively low prices.

It is a matter of controversy within Japan and elsewhere whether MITI is entitled to the full credit for planning the Japanese success. MITI influence runs far beyond its formal plans, through to informal links with the banking system, which provides capital for investment in a highly regulated way, and with senior managers, many of whom are ex-MITI civil servants. The Japanese have developed a complex balance between competition and collaboration, which appears to be managed by MITI on behalf of the whole economic system.

CONCLUSION

In summary, competition policy in the EEC was designed to bind countries together into a community. The initial impulse in the US was to provide countervailing power to big business, in Japan to facilitate the working of the economy as a balanced whole and in the UK as a need to create a post-war environment appropriate to full employment.

The domestic and international success of Japan's processing industries must be attributed in large measure to the competitive environment in which they operate. The industrial policy pursued in the UK (and, to a lesser extent, in the US) has failed to provide the competitive environment for its processing industries to achieve domestic and international success. The relative failure of monopoly, merger and anti-competitive practice legislation to deal with the 'commanding heights' of the economy have resulted in high levels of concentration and sluggish growth in the UK. A much tougher industrial policy (based on heavy fines, dismantling of corporations and possible imprisonment if the law is not complied with) is required.

One encouraging aspect of recent UK policy must be the avowed aim of the government to enhance the general environment for small businesses, which is a movement towards the Japanese approach.

POSTSCRIPT: COMPETITION AND THE SINGLE EUROPEAN MARKET

The public commitment by the UK Government to the single European Market by the end of 1992 adds political force to the legal agreement already entered into, under the European Communities Act of 1972, that states that Community Law would be binding on the national courts. In particular we may expect increasing challenges in the courts under Article 30 to government and other regulations which are 'capable of hindering, directly or indirectly, actually or potentially, intra-community trade' (Dassonville, 1974, ECR 837).

Here the central competition issues are concerned with allowing trade to flow freely between member states and with resisting those things which tend to partition the single market into local, regional and national sub-markets, as opposed to the established prohibition on measures which directly or indirectly discriminate against goods from other member states. The second new thrust in EC competition policy lies in the development of an active Europe-wide industrial policy concerning monopolies and mergers.

The Cecchini Report (1989) builds the case for the removal of barriers to competition on a proposition by Jacques Delors, President of the Commission, that 'This large market without frontiers, because of its size and because of the possibilities that it offers for scientific, technical and commercial co-operation, gives a unique opportunity to our industry to improve its competitivity' (p. xi).

The Cecchini Report was limited to a consideration of those barriers identified in the Commission's White Paper on Completing the Internal Market, adopted at the 1985 European Community summit, although a reading of the report suggests a much broader approach to competition.

Lord Cockfield, vice president, in his foreword to the report enlarges the point (p. xiii):

> The importance of this study, and what it reveals and confirms, cannot be overestimated. Mr Cecchini and his team have laid before us, in terms which will be clear to every citizen of Europe, the full magnitude of what needs to be achieved in cutting out red tape, in breaking down protectionism and removing blocks on cross-border activities.
>
> But it does not just demonstrate the heavy cost of having 12 separate markets divided by frontier controls. More important by far, it also demonstrates the immense opportunities for the future which the completion of the internal market will open up: opportunities for growth, for job creation, for economies of scale, for improved productivity and profitability, for healthier competition, for professional and business mobility, for stable prices and for consumer choice. In short a prospect of significant inflation-free growth and millions of new jobs.

The Cecchini Report gives as its purpose the desire 'to provide a solid body of scientifically-assembled evidence as a means of judging the extent of the market fragmentation confronting European business and Community policy makers alike. In the process, the research has thrown up a vivid illustration and rigorous analysis of the cost imposed on Europeans by the mosaic of non-tarrif barriers, which – 30 years after the Community's birth – continue to mock the term common market,' (p. xvii/xviii).

The Report continues: 'Thus when EC political decisions are taken and the business community has fully adjusted to the new competitive environment, gains of this order of magnitude (ECUs 200 billion) would be acquired once and for all, meaning that the European economy would be lifted onto a higher plane of overall performance.'

The report estimates the potential gains at ECU 200 billion, that is, £134.2 billion by mid-March 1988 (p. xviii). It may well be that the report understates the potential as many of the effects are likely to be dynamic in character.

The proposed mechanism for realising these gains is through the removal of non-tarrif barriers. We read on p. xix:

> The release of these constraints will trigger a supply-side shock to the Community economy as a whole. The name of the shock is European market integration. Costs will come down. Prices will follow as business, under the pressure of new rivals on previously protected markets, is forced to develop fresh responses to a novel and permanently changing situation.
>
> Ever present competition will ensure the completion of a self-sustaining virtuous circle. The downward pressure on prices will in turn stimulate demand, giving companies the opportunity to increase output, to exploit resources better and to scale them up for European, and global, competition.

And on p. xx:

> For business, removing protective barriers creates a permanent opportunity, but signals a definitive end to national soft options. Cost reductions will be good news, but market opening means also the permanent threat, actual or potential, of competition. This is also good news for the company which is gearing up to capitalize on the enlarged market's enhanced opportunities for innovation and economies of scale. But profits derived from cashing in on monopoly or protected positions will tend to be squeezed. The situation will be one of constant competitive renewal' (p. xx).

Unless something is done, firms, especially smaller firms, are likely 'to a significant extent [to find themselves] debarred from trans-border activities by administrative costs and regulatory hassles' (p. 3). We can extend the concept of border barriers to differing trading regulations and practices, making some markets less attractive than others, and thus contributing to the 'costs of non-Europe', to use a favourite Cecchini phrase (see p. 4).

The context is again given by the Cecchini report (p. 31):

> A real home market is not just a place where companies trade without hinderance, but also one where they can operate in a cohesive regulatory environment. It is a market where the laws controlling firms and the incentives encouraging their activity are

not so out of line as to make its unity a polite diplomatic fiction rather than a hard economic fact – one where the rules of the game, if not the same, are not so different as to add major costs to doing business on a Europe-wide basis.

6 A Practical Guide to Anti-competitive Practices

Earlier chapters have shown that competition can be defined in a number of ways. It follows that it is not possible to make a definitive economic statement as to whether a particular practice is 'pro' or 'anti' competitive. However, this theoretical difficulty has not prevented nation states legislating against 'anti-competitive practices', as Chapter 5 explains. The purpose of this chapter, therefore, is to seek to provide some insight into practices which have been deemed to have, or likely to have, 'the effect of restricting, distorting or preventing competition in connection with the production, supply or acquisition of goods or services' (Competition Act, 1980, s.2).

PRICING POLICIES

This first set of practices are those which are arguably the most clearly anti-competitive yet are frequently the most difficult to detect. The laws of supply and demand require that manufacturers manipulate the output level to ensure profit maximisation within changing markets. While the theory of monopoly predicts that single producers will restrict output to ensure the maximisation of monopoly rents, the position of a dominant supplier with perhaps a 30 per cent market share is less clear-cut.

Price fixing

Price fixing is the practice of firms agreeing either formally via some form of collusive agreement, or informally, to set prices at a particular level. Horizontal price fixing (collusion, cartels and like agreements) and vertical price fixing (resale price maintenance) are *per se* illegal within the United States, Japan, the UK and the EEC, but in the last three legislatures opportunities exist for certain types of agreement to be granted an exemption.

Horizontal price fixing enables manufacturers to reduce competitive pressures and risk. Thus the European Commission has invariably taken the view that price fixing benefits only producers, and all attempts to claim consumer benefit – the primary basis for exemption under Article 85(3) – have so far been rejected. Parallel pricing is regarded as part of the same type of conduct, with the EEC regarding gatherings of industrialists in the same line of business as sufficient proof of prohibitable conduct – a most recent example is the Commission's decision against six polypropylene manufacturers (OJ L230, 18.8.86). Neither UK or Japanese enforcement has been quite so scrupulous.

The UK's Restrictive Trade Practices Court has produced certain notable decisions in favour of price fixing. Black Bolt and Nut (1960) allowed price fixing on the grounds that the price of bolts and nuts was such that common pricing by manufacturers favoured consumers by obviating any necessity for them to incur search costs. More significantly, in 1961, the Cement Makers Federation persuaded the court to uphold a price agreement on the grounds that as a new industry, it required stability and high profits, and could not expand effectively if it were to be required to compete on price. Despite attempts by the Director General of Fair Trading to have the agreement reconsidered in 1974 – on the grounds that the industry was no longer new or expanding – the agreement ceased only in 1987, when the cement manufacturers voluntarily agreed that it no longer served their interests.

Japan's purposive use of exemptions had, by 1972, created nine 'authorised depression cartels', ten 'rationalisation cartels', 175 export and two import cartels, and 604 small business cartels (Caves and Vekusa, 1976, pp. 141–8).

Vertical price fixing – or resale price maintenance – has both defenders and detractors. It aims to achieve uniformity in the selling prices of branded goods. Manufacturers impose RPM by setting and stipulating the price at (or above) which the retailer must re-sell his brand if he is not to risk the imposition of sanctions against him.

Until 1956, the UK placed no restrictions on the stipulation of resale prices. But the Restrictive Trade Practices Act prohibited agreements to maintain prices and collectively apply joint sanctions. Individual RPM by a manufacturer, who could withold supplies to a price cutting retailer and/or seek damages through the courts for breach of contract, was prohibited under the Resale Prices Act 1964, later amended to the Resale Prices Act 1976.

Dealers frequently favour RPM on the grounds that it reduces competitive pressures and enables them to compete on quality and service. Manufacturers frequently make the same claims. However, consumers may not require the service thus provided. Under such circumstances, consumer welfare is substantially reduced. As the UK approach to RPM is discussed in greater detail in Chapter 5, reference to the practice here serves only to underline the point that within the UK the gateways or opportunities for exemption under the Restrictive Trade Practices Act have had, and continue to have, the capacity to permit the establishment of price fixing agreements.

Price discrimination

Price discrimination is the practice of selling goods or services to distinct and separate groups of customers at different prices, where such pricing cannot be justified on the grounds of cost differences. In theory, it requires the presence of three conditions: manufacturers must be able to identify and distinguish clearly between different classes of consumer; these different classes should each have a different scale of preferences for the product; there must be no opportunity for consumers to trade between the two markets – i.e. to buy in the cheaper market and sell in the more expensive.

Examples of price discrimination are many, for whilst its defenders may justify the practice on the grounds that it has the potential to increase output by creating a new class of customer at a lower price, the primary objective is the private gain of a dominant firm. The attempt to isolate markets for the purpose of increasing the gains available under monopoly conditions is outlawed in each of the four legislatures described in Chapter 5, yet within the UK and the EEC the practice continues to be sufficiently widespread to enable us to break it down into three types.

Differential pricing

British Rail's policy of offering reduced rates for certain classes of traveller at certain times of day is differential pricing and said to create a new class of consumer. BR's objective is the reduction of costs borne whether anyone travels on the trains or not. The same argument applies to discounted air fares and cheap theatre tickets. Purchasers of beer in the north of England benefit from lower prices than those buying beer in the south. And producers benefit from increased sales. In theory, firms increase their output to meet this new demand. Increased output may have the effect of generating economies of scale and reducing the total price paid by all consumers, thus suggesting that price discrimination under monopoly may have benefits in extending supply otherwise unobtainable under competition.

In reality the results are somewhat different. Any potential increase in output under price discrimination is wholly dependent upon individual elasticities within the overall market. Equally, the theory only predicts increased output where the supplier can calculate individual demand and fix his price accordingly. In practice, therefore, successful price discrimination, where success is measured by increased output, is never assured. In some markets lower prices might increase demand, but the companion, higher prices elsewhere, might be too high. Thus in the aggregate, demand could be reduced below the competitive level. Further, costs incurred in seeking to measure the elasticities of individual customers or markets might actually result in costs outweighing gains obtained through increased output.

Certainly Distillers' decision to remove Red Label Whisky from the British market rather than allow British distributors the opportunity to take advantage of promotional investment in the French market without contributing to costs, suggests that the decision to engage in differential pricing is far from costless, either to the producer or to the consumer. The misallocation of resources which occurs as a result is unambiguous.

Level pricing

The other side of the discriminatory coin is where manufacturers charge the same price irrespective of differences in cost. The practice of spreading costs – most commonly transport – evenly across all customers so that those nearer to the supplier's depot effectively subsidise those further away is rather more difficult for its defenders to justify. In theory, cost savings arise from the absence of any necessity to calculate the real cost to each individual consumer, and in Chemical Fertilizers (MMC, 1959–60) and Wire Rope (MMC, 1973–4), the Monopolies and Mergers Commission found transaction costs and the impact upon consumers in remote areas outweighed the theoretical desirability of charging the economic rate.

Despite such examples, it would appear self-evident that requiring certain consumers to subsidise others, places them at a competitive disadvantage and misallocates resources unless, as in Chemical

Fertilizers, the benefits to society as a whole are deemed to outweigh the reduction in social welfare which occurs as a result.

Discounts and rebates

The Office of Fair Trading's guide to the provisions of the Competition Act states:

> Some variants of price discrimination take the form of differential rates of discount or rebate from list price – perhaps in return for loyalty or exclusive supply arrangements. An important variant arises where a purchaser's buying power enables him to insist that suppliers grant him advantageous terms, so artificially enhancing his ability to compete on price in the market in which he sells (OFT, 1980, pp. 8–9).

However, it is important to remember that discounts to certain large customers can be entirely justified by cost savings to the manufacturers. Savings which arise from bulk ordering, transport and account handling, etc., entitle the customer to receive a proportion of those savings in lower prices. Yet such costs are very often difficult, if not impossible, to quantify.

> The MMC in its general report on Discounts to Retailers [found] that most suppliers did not undertake detailed costings while those that did placed little faith in them (Merkin and Williams, 1984, p. 166).

Thus while in theory prohibition of discriminatory conduct which can have the effect of locking consumers into an exclusive supply agreement ought to be fairly straightforward, in practice it can be almost impossible to detect. In extreme cases, such as the agreements between Hoffman-La Roche and customers for vitamins, the effect of the company's system of discounts made it irrational for customers to purchase any of their requirements elsewhere. Yet had Stanley Adams, then one of the company's marketing executives, not provided the Commission with copies of contracts and other information, the practice might still be going on today. The Hoffman-La Roche case involving the free supply of tranquilisers to the UK's National Health Service and armed forces was a rather more transparent attempt at market foreclosure via price discrimination and hence was easier to prohibit (MMC, 1973, p. 12).

While legislators appear clear that price discrimination misallocates resources, results in welfare losses, and should be prohibited, not all economists agree. Schwartz and Eisenstadt, economists at the US Department of Justice Anti-Trust Division, recently wrote that:

> The welfare economics of price discrimination are always tricky. In the case of exclusive territories, one should be particularly careful before condemning price discrimination. Since distribution technology is often a natural monopoly in the local market, a single price equal to marginal cost would often fail to cover total cost. The (second best) efficient pricing structure that meets breakeven requirements . . . involves different mark-ups over marginal cost, with the size of the mark-up inversely proportional to the elasticity of demand of various groups; i.e. (second best) efficiency pricing requires price discrimination (Department of Justice, 1982, p. 61).

However, their report acknowledges the larger monopoly rents that price discrimination facilitates.

Predatory pricing

Predatory pricing is usually defined as the practice of selling below cost with the intention of driving equally or more efficient competitors from the marketplace. Once that has been achieved, prices can then be raised and monopoly profits taken. Firms most adept at achieving the desired results are large, diversified, dominant suppliers, within markets characterised by high barriers to entry. These particular conditions may be neither necessary nor sufficient but essentially they direct attention to the problems facing the intending predator.

Below-cost selling requires a 'deep pocket' – the ability to fund losses in one market either from previous years' profits or from profits taken within other markets. Resources must be far greater than those of the intended victim or victims, because losses will be sustained over an increasing level of output as the pricing strategy takes effect. Equally, therefore, the predator must either have excess capacity to meet the increasing demand or an ability to switch resources from an alternative use. The latter action suggests a determination to monopolise the market whatever the short-run cost. Finally, barriers to entry must be high. If entry costs are low, the lure of monopoly profits will require the monopolist constantly to repeat the predatory process as new companies move in to the market.

The fashionable approach to predatory pricing in the late 1980s is to claim that it is a complete fiction. In making such a claim, economists and regulators refer to the theory of contestable markets (Baumol, 1983, p. 14) and the work of John McGee who concluded first in 1958, and again in 1980, that 'predatory pricing is rare and is not an important problem for competition'. The approach rests upon the assumption that firms choosing to sustain losses are acting irrationally. However, as Irwin Stelzer suggests, that view is not universally accepted:

> Predation is said to be irrational because in the end, most markets are contestable. Drive out a competitor with below-cost (somehow measured) price cuts, or costly advertising, or some other tactic, and a swarm of new entrants will appear before the foregone profits can be recouped . . . Would they? Only if this swarm of entrants, and their backers were unaffected by the previous practices of the incumbent firm. As I have said before, a hiker might not pay much attention to a no trespassing sign, standing alone; but if the field behind it is littered with the corpses of previous trespassers, he would most likely decide the poster of the sign means business. And it would matter very little whether the poster of the sign had clear legal title to the field (Stelzer, 1987, p. 3).

Proponents of the irrationality argument also presume that consumers will realise that by accepting price cuts now they will sustain a net loss. The lower price paid today, will be more than offset by the higher price paid later when the company, with the consumer's help, has gained a monopoly. The consumer would be better off continuing to patronise the higher priced competitor, and ought to realise that. Equally, it is argued that intending predators are aware of far easier ways of achieving their desired goal, merger being the most often cited route. The problem here, of course, is that horizontal merger is generally discouraged, if not actually illegal, within the vast majority of Western developed nations and contested take-over may ultimately prove as costly as predation. While predatory pricing is also illegal, it is far more difficult to detect.

Detection requires that regulators are able to differentiate between efficient pricing and predation – frequently on the basis of evidence supplied by the companies involved. If a company reduces its prices in response to a new entrant, is the company responding to competitive pressure by reducing the monopoly price to a competitive price, or engaging in predatory behaviour? Posner (1976, pp. 188–96) provides a useful analysis of various methods appropriate to the determination of the problem. In his view, the most useful definition which overcomes the difficulty of determining whether or not a particular pricing policy may be termed 'predatory' is: 'pricing at a level calculated to exclude from the market an equally or more efficient competitor'. To make that workable, Posner regards 'average balance-sheet costs . . . a tolerable proxy' to determine whether or not firms are pricing below cost. 'Proof of sales below average balance-sheet cost with intent to exclude might be enough to establish a prima facie case of predatory pricing' (Posner, 1976, p. 190).

The most recent, blatant example of predation within the EEC, is the ECS v AKZO case. Where AKZO UK (a subsidiary of the Dutch chemical multinational) warned the relatively much smaller British company ECS, that if it continued to supply the EEC market for organic peroxides, AKZO would put ECS out of business in its main market, flour additives. AKZO then – crucially – drew up a plan to achieve that end and undercut ECS flour additive prices by 10 per cent – cutting its own prices by 20 per cent to do so. The EEC's test of predation as expressed in its decision, provides strong support for the preferred solution offered by Posner.

> The infringement in the present case involved the making of direct threats to a small competitor in order to deter it from expanding into a new market and providing an important element of competition to AKZO's position of market dominance. When AKZO's threats were ignored, AKZO sought in a systematic and determined manner to implement a plan to damage the business of ECS. AKZO employed its substantial resources to subsidise over a long period of time a course of conduct designed not only to harm ECS specifically but also to serve its policy of retaining by any means its dominant market position in an important industrial sector . . . The Commission also considers it a further aggravating factor that AKZO had given a totally misleading version of events . . . and that given the difficulties of proof it would probably have succeeded in achieving its purpose of eliminating ECS had the Commission not discovered the evidence on which this Decision is based. It is further apparent that the aggressive behaviour against ECS was not an isolated event but occurred in the context of a settled corporate policy by AKZO to use its market power to discipline or destroy unwanted competitors (Commission Decision, 1985, p. 25).

As the Commission pointed out, proof of predation relied on evidence of intent as well as price. The Commission's ability to launch a 'dawn raid' and find the AKZO blueprint on file, provides a useful reminder of a significant difference between UK and EC powers of enforcement.

In assessing the bases for determining an acceptable analysis of 'pricing below cost', the Commission referred to the marginal cost pricing rule propounded in 1975 by Areeda and Turner in relation to

US anti-trust legislation (in 88 Harvard Law Review 697). The Areeda and Turner rule presents a *per se* test of legality: pricing at or above marginal cost is presumed lawful, pricing below marginal cost is presumed abusive. The problem with such an analysis is the determination of marginal cost. Using average variable cost as a proxy requires – according to Areeda and Turner's analysis – that variable costs must include such direct manufacturing costs as labour, repair and maintenance. They specifically exclude from variable costs only capital costs attributable to investment in land, plant and equipment, property and other taxes unaffected by output, and depreciation on plant attributable to obsolescence (III P. Areeda and D. Turner, Anti-Trust Law, 715c).

However, in its decision the Commission provided a clear version of its assessment of the theoretical arguments:

The Commission does not accept the argument that the incidence of Article 86 depends entirely on the mechanical application of a *per se* test based on marginal or variable cost. The standard proposed by AKZO based on a static and short-term conception of 'efficiency' takes no account of the broad objectives of EEC competition rules set out in Article 3(f) and particularly the need to guard against the impairment of an effective structure of competition in the common market. It also fails to take account of the longer-term strategic considerations which may underlie sustained price cutting and which are particularly apparent in the present case. Further, it ignores the fundamental importance of the element of discrimination in seeming to permit a dominant manufacturer to recover its full costs from its regular customers while tempting a rival's customers at lower prices . . . it is not only the 'less efficient' firms which will be harmed if a dominant firm sells below its total cost but above variable cost. If prices are taken to a level where a business does not cover its total costs, smaller but possibly more efficient firms will eventually be eliminated and the larger firm with the greater economic resources – including the possibility of cross-subsidisation – will survive (OJ L374, 31.12.85, p. 20).

It is thus not suggested that those who regard predatory pricing as fictitious are in some sense 'wrong', but simply that the criteria applied to support such a hypothesis may be inappropriate to the attainment of freely competitive markets, and inapplicable within the EEC where pricing average above total cost would appear to be required.

To refute any notion that AKZO is the 'exception which proves the rule' we would refer to two other recent cases where predation was considered to have been attempted. In Grey Green Coaches (1985) informal enquiries by the Office of Fair Trading encouraged Grey Green to withdraw its free bus service, offered as a competitive response to a new service on one of its routes introduced by a competitor. The OFT concluded that the conduct 'might have been intended to eliminate new competition, or might have had that effect'. In Prosper de Mulder Ltd, [MMC, 'Supply of Animal Waste', 1985] the MMC emphasised that predation might be both monopsonistic as well as more commonly monopolistic. (Director General of Fair Trading, 1986).

Vertical price squeezing

Vertical price squeezing can arise where a vertically integrated firm controls all or a substantial proportion of total supply of an input which is essential to the production requirements of its subsidiary and also its competitors. The input price can be raised and the downstream price reduced, so that the profits of competitors are squeezed. One possible result may be to drive competitors from the market, a second may be simply to increase the profitability of the dominant firm.

A purely hypothetical example of such practice might be that of a dominant bread and flour producer. Smaller competing bakers must buy their flour from the dominant supplier and set their prices accordingly. The dominant firm's baking subsidiary buys flour at substantially lower prices and yet sells its bread at the same price as its independent competitors. In such circumstances, the problem for the competition authority would be the determination of whether such a practice could be considered to be anti-competitive. Only if the manufacturer were selling its bread at prices below those of its competitors would the position be clear cut. In the report on man-made cellulosic fibres, the MMC drew attention to Courtaulds' practice of supplying fibres to certain customers on terms which were not obtainable to others. The Commission found the practice to be against the public interest on the grounds that the company held an almost complete monopoly in the supply of that particular good.

Whilst the UK's MMC has shown an interest in firms making 'unduly high profits' (Credit Cards, Cmnd. 8034; Contraceptive Sheaths (no.1) 1975–6 HC. 135; Chlordiazepoxide and Diazepam, 1972–3, HC. 197, etc.), the EEC would appear to prefer to use other criteria for prohibiting action which effectively discriminates between traders. Equally, while the MMC has recourse to the remedy of requiring the OFT to monitor profits – virtually in perpetuity – the EEC has no equivalent powers.

DISTRIBUTION PRACTICES

The variety of distribution practices which fall into the category of vertical restraints are those surrounded by the greatest degree of controversy. Many more eminent economists than those we shall refer to here have spent a great deal of time attempting to prove either the 'pro' or 'anti' competitive impact of such conduct. Within the US, the result of such controversy has been the establishment of the 'rule of reason test', which essentially mirrors the UK's procedure of seeking to determine the competitive nature of each practice on its merits.

Refusal to supply

Refusal to supply is frequently regarded as a sanction against dealers failing to comply with an agreement or a means of enforcing exclusivity rather than a vertical restraint in and of itself. However, there are examples of its use as an attempt to reinforce or maintain brand image.

A prestige manufacturer may not want its product sold at a discount for fear that its brand image might be harmed and that as a consequence sales elsewhere would be reduced. TI Raleigh made such a claim when seeking to justify its refusal to supply bicycles to a number of UK discount stores. The company also claimed that sales through such outlets would deny customers necessary pre-sale quality checks and after-sales service – services which specialist cycle shops could only offer if they were not required to compete with discount stores. Essentially, Raleigh sought to prevent discount stores taking a 'free ride' on the service provided by small independent cycle shops – a service which the company considered necessary for the protection of its reputation for quality.

The free rider justification can be applied to many forms of exclusive distribution activity, of which refusal to supply forms simply one part. Its theoretical acceptability rests upon the notion that consumers visit stores offering technical expertise, a full range of equipment, and other services to reduce search costs. Having decided on their purchase they then buy from stores which as a result of offering none of these services are able to sell at a discount. A further justification relies upon the possibility that a non-exclusive dealer who has been provided with the use of equipment, training or reputation by one manufacturer will use those services to sell the goods of another who as a result of not having incurred the costs of providing such assets is able to offer the dealer a higher mark-up. In the view of Schwartz and Eisenstadt (1982), activity aimed at overcoming the free rider problem is generally welfare enhancing 'since it leads to increased investment in valuable assets'.

Given that there is a substantial body of opinion which regards refusal to supply as potentially of benefit to competition rather than deleterious, what is the rationale for its clearly being regarded as anti-competitive?

Essentially the roots of objection to refusal to supply lie within the prohibition upon resale price maintenance and dealer cartels. Refusing to supply a distributor who has previously re-sold to a price-cutter and operating an internal enforcement procedure against any dealer not conforming to stated prices amounts to resale price maintenance. Dealers agreeing to refuse to supply cost-cutting rivals are engaging in the same activity. While the form-based nature of the UK's legislation requires substantial proof of resale price maintenance, the EEC's legislation in paying heed to effect will regard such activity as falling within the terms of Article 85(1). Thus whether or not conduct is aimed at nullifying the impact of the free rider the effect is resale price maintenance and thus a reduction in consumer welfare.

On the basis of this analysis, there are economists who perceive the free-rider argument as a sophisticated defence of manufacturers' attempts to circumvent the prohibition of resale price maintenance and thus regard it as an apology for firms who would prefer not to be required to compete on price.

Exclusive dealing arrangements

Exclusive dealing arrangements form a single genus of bilateral trade agreement between manufacturers and distributors. They are frequently regarded as encompassing such conduct as the granting of selective distribution agreements, exclusive territories, and entering into exclusive purchase and exclusive distribution or supply contracts.

In general, exclusive distribution contracts denote the granting of exclusive territories. That is, where manufacturers grant authorised dealers the exclusive right to serve a particular territory and agree to supply no other dealer within that area. Exclusive purchasing contracts arise where a dealer agrees to take supplies from one supplier only. Selective distribution agreements involve agreements whereby manufacturers use selective qualitative and quantitative criteria to choose outlets for their products.

Within the United States, exclusive dealing is expressly prohibited under Section 3 of the Clayton Act subject to the proviso that the practice be found 'substantially to lessen competition or to tend to create a monopoly'.

The UK OFT's outline of potentially anti-competitive practices includes reference to exclusive supply, selective distribution and exclusive purchase. All are deemed to have the capacity to limit competition – notably by reducing competition between the distributor and his competitors. In the MMC's Report on the Supply of Asbestos and Certain Asbestos Products, the Commission did not accept that there were any special features of the markets concerned which made it desirable to set up artificial barriers against access by competitors to particular customers of the company concerned, and against potential competition by the customers themselves (MMC, 1972–73, HC3). However, as vertical restraints are not covered by the Restrictive Trade Practices Act, and the UK's civil law precedent suggests that such contracts can only be deemed to be a restraint of trade where they are either improperly drawn or entered into, the competence of the OFT to prohibit such agreements extends only as far as the Fair Trading and Competition Acts will permit and thus requires dominance before such agreements would be considered worthy of investigation.

Furthermore, the particular view expressed by the MMC in Asbestos pre-dates work conducted at the Office of Fair Trading by the economist John Chard, who in an article published in 1980 challenged the generally accepted view of UK regulators, by suggesting that vertical restraints were probably pro-competitive. In a series of rhetorical questions, Chard suggested (1980, p. 407) that by agreeing to enter into such agreements manufacturers ran the risk of reduced sales and hence profits. Firms do not behave irrationally, therefore there must be circumstances which ensure that by entering into such agreements manufacturers are able to increase profitability and efficiency. Essentially, Chard claimed that bi-lateral agreements increase the provision of distribution services, improve levels of information to consumers by increasing product differentiation, and by facilitating price discrimination encourage increased output.

In a rather more sophisticated analysis of exclusive dealerships (referring only to contractual requirements by which retailers or distributors promise a supplier that they will not handle the goods of competing producers) Howard Marvel perceives such agreements as a means by which manufacturers create and retain, 'property rights in information concerning potential customers' for their product – or promotional investment (Marvel, 1982, p. 2).

> Exclusive dealing arrangements are interpreted . . . as devices to ensure that dealers do not act opportunistically so as to avoid paying the manufacturer for valuable ancillary services provided in a tie-in to the product sold.

Essentially, the analysis replicates the free-rider argument and suggests again that investment in advertising, warranties and so on, necessitates the creation of contractual obligations upon dealers to prevent them from using such investment to their advantage but against the best interests of the manufacturer who supplied those services.

Until the implementation of the European Commission's Regulation 1983/83 (OJ 1983, L173/1) all agreements between undertakings within the Common Market had to be notified to the Commission and wait to receive either negative clearance, exemption, or indeed prohibition before being put into effect. However, the 1983 Regulation introduced a block exemption for certain types of agreement between dealers and suppliers which facilitated resale of goods within the EEC. Bilateral agreements between manufacturers and dealers must still be notified, and are likely to find the terms of their agreement on the 'black list'. However, the weight of agreements requiring investigation forced the Commission to agree to exempt resale agreements and to publish a 'white list' of acceptable supplementary restrictions (Merkin and Williams, 1984, p. 189).

Despite the new regulation the analysis provided by Marvel, Chard, Bork and others, suggests that the conservative approach taken by the Commission is not simply unreasonable but militates against the promotion of competition. And because the Commission takes no action against vertical integration *per se*, certain observers suggest that the Commission's conduct is contradictory. If vertical integration is not deemed to be anti-competitive why are vertical restraints?

Vertical restraints have the capacity to create and reinforce all those services and opportunities for profit-maximisation outlined by both Marvel and Chard. As Scherer suggests:

> For manufacturers, exclusive dealing arrangements are often appealing, because they ensure that their products will be merchandised with maximum energy and enthusiasm. The dealer confined to a single manufacturer's line can scarcely be indifferent as to whose brand consumers purchase (Scherer, 1980, p. 590).

However, Scherer's analysis (and indeed that of Comanor, 1968), is rather more circumspect. Scherer, for example, suggests that the strengthened product differentiation facilitated by exclusive distribution does not necessarily increase consumer welfare. The responsiveness of such differentiation to consumer wants is the determining factor. Equally an escalation of advertising encouraged by vertical restraints will only help consumers make better decisions if it is informative. High-quality service is desirable 'especially when consumers retain the option of buying the same brand or equivalent products with less service at lower prices'. Where vertical restraint makes that impossible, its desirability is less clear-cut. Distribution costs may be reduced if dealers are by virtue of the agreement able to take advantage of scale economies. But, as Scherer suggests, if territories are too small, costs may be increased. 'The blunting of intrabrand price competition does not necessarily arouse concern as long as interbrand competition remains vigorous. Whether this condition is satisfied depends mainly upon how entry opportunities are affected' (Scherer, 1980, p. 591).

Obviously, as far as the EEC is concerned any agreement which has, or is likely to have, the effect of increasing barriers to parallel imports must be regarded as distorting competition within the Common Market. Thus their conservative stance has at least one substantial justification.

For others who also accept the inevitability of vertical integration but reject the arguments suggesting a pro-competitive analysis of vertical restraint, Scherer's set of arguments lends some weight. There is, however, a further argument which does not immediately spring from the literature, but which we regard as a justifiable cause for questioning the competitive nature of these agreements.

Exclusive distribution agreements are not employed by manufacturers of everyday consumables. They are specifically used by the manufacturers of durable and frequently luxury goods – goods that are only infrequently purchased and about which consumers will have scant amounts of information. By allowing selective distributors a high mark-up as recompense for their investment in display space, technical service, etc., manufacturers allow themselves and their dealers to take supernormal profits. Consumers pay what they are given to understand to be the going rate – which in the absence of competition in that highly differentiated product – is the only rate in a large, specified territory. The difference between vertical restraint and vertical integration is that consumers know that they will be sold 'Smith's brand' if they walk into 'Smith's store'. But when they walk into Harrods, or Bloomingdales, for example, they are entitled to believe that they will be offered a range of a particular class of good. If there is only one make on offer, the low level of information available may suggest to them, as indeed it is intended to, that this is 'the best', when indeed it may not be.

The argument against exclusive agreements within this example is not the same as that against luxury goods, such as expensive perfume and watches, which many regard as fully entitled to seek to preserve brand image by narrowing availability. One would have thought that on price alone, brand image for many of these products is assured, and that by allowing Rolex watches to be sold in Woolworths, Rolex succeed in serving that rare provincial customer who might prefer to buy locally rather than travel to London. However, any welfare loss arising from an inability to obtain a premium product close to one's home is likely to be sufficiently small to be hardly worth arguing about.

However, losses arising both to the companies involved and consumers from indulgence in agreements which ultimately serve only to increase costs to the consumer have the capacity, in the long term, to reduce levels of discretionary purchases. As a consequence, outlined in Chapters 8 and 9, they are potentially a cause for concern on an international scale, but more particularly for their impact upon national economies.

Tie-in sales

Tie-in sales involve a stipulation that a buyer must purchase part or all of his or her requirements of a second (tied) product from the supplier of a first (tying) good. Or as the Rome Treaty puts it within the context of prohibited agreements between undertakings:

> the subjecting of the conclusion of a contract to the acceptance by a party of additional supplies which, either by their nature or according to commercial usage, have no connection with the subject of such contract.

Economists who encourage prohibition of tie-in sales do so on the grounds that they are a relatively transparent attempt by dominant manufacturers of one product to apply leverage within a second market where their market power is substantially less. As Scherer notes:

> Businesses have diverse reasons for attempting to tie the sale of one

product to that of another. First, a firm may have monopoly power over one product by virtue of patent protection, strong product differentiation, or scale economies; and it may try to exploit this leverage in a second market where, without the tie, it could earn no more than a normal return. Thus, it adds to its monopoly profits in the tying good market the profits it can realise by exercising power over price in at least part of the tied good market . . . Second . . . the profits attainable from co-ordinated monopoly pricing of two goods which, for example are complements in use, will generally be higher than those realised by setting a monopoly price for each commodity separately (Scherer, 1980, p. 582).

Tying is also a convenient way of engaging in price discrimination by extracting more revenue from intensive users of equipment. The example of photocopiers and photocopy paper is that most frequently used to define the conduct under these circumstances, although tying toner and allied goods has also been investigated (MMC, 1976, pp. 28–9).

However, firms may justify engaging in tying where technically complex machines require quality controlled materials and supplies to ensure no-fault operation. The firms' reputation and future sales may depend upon only certain specific secondary products being used as complements to the primary good.

Equally, there may be rare situations where distribution costs are reduced by supplying the tied and tying goods simultaneously, although any such savings where they occur are not likely to be very great.

Finally, tying contracts may be employed as a means to circumvent governmental price controls. Certainly the UK's British Telecom had, until privatisation in 1985, the supply of telephone handsets, cable and other equipment fully under its control while telephone call charges were not.

Richard Posner begins his analysis of exclusionary practices with tying arrangements and opens the section with the statement:

I begin with a practice that has been incorrectly classified as exclusionary . . . The traditional objection to tying arrangements is that they enable a firm having a monopoly in one market to obtain a monopoly in a second market . . . One striking deficiency of the traditional 'leverage' theory . . . is the failure to require any proof that a monopoly of the tied product is even a remotely plausible consequence of the tie-in (Posner, 1976, p. 172).

Added to this, Posner finds a 'fatal' flaw in the leverage argument arising from the fact that tied goods will ultimately prove more expensive than their competitors on the open market. The difference will represent an increase in price of the final product or service to the consumer and he or she will demand less of it. 'In the absence of price discrimination, a monopolist will obtain no additional profits from monopolising a complementary product' (p. 173). However, Posner regards that qualification as crucial for he regards price discrimination as enabling a monopolist to earn higher profits.

While Posner may not regard tie-ins as exclusionary, that has frequently proved to be their effect – as much in the field of services as in goods. Schwartz and Eisenstadt (1982) equally regard the impact of tying as benign, essentially on the grounds that tying does not appear to facilitate collusion or market foreclosure.

> Since collusion and foreclosure are the main concerns of anti-
> trust and tying is relatively benign in these respects, and since tying
> does have various efficiency motivations, the current law towards
> tying appears too harsh (Department of Justice, 1982, p. 88).

In the MMC's report on Full-line Forcing and Tie-In Sales (1980–81, HC. 212), the findings were considered broadly to reflect the view that where barriers to entry exist, tying contracts should be considered with particular care, but that ties should not be regarded in themselves as particularly likely to be either exclusionary or harmful.

However, their potentially exclusionary nature makes them unpalatable both to the US courts and to the European Commission and their potential for reducing consumer welfare by artificially increasing the price of an initial good, suggests that, where they are attempted, such ties are unlikely to be permitted for long.

Full-line forcing, or total requirement contracts, is simply an extreme form of the tie, such that the producer of good A requires that purchasers buy the complete range of goods produced before A will be supplied. They are a much more transparent attempt at market foreclosure and thus with the increasing sophistication of business strategists ably supported by competition lawyers, the practice – if it takes place – has become increasingly difficult to detect.

Whilst the practices outlined above are those which the competition authorities specifically pinpoint as anti-competitive, there are much more insidious practices which regulatory authorities prefer either to ignore or refuse to acknowledge as capable of occurring within their particular national economy. As we seek to show within the case studies that follow, anti-competitive practices which are defined as such are merely one aspect of anti-competitive conduct in which businesses engage on a regular basis.

7 Four Study Areas

INTRODUCTION

In the latter part of the twentieth century there exists a spectrum of political *qua* economic opinion running from calls for the complete deregulation of industry through to demands for tight control: an on/off condition, understanding of which is deeply muddied by both sets of calls often arising from the same people. Within a three-year period from late 1983 to mid-1986, the Conservative government published and implemented plans to break up state monopolies; published plans to exempt small firms from health and safety regulations; planned to deregulate shop opening hours; but introduced stringent regulation of financial services markets; stringent control of the agricultural sector through its Environmental Control Act; and much more besides. The *raison d'être* for each separate piece of legislation varied between dogmatic faith in the efficacy of the free market, through to the necessity to protect consumers from themselves.

In an attempt to draw out any comparisons which may exist between the numerous disparate areas in which one government saw fit either to involve itself, or not, we present these four case studies.

INTELLECTUAL PROPERTY RIGHTS – THE FORD CASE

In February 1981 the Ford Motor Company's strategy of tolerance towards unauthorised production of copy car body panels took a sudden, and wholly unexpected, change in direction. Having just nine months before informed the Society of Motor Manufacturer's and Traders (SMMT) '. . . that we do not attempt to exert our rights under the British Design Copyright laws in the parts market', Ford wrote to eleven manufacturers or suppliers notifying them of its legal rights

under the 1956 Copyright Act demanding an undertaking that manufacture or supply of infringing copies cease.

Ford claimed that artistic copyright in its design drawings was
infringed by production of copy body panels and that the law afforded
the company the right to sue each independent manufacturer or
supplier. If successful, Ford would be entitled to 'conversion damages':

> all such rights and remedies, in respect of the conversion or
> detention by any person of any infringing copy . . . as . . . if . . . he
> were the owner of every such copy . . . and had been the owner . . .
> since the time when it was made (Copyright Act, 1956, S.18).

These exclusive rights had existed from the moment the copies first
entered the market in the late 1960s, when the introduction of the
Ministry of Transport roadworthiness test (the MOT) stimulated, if
not actually created, demand for corrosion part panels. Yet it was not
until 1981 that the company chose to exercise its rights. If its claim
could be upheld in court the level of damages likely to be awarded
against the independents would be substantial. It is hardly surprising,
therefore, that Ford's new strategy was viewed as an attempt to
foreclose a market by destroying the competition, rather than simply a
decision by one company to exercise its legal rights.

If Ford had contained its new strategy within litigation, the case
would have mirrored BL v. Armstrong Patents, in questioning only
the appropriateness of a law which appeared to afford companies
exceptional monopoly rights in mass-produced spare parts and had
the capacity to award punitive damages for infringement.

However, Ford's decision to prosecute was followed by a blanket
refusal to negotiate independent production under licence. While the
company may have regarded this as a logical extension of its new
strategy, the Office of Fair Trading declared it to be anti-competitive
(OFT, 1984) and referred it to the Monopolies and Mergers Commission (MMC) to determine whether the practice operated against the
public interest. In the summary of its findings, the MMC held that:

> the principal effect of Ford's anti-competitive practice is in the area
> of competition. The practice tends to keep prices up. It was the
> independents who introduced corrosion part panels and we can only
> speculate whether, if the independent's competition had not existed,
> such panels would ever have been introduced by Ford. The practice
> which was referred to us is thus clearly adverse to the public interest
> (MMC, 1985, p. 41).

The MMC was denied recourse to any legal remedy because the law confers exclusive rights on copyright owners. If the works were copyright (and certainly at the time, the MMC understood them to be so) no one could demand that Ford grant licences to competing manufacturers. Even if the MMC could have granted a compulsory licence, it did not consider that to be a solution to the clear conflict between the exclusive right of the copyright owner and the public interest. Rather, in the MMC's view:

> the adverse effects which we have found could . . . be remedied by a change of the law . . . In particular, if the protection of artistic copyright were to be removed from purely functional designs . . . or from industrial designs generally (MMC, 1985, p. 45).

Less than a year later, the House of Lords achieved precisely that end without recourse to any time-consuming legislative process via the British Leyland decision.

The European Commission's competence to act in the Ford case arose from complaints by independent panel producers to the Competition Directorate (DGIV) under Article 86 of the Rome Treaty. That is, the independents accused Ford of abusing its dominant position.

Articles 30, 85 and 86 of the Treaty govern the whole of the Community and take precedence over national law *except* where Article 36 states that they shall not, viz:

> 36. The provisions of Articles 30 to 34 shall not preclude prohibitions or restrictions on imports, exports or goods in transit justified on grounds of public morality, public policy or public security; the protection of health and life of humans, animals or plants; the protection of national treasures . . . or the protection of industrial and commercial property. Such prohibitions or restrictions shall not, however, constitute a means of arbitrary discrimination or a disguised restriction on trade between Member States.

Within that context the EEC had long perceived UK copyright law as problematic. The duration of protection afforded mass-produced spare parts (the life of the artist plus 50 years) was unique within the EEC and considered excessive; the penalties punitive (the EEC's particular concern was with conversion damages); there is no form of registration; and no requirement for novelty or originality. The combination of protection for objects of a functional character was considered unreasonable for the level of 'original intellectual thought' contained within them. Thus the European Commission's investigation of Ford arose from the extent to which artistic copyright protected UK-based manufacturers from EEC competition.

The Commission's concern arose from the company's sudden and unannounced change of policy. Having permitted the creation of an industry and tolerated its existence for more than ten years, and given assurances that it would not enforce its rights, Ford's decision to prosecute body panel producers without adequate warning, was perceived as an abuse of its dominant position. Added to this Ford's pricing pattern was, according to the Commission, 'sufficiently bizarre' to provide a clear indication of abuse (i.e. parts for which demand was greatest were the most highly priced – a reversal of expected pricing strategy according to standard demand and supply analysis).

The market for spare parts is unusual in so far as the decision to buy a particular make of good, locks the consumer into the market for that good's spare parts. In the market for Ford spares, Ford held a dominant position and information on pricing of parts led to a clear indication of abuse. Ford's refusal to license simply confirmed the company's intention to enforce its legal rights. If there had been no indication of abuse, the EEC (unlike the OFT) would have found such refusal to license quite acceptable, and consequently regarded it as of only minor significance to their investigation under Article 86.

The Commission believed that Ford's sudden change in policy arose initially as a result of recommendations made by the MMC in its Car Parts Report (MMC, 1982) and the Restrictions on Agreements (Manufacturers and Importers of Motor Cars) Order (1982). This made it illegal for a manufacturer or importer to make or carry out an agreement with a franchisee if the agreement contained an 'exclusive buying' provision relating to replacement car parts. The order clearly included replacement body parts and panels. At almost the same time, the EEC were investigating Ford's exclusive agreements with its authorised dealers elsewhere within the Common Market. In November 1983, the Commission found certain provisions in Ford Werke AG standard distribution agreements to restrict competition, and prohibited them. The clause of most immediate relevance to this case was that which denied dealers the opportunity to engage in distribution and servicing agreements with third parties regarding competing products. In the Commission's view there had until then been no necessity for Ford to exercise its intellectual property rights – its exclusive agreements with its distributors made such action unnecessary. But the prohibition of these contracts both by the EEC and the UK forced Ford to change course if it was to retain monopoly control over the market for Ford spares.

Economic framework

In November 1985, the *Financial Times* reported:

> Record figures for new car sales for 1985 seem even more certain, with registrations last month 5.3 per cent higher than in October 1984, boosted by heavy promotion and special dealer incentive schemes. This rise brings the total for the first ten months to a record 1.63 million or 4.4 per cent more than the same period of last year.

Market leaders with 26 per cent market share were the Ford Motor Company, with nearest rivals, British Leyland, accounting for 18 per cent of total UK sales.

In its evidence to the Monopoly and Mergers Commission, Ford stated that it regarded its automotive activities as forming a total business which included the supply both of new vehicles and of replacement parts. Its justification for the substantial price differential between its panels and those of the independents was that this 'total business' required heavy investment in design development, manufacture and distribution, together with the necessity to maintain stocks of all parts. However,

> The independents, Ford said, were interested in only the comparatively few fastest-moving spare parts, and reaped the benefits of Ford's innovation investment, having made no contribution to it. The independents were, according to Ford, thereby enabled to undercut Ford's prices (MMC, 1985, p. 21).

The standard economic arguments supporting Ford's demand for protection are:

(i) Companies require monopoly rights over inventions because only then are they guaranteed a return on investment in research and development. Without such a guarantee there is little or no incentive to engage in research.

(ii) Society requires that innovation takes place. It therefore agrees to reward inventors with a period free from competition. Society's welfare is said to increase by additions to the store of knowledge – hence the insistence on publication of all details relating to patentable inventions.

(iii) Intellectual property protection is an exchange relationship – i.e. in return for a company's investment in research and development, society 'pays' by allowing the owner of that invention a maximum 20-year monopoly. In the case of a design registrable under the Registered Designs Act, society acknowledges improvements to the aesthetic quality of life by protecting the designer's monopoly over reproduction for 15 years, and in the case of copyright affords protection for the lifetime of the artist plus 50 years.

To suggest that design drawings for car spare parts conform to one or all of these theoretical constructs, requires a particularly wide interpretation of the arguments.

From an economic viewpoint, the right to protection of intellectual property turns on the question of whether anything about the particular good can be said to be the result of original thought, or indeed if there can be said to be anything innovatory about a car body panel. As J. A. Menge (1962) pointed out, over 20 years ago motor manufacturers must innovate or die. Research and development is a continuous part of their production process, arising from the need to maintain or increase market share. Style changes do not necessarily produce 'better' (in the sense of 'functionally superior') cars. They are generally introduced to ensure that the public desire for the newest, best, most fashionable, or fastest, is reinforced and constantly fed. Such innovation, linked not to more efficient or safer cars, increases social welfare only in so far as it meets the need of the fashion-conscious consumer, who, to quote J. K. Galbraith, 'has been made to want the particular blend of originality and banality so provided' (Galbraith, 1981, p. 516).

Ford claimed that it offered consumers a package of quality and service. But sales warranties and service agreements are simply an unsophisticated form of tie-in sale, much favoured by producers seeking to extract monopoly profits from secondary markets. In its evidence to the MMC, Ford claimed that its 'total automotive business' required:

a very large investment both by Ford itself, for example, in design, development, manufacture and distribution, and by Ford's nation-wide network of dealers through whom new vehicles and parts were distributed (MMC, 1985, p. 20).

According to the company, anyone buying a Ford car, whether new or second-hand, did so in the knowledge that they could rely upon a comprehensive dealer network which could service and repair customers' vehicles and which could supply a full range of parts, both fast-moving and slow-moving.

However, according to 'irresistible evidence from extensive surveys and researches . . . Ford garages are no more reliable though they are always more expensive than the independents' (Genn-Bash *et al.*, 1985b, p. 24). Thus the promised benefits of tie-in sales were illusory. Ford claimed that its spare parts were competitively priced to ensure that Ford cars were able to take advantage of lower insurance classes (the price of car insurance takes account of the price of spares). Yet the Office of Fair Trading found that Ford spares were often as much as four times more expensive than the same item produced by an independent.

Even without such evidence, it was only new car buyers who were offered this package of 'quality and service'. Second-hand car purchasers were offered only high prices or, as implied by Ford through its refusal to license, parts produced by an independent which might be inferior. Forty per cent of all new Ford cars are sold to fleet owners – none of whom keep their cars longer than, on average, three years. Clearly, Ford's refusal to license sought to extend the tied relationship beyond purchasers of new cars to second-hand buyers by preying on the fears of those consumers most keenly aware of the necessity to meet the requirements of the MOT test and most likely to be conscious of the need to keep down the costs of their insurance.

The insistence upon monopoly profits in spare parts is emphasised by Ford's attempted suppression of the emergent market in corrosion part-panels by refusing to supply. It was Ford's insistence that repairers buy full body panels, which originally encouraged independents to meet the new part-panel demand in 1967. Those part-panels were clearly new goods for a separate market which, until February 1984, Ford failed to produce. In its evidence to the MMC, one independent panel producer claimed that were Ford to agree to license independent production, no royalty could be claimed for corrosion part-panels because Ford had had no part in their design or development.

In seeking to justify its strategy Ford argued that the viability of its business was dependent upon revenue from the sale of spare parts. Only a fully compensatory royalty could safeguard its future investment in new models, and this, the company claimed, would be considerably greater than any amount independents would be prepared to pay. Ford calculated that only a royalty of 60 per cent of the net sale price of panels at 1983 prices could compensate for the 'loss of contribution to the unavoidable costs of its total business' and 'the competitive profit of the total business, resulting from the loss of turnover to licensees' (MMC, 1985, p. 28). A licensee of a British patent for mechanical equipment would not normally expect to pay a royalty of more than 7 per cent on the net sale price of the article concerned.

The core of Ford's case was that without the sales of spare parts to domestic car users, the company would have insufficient revenue to engage in research and development. There is a Schumpeterian argument which suggests that only companies in receipt of super-normal profits are in a position to fund innovation. The outline of Ford's view of its total business, suggests that the 'sunk costs' in research and development leads to a requirement for supernormal profits.

It is only in the UK that motor manufacturers are protected by design copyright. Throughout Europe a free market in mass-produced spare parts exists, yet Ford cars sold in the UK are often considerably more expensive than similar models sold elsewhere in the EEC. All motor manufacturers engage in continuous research and development, but not all have the opportunity to extract monopoly profits from spare parts. It would thus seem reasonable to suppose either that the European motor manufacturers are vastly more efficient than Ford, or Ford has been greedy.

Behavioural framework: corporate strategy – reasons for change

There would appear to be a reasonably straightforward explanation for Ford's refusal to license independent production of body panels. The UK design copyright laws permitted Ford the opportunity to retain control over sales of Ford parts which the EEC and UK government had taken away by prohibiting exclusive agreements with its distributors. The necessity to exercise its intellectual property rights became evident only during 1981 when the EEC began its investi-gations of Ford Werk AG and legislation followed the MMC's investigations into the supply of car parts. Until that time Ford had its distributors tied in to exclusive purchase and supply agreements and could tolerate copies in its market for spares. Once that tie was broken, another route to foreclosure of the spare parts market had to be taken.

If we accept the Chicago School theory that monopoly profits can be taken only once, then the irresistible conclusion to be drawn from Ford's strategy is that the company, having no monopoly in motor cars, had to create and maintain a monopoly in the spare parts market if it was to have sufficient funds to finance research and development of new models.

On the basis of this analysis, forcing Ford to license production at any level below that which Ford claimed to be economically viable (i.e. 60 per cent) would sign the company's death warrant. If Ford genuinely believed that, it would have closed down its UK operations and transferred them outside the EEC before it would have bowed to government pressure to license. Yet in 1986, the company announced the grant of licences for the manufacture of Ford spare parts. The royalty was set at 'not more than 2 per cent to the licensor in respect of each replacement body part . . . calculated on the net, arm's length, sales price thereof excluding VAT' (OFT, 1986, p. 7).

The evidence suggests either that the theory that monopoly profits can be taken only once, is incorrect, or that the facts presented by Ford to the MMC were skewed. In view of Ford's reputation, the only reasonable conclusion is that Chicago has it wrong. On the basis of this case, the analysis presented by Scherer (Scherer, 1984, p. 582) suggesting that companies can take monopoly profits once on the primary product and then again on a tied product would appear to be much more realistic.

Whilst it is possible that Ford agreed to license under unified pressure from the EEC and UK legislatures, there is also the possibility that their preemptive decision arose as much from the government – or some other source – warning that the House of Lords was due to find against BL in its action against Armstrong Patents, and that Ford's parallel actions would fail. Taking Scherer's paradigm as the most appropriate to this case, any level of royalty is better than the possibility of no royalty at all.

Conclusion

The Ford case provides one example of a company using one set of laws to circumvent another. In this particular instance the UK Copyright Laws provided the means to subvert UK and EEC competition legislation designed to open up and prohibit monopolistic practice in the market for motor car spares. Why they chose to do so now seems clear. How it was possible for them to achieve their desired end is clear also. Why it was left to the House of Lords to force their hand via the somewhat eccentric BL judgement demands further thought.

In 1980 the new Conservative administration introduced its Competition Act which clearly established anti-competitive practices as a major block to economic growth. The next step on the road to increasing the competitiveness of British industry and reducing barriers created by government regulation was reform of the intellectual property laws. In 1983, the government published its Green Paper on Reform of Copyright and Design Law. The major recommendation of that report was that urgent reform of the protection afforded mass-produced functional objects was required. The report was set within the context of a government wedded to a free market philosophy and to raising levels of economic growth through increased competition and reduced government regulation. Yet four years and a White Paper later, its recommendations have still to be placed upon the parliamentary agenda.

To some, the Ford case merely highlighted governmental inability to order its priorities. Reform of design copyright law has been badly delayed by government procrastination over associated reforms. The attempt to reform the gamut of intellectual property laws at one time, appears to have made it impossible to reform that aspect most urgently in need of reform – design copyright. Thus it fell to the Law Lords – those who theoretically at least hold a position above politics – to change the law. The BL/Armstrong case provided the opportunity and the Law Lords complied.

For others, there are a number of alternative hypotheses available to explain the apparent inability of one government to support and sustain a commitment to prohibit anti-competitive conduct within the economy. Certainly, as the political model set out in Chapter 3 suggests, politicians actually possess a very low commitment to competition policy *per se*. Their allegiance is first to the particular needs of the voters in their constituency, and secondly to a dogmatic adherence to the tenets of their particular political ideology. Historically high levels of unemployment, coupled with low levels of manufacturing output within the UK in the period 1981–6, would almost inevitably have encouraged a reluctance to hit out at a substantial multinational such as Ford. A company perfectly capable of folding its tents and moving to a location more amenable to the extraction of monopoly profits in two markets, is not to be harrassed in such difficult times.

Such a hypothesis suggests that the problem of UK consumers being denied efficiency in consumption, and independent metal manufacturers being subjected to threat of bankruptcy through copyright litigation, was considered insufficiently important to the UK government to prioritise reform of the law which made such anti-competitive conduct possible. Certainly urgent calls for reform emanating from the regulatory authorities and indirectly from the House of Lords, were ignored.

The dislocation between the theory and practice of competition policy as exemplified within this study, is clearly set within a political context – one wherein the need for free and fair competition is placed well below the need to win the next election in the order of priorities. More significantly, the case suggests a context wherein sympathy for the needs of major conglomerate corporations stays the legislative hand and thus, indirectly, is given highest priority of all.

RETAILING

Food production throughout continental Europe and the USA is a multi-million pound business, characterised by conglomerate engagement in high levels of vertical integration, monopsonistic and monopolistic purchasing power and transnational market operations. The size of the relatively small number of major companies involved in food production and the scale of their operations has, to a very great extent, blinkered legislators to the significance of monopsonistic purchasing power at the point at which food reaches the final consumer: supermarket retailing.

In 1964, the introduction of the UK Resale Prices Act prohibited resale price maintenance, to the considerable satisfaction of economists who believed that RPM had forestalled competition, forced costly non-price competition upon consumers and consequently hindered expansion of UK retail markets. They agreed, at that time, that the abolition of RPM would increase economic growth by improving allocative efficiency, notably by reducing monopoly power over final prices. However, the prohibition of RPM also provided producers with a substantially increased opportunity to price discriminate, and while potentially increasing product availability, increase the gains from monopoly. More significantly, it also provided monopsonists with the opportunity to exert their power over producer final prices and determine producer levels of profitability.

Within the UK, the exercise of that power was most overt amongst the major multiple food retailers and in 1977, the Monopolies and Mergers Commission began an investigation under the Fair Trading Act into 'the general effect on the public interest' of discounts to retailers. The competence of the inquiry extended to:

the practice of the acquisition by or the supply to retailers of goods –

(a) at prices less than those charged to other retailers by the supplier whether the reduction is by means of a discount, rebate or allowance or by means of prices specially negotiated, or

(b) on terms which involve the provision of any special benefit in money or money's worth by the supplier to those retailers in connection with the supply of the goods by or to the retailers, not being a benefit provided to other retailers, where the reduction or the value of the benefit cannot be attributed to savings in the supplier's costs.

The Commission agreed, in the interests of expediting the inquiry, to concentrate on those areas 'where large discounts are known to be given (such as groceries and petrol) . . .'

Five years later, the Commission reported that while all of these practices had been found to exist, they were not against the public interest because the discounts wrested from the manufacturers by multiple supermarket chains were passed on to the consumer. Thus the MMC vindicated the government's specific requirement that the 1980 Competition Act should acknowledge that certain practices – in this case price discrimination – have the characteristic of enhancing competition in certain circumstances, whilst reducing it in others. By insisting on price discrimination, the majors were considered to be reducing food prices to the consumer and thus increasing efficiency.

In 1984, the Office of Fair Trading undertook to update the findings of that investigation, and in its report on Competition and Retailing (which took just a year to complete) came to much the same conclusion despite one rather substantial difference in the evidence. In the course of its investigation, the OFT found that:

food manufacturers' profitability is broadly in line with the average for all sectors (excluding oil), although large food retailers' profitability is well above average.

Using the current cost return on capital employed as a proxy variable, the OFT found that also to have increased between 1981 and 1983 and to be: 'well above the level for food manufacturing and for all sectors, excluding oil'. In investigating company profitability it is common practice to use historic and current cost return on capital employed as proxies for determining the extent to which monpolistic or monopsonistic profits are being taken. Under the circumstances it is difficult to understand the logical step taken to conclude as the OFT did, that food manufacturers' average profitability, and food retailers' well above average profitability, arose within a context wherein retailers were engaging in historically high levels of investment and passing on the full value of discounts to the consumer.

The findings of the original MMC investigation alarmed independent retailers sufficiently for them to call for another investigation. The Scottish independents' response to the OFT's repetition of the initial conclusion was to seek help from the European Commission. The fact that the complaint came only from a single region of the UK, moved the case outside the competence of the EEC, which as a consequence could offer no help.

Economic theory of price discrimination suggests that monopolists charge differential prices to consumers (intermediate or final) in an attempt to maximise monopoly profits. The evidence obtained by the OFT, however, does not appear to suggest that producers are appropriately placed to take advantage of their monopoly position. Indeed, the figures suggest that it is the very real muscle or monopsonistic power of the retailers within an industry noted for its small number of major multiples, which appears able to distort the free market mechanism.

On this analysis, the OFT's decision to question the manufacturers rather than the retailers appears to have been asking questions of the wrong group. This is not to suggest that the OFT was unaware of the requirement for an investigation into the purchasing power of the major multiples, rather it is suggested that their investigation failed to address the central economic question surrounding the issue: whether the observed demise of the small independent grocer was a consequence of the food manufacturers forcing them to cross-subsidise the substantial discounts to the major multiples, and in so doing, were denying the independents any opportunity to compete with the majors on price.

In the period from 1961 to 1983, the total number of retail grocery outlets within the UK fell by almost 95,000 or 65 per cent. While not all of this loss was sustained by the independent sector, 63 per cent of independents left the market. More significant however, are the figures showing changes in percentage shares of the groceries and provisions markets. In 1966, the shares were:

Independents	44.2 per cent
Multiples + Co-operatives	55.8 per cent

By 1982 that had changed to:

Independents	25.1 per cent
Multiples + Co-operatives	74.9 per cent

In a period when the number of independent outlets had reduced by 65 per cent and their market share had fallen by 43 per cent, the 71 per cent reduction in multiple outlets which occurred throughout the same period led to an 82 per cent increase in market share. However, the change in numbers of multiples does not reflect a reduction in the number of outlets owned by the four major companies – although with the rise of the hypermarket or superstore many small outlets were being replaced – rather it reflects the fact that smaller multiple chains, including the co-operatives, were losing market share to the multiples, and leaving the market with the independents. It was within this time frame that the structure of the market changed to the highly concentrated form that it now takes.

The extent to which cross subsidy has been the cause of such a change in the pattern of distribution and structure of the UK market, is effectively unquantifiable. So many potentially significant variables have affected the pattern of consumption within the same period that any attempt at a mono-variate analysis would be naive. It would seem safe to suggest, however, that the presumption of such reductions in independent shopkeepers arising as a result of unfair trading practices has provided the rationale behind the prohibition of price discrimination in France since 1973, Canada since 1960, the USA since 1936, Australia since 1974 and indeed within the EEC since the passage of the Rome Treaty in 1951.

In justifying such protection of small retailers, and by extension consumers, economists in those countries emphasised the role of the small store to their communities; the service provided to the aged, infirm and indeed those without private cars. Without a specific prohibition upon price discrimination such small stores would be unable to compete with the majors and would be forced to close. The resultant isolated communities would encounter higher prices for food with costs artificially raised by the necessity to purchase public transport. Where these effects have materialised within the UK, the local corner shops have often been replaced, most frequently by ones run by members of ethnic minority groups. Their success is often dependent upon their workers being members of the family and accepting below market level pay rates, and certainly within the UK operating outside the law in relation to opening hours. Both activities suggest that the self-employed have to operate illegally if they are to compete with the major multiple retailers. A sharp description of market failure.

This short example of the UK retail food market provides an example of a substantial contradiction between competing economic orthodoxies and the political views of the purpose and benefits attainable from anti-trust.

The Chicago School of economic thought holds allocative efficiency as the primary goal of anti-trust. Within that framework, protecting small businesses for the sake of some social benefit or political purpose is wholly inadmissible. If scale economies and minimum efficient size determine (in the extreme case) that only one company should supply total demand, then that is the most efficient allocation of resources and it is to the attainment of that level of concentration that market forces should be permitted to operate. Any intervention to deflect markets from that goal will result in efficiency losses and should thus be avoided at all costs.

From this standpoint, it becomes clear that the major multiple retail chains are substantially more efficient than their competitors. Their continuing levels of profitability during a period of recession, and their ability to expand through internal growth, suggest that they have identified and built upon the MES appropriate to retail stores and taken advantage of scale economies available to them in supply. They are to be regarded as a model of efficiency, a clear example of the gains available from the exercise of market power.

However, there is some difficulty with the UK, or any other government, through its regularity authority, finding such conduct to be not against the public interest. Governments of all shades tend to promise support for the small businessman and to seek to encourage the individual entrepreneur. Self-employed small business people (amongst whom shopkeepers invariably constitute a large number) have always been promised very special protection by UK Conservative governments, the current government to an even greater extent than its predecessors. However, such protection, if it were to be forthcoming, would directly contradict prevailing Conservative economic thought and would require government to find a legal remedy to the legitimate use of market power exercised by the multiples.

Of equal political importance is the contribution made by major retailers to the UK economy – an economy whose future appears wedded to the growth of the service sector.

With unemployment and other factors holding substantial sway over the minds of the bureaucrats and the election chances of the politicians, the problem then devolves upon the pensioners, the disabled, the carless, the 45 per cent of all married women who don't work full time outside the home, and other disadvantaged groups within society who are dependent to a greater or lesser extent upon their corner shops.

Evidence presented to the MMC by consumer groups expressed concern that if small retail outlets were forced to leave the market, these are the consumers who would suffer the greatest welfare loss. The dichotomy for government stems from the necessity to balance the needs of these voters against those of the workers and industrialists. Can the social and economic value of local shopping and the needs of these marginalised members of society be considered to be of such significance that they should be included within any substantive analysis of the problem? Associations of local traders, and indeed the government's own schemes to encourage the establishment of small businesses, would suggest that they should. But in preparing its report, the OFT took no consumer evidence, nor appears to have considered this question relevant to an economic analysis of the issue. However, the explicitly narrow terms of reference of the OFT report precluded it from a consideration of this issue.

The contradictory needs of small and large businesses, relatively advantaged and disadvantaged consumers, represent the major dichotomy facing both bureaucrats and politicians in any attempt to support and enforce a rational competition policy. Whilst ill-defined public interest criteria, rather than clear targets of policy, provide the only rationale for intervention, such action will continue to be open to criticism.

INSURANCE

We include the life assurance industry amongst our case studies as a most striking example of a highly competitive, efficient industry made anti-competitive and inefficient by government – a government responsible for introducing the Competition Act and which won power on the basis of its declared dedication to reducing waste and increasing the competitiveness of British industry.

Yet in 1986, after two years of Herculean efforts to stop it, the UK government forced the Financial Services Act upon an unwilling Parliament and subjugated life assurance industry. In doing so, it created the Securities and Investment Board, a self-regulating umbrella organisation with delegated statutory authority from the Secretary of State for Trade and Industry. Its role was to police all financial services via the delegation of its authority to five self-regulating organisations, trade associations set up by each sector of the financial services market to regulate their part of the industry in accordance with the rules and regulations initially laid down by SIB. The five were: FIMBRA (Financial Intermediaries, Managers and

Brokers Regulatory Association), LAUTRO (Life Assurance and Unit Trust Regulatory Organisation), AFBD (Association of Futures Brokers and Dealers), IMRO (Investment Managers Regulatory Organisation), and the Securities Association (encompassing the Stock Exchange and International Security Dealers). Of these only FIMBRA, LAUTRO and IMRO are of direct relevance to the life assurance industry, with FIMBRA and LAUTRO being of most immediate importance to the sale of life policies.

However, these regulatory bodies did not replace the Insurance Brokers Registration Council created under the 1980 Insurance Companies Act, or other professional organisations such as the Association of British Insurers, the British Insurance Brokers Association, and so on. In creating SIB and its attendant SROs the government simply added another layer to the panoply of rules and regulations to which insurance companies and intermediaries were already subject, and increased the number of organisations to whom brokers and insurers had to make annual returns and pay subscription fees.

The call for regulation which gave rise to the Financial Services Act arose as a result of a number of factors, but was justified by government as an attempt to protect the investor as proposed by Professor Gower in his 1984 Review of Investor Protection. The history of all UK life assurance regulation is the history of government seeking to plug a hole in its legislation after an undercapitalised or dishonest company has fallen down it – pulling a number of large and small investors with it. The Signal and Cavendish Life scandals, the Lloyds fiasco and the continued calls for regulation coming from consumer bodies, ensured that the 1980s would see yet another piece of legislation constraining the activities of the life assurance industry, despite the apparent prevalence of Austrian economic thought encouraging the view that where companies fail it is the free play of market forces clearing the inefficient from the marketplace.

As described earlier in the political model of competition (Chapter 3), politicians had to do something despite the prevailing economic orthodoxy. They had to protect those who had gambled and lost on investments in offshore funds – even though such investment was often aimed primarily at tax avoidance. They had to protect the industry itself from further scandal and loss of confidence if they were to protect national income and the important contribution made to it by invisible earnings. And they had to be seen to be protecting the small investor because small investors expect to be protected, particularly when they are being encouraged to enter the investment market through the flotation of a number of denationalised industries (e.g. the TSB, British Gas and British Telecom public flotations).

Many of the areas identified by Gower within that part of his report dealing with the life assurance sector, were problems which the industry had itself been trying to solve for many years without much success – problems which arose from the necessity for new entrants to overcome substantial barriers to entry.

The UK life assurance industry is dominated by a number of very large companies, some of whom have existed for a substantial amount of time and form an essential part of the British establishment. The scale of their influence is vast and commensurate with the level of pension and other funds they manage. Their size and longevity presented substantial barriers to entry arising from scale economies, consumer loyalty, and the very fact of their stability, which in an industry responsible for protection against destitution on death, is of some considerable importance. More significantly their position within the market required that to ensure effective distribution of their product, new entrants would either have to establish equivalent relationships with independent intermediaries or set up new channels of distribution.

The 1960s and early 1970s saw a rash of new insurance companies solving the problems of entry by introducing the first genuinely new insurance products that century, and breaking with established methods of distribution. The new companies encouraged the traditionally conservative and apathetic brokerages to sell their 'bright, new, innovatory' policies by offering them a variety of financial inducements, such as volume overriders, exotic holidays for achieving specified sales targets, and high rates of commission. Simultaneously, however, they showed their ability to circumvent the broker market by introducing direct sales forces composed almost entirely of self-employed people whose earnings were wholly dependent on the commission they earned from sales.

The response from the major insurance companies was predictable. Contemptuous of the 'superfluous and superficial' product innovation, which substantially altered the industry's marketing thrust, and unable to differentiate between their own wholly employed company representatives and the new breed of tied agent, the majors attacked the change in conduct rather than structure which had occurred. Practices which encouraged independent intermediaries to bias their advice towards the products of one company, were ungentlemanly, bad for the consumer and consequently bad for the industry. Thus the majors through their Life Offices Association called for a maximum commissions agreement, believing that by putting an end to price competition they could reinstate the primacy of their product. The wide publication of the LOA's case for that agreement and its inevitable demise encouraged the view that these new products were only ever recommended for 'the money' and that any problems within the industry arose from these inflated commission levels. To predicate regulation upon such a premise in 1970 and to repeat the process in 1986, as the government has done, is to belie the experience of both consumers and producers, and negate the importance of structure to product innovation, conduct and performance.

The dramatic changes in distribution which took place in the 1960s and 1970s, created entirely new structural problems within the industry which, in our opinion, were far more significant in terms of consumer protection than any problems associated purely with brokers' commission. In listening to the siren calls of lobbyists such as the Consumers' Association, and indeed the LOA which concentrated on such payments, regulators appear to have overlooked the rather more intractable structural problems which characterise the intermediary market.

Although in UK law the independent intermediary or broker is the agent of the client, it is the insurance company who pays the broker commission on the sale of one of its policies. While a sizeable proportion of insurance companies use brokers and wholly-employed company representatives to sell their products, two or three claim to pay no commission and thus are rarely, if ever, obtained through an independent advisor. Many of the companies who entered the market in the 1960s and early 1970s retain 'tied agent' sales forces, and where they can, sell through brokers too. In this context, the 'tied agent' has self-employed status but in fact lives off the commission he earns from his employment as an agent of one company. While he may sell non-life insurance policies from other companies, he will be contractually tied to sell the life policies of only one. Other forms of 'tied agent' were, until the introduction of the SIB's rules outlawing them, solicitors, accountants, bank managers, etc., who in the course of their primary professional activity might be required to advise on appropriate life assurance policies. They would have an agency relationship with perhaps one or two companies and would earn commission on such sales.

Thus the industry supports company representatives who officially earn no commission but whose salaries and level of perks are, in practice, linked to their productivity – their level of sales; direct sales forces made up of self-employed tied agents hungry for commission, who frequently represent themselves as the agent of many life companies but are in fact sole agents of one; and independent intermediaries, insurance brokers whose continuing profitability, in theory, depends upon their ability to represent many companies and offer their clients the most appropriate product, 'best advice'. The majority of old-established companies such as the Prudential, Scottish Widows and Legal and General, sell through employee company representatives and brokers. Their involvement with self-employed tied agents (other than professionals with agencies), is limited where it exists at all. The newer entrants such as Abbey Life, Crown Life, Imperial Trident, Target Life and Allied Dunbar, are almost entirely dependent on large, aggressive tied agent direct sales forces, but also use brokers, particularly those who themselves employ direct sales forces and offer the potential for high-volume sales.

The brunt of the criticism levelled against intermediaries has been taken by insurance brokers and stems from their need to pay their sales forces the same rates as those available to self-employed tied agents. In order to defend their business and their investment in recruitment and training from predatory insurance companies, all the perks, overrides and expenses available to the 'tied agent' and company representative have been demanded by the broker seeking to ensure that rates of pay in that sector are commensurate with those paid by the insurance companies direct. It was inevitable under these circumstances that insurance brokers would bias their advice towards those companies who responded positively to their demands for equal rates of pay. The dogged refusal of the old-established companies to compete on pay and their contempt for the type of product innovation that the direct sales companies brought with them in the 1960s led inexorably to the newer entrants taking a substantial slice of the broker market and encouraging other insurers to enter.

It is hardly surprising, therefore, that in 1984, when the first hint of an opportunity to legislate against these 'new boys' was offered by government, an organisation dominated by representatives of the LOA companies emerged almost overnight with the one intention of regulating commission. The preferred solution to the long-standing problem of product bias, showed no signs of the majors having learnt from their previous mistakes. They set up ROLAC – the registration of life assurance commissions – a highly restrictive and discriminatory maximum commissions agreement. While the organisation and agreement were overtaken by the government's own proposals for SROs and SRAs, it still formed the underlying basis of the maximum commissions agreement to which LAUTRO members had to adhere.

Failure to comply, or refusal to join LAUTRO, results in companies being required to disclose to clients the precise amount paid to the intermediary as commission on each individual sale – a prospect which all companies find unacceptable, for a variety of reasons.

The discrimination between classes of intermediary, central to the original ROLAC proposals, was deemed unnecessary by SIB. Instead, product bias was to be prohibited by saddling FIMBRA with the job of confirming that its members sold across the complete range of available life contracts (including those which paid no commission), by auditing brokers' annual sales records.

Much more to the point, can market entry conduct such as that which SIB's conduct of business rules now prohibits, be categorised as anti-competitive? Insurers were guilty of having sought to maximise sales via various forms of distribution agreement, bonus payment and the like; brokers sought to maximise profits by seeking to guarantee a return on their investment in human capital. These activities were apparently sufficiently reprehensible to warrant prohibition by SIB. Yet economic theory would suggest that this is precisely the type of conduct that the rational firm must engage in if it is to survive within the market. What then is the economic detriment that self-regulation is required to overcome?

Applying the model of perfectly competitive markets, it appears that until 1986, the UK life assurance market exhibited a certain closeness to the model except in two particular respects. While there are certainly many buyers and many sellers, the product is not homogeneous and information is not simply imperfect but asymmetric. While sellers are well-informed, buyers suffer from an uncommon degree of ignorance. Thus according to one theory, brokers can sell any old rubbish, and will, if the commission they receive on the sale enables them to maximise profits. In practice, however, levels of consumer ignorance fall with consumption, and where brokers sell rubbish in the short term, long-term profitability will suffer as consumers refuse to repeat the exercise. In reality therefore brokers seek to maximise long run profits through maximising sales – the two are mutually dependent.

Applying this analysis to the industry, it would seem that holding brokers responsible for a substantial loss in consumer welfare – the 'bad' which the Consumers' Association, for example, claim has occurred as a direct result of high commissions flooding the market with bad business – is not simply unfair, but irrational.

Indeed if this were such a self-evident truth, SIB would have welcomed rather than rejected the OFT's proposal that the agency relationship which exists in theory, be formalised in practice. That is, that brokers should receive a fee from their clients for their professional advice. But neither SIB, LAUTRO or FIMBRA could ever accept such a proposal for the insurance industry's primary axiom is that insurance is sold not bought. If this is the self-evident truth, then the more obvious culprit is the often untrained self-employed tied agent who having responded to a newspaper advertisement offering substantial earnings, finds that his or her ability to eat in any one month depends entirely upon selling the product of one company – whether it be good, bad or indifferent. Yet it has never been suggested that this practice should be prohibited.

What has been prohibited is the right of companies and brokers to compete on price. The FIMBRA rules and LAUTRO maximum commissions agreement effectively prohibit price competition, specifically discourage discounting, and encourage independent intermediaries to perceive their interests as being best served by becoming tied to one company. Certainly, there are substantial disincentives to those seeking to remain within the independent broker market but who will be required to compete with tied agents and company representatives without being able to offer equivalent earnings.

By fixing commission at maximum levels, the SRAs appear to make a number of erroneous assumptions. First, they assume that insurance contracts are bought on the same basis as other commodities. Second, they appear ignorant of the fact that a range of contracts all offering life assurance plus a variety of different optional extras for 'just £15 a month' offer a very varied degree of product for that price, with the scale of 'management charges' and 'front-end loading' making a substantial difference to the price in real terms. And finally, they appear ignorant of the significance of the competition rules contained within the terms of the Rome Treaty to their deliberations.

Yet the SRAs and SIB are not ignorant of any of these facts for their boards are peopled by representatives of the industry. And here we have the essential element of the anti-competitive, wasteful nature of the government's self-regulation with statutory authority. Those representatives of industry who dominate these new authorities represent the establishment of the British insurance industry. Others within the same group are considerably newer, but by dint of their size and capital asset base have been granted entry to these exceedingly powerful ranks. Abbey Life and Allied Dunbar (previously Hambro Life), originators of self-employed direct sales forces within the UK, have substantial influence and positions of authority within SIB and the SRAs, as do representatives of companies who refused or failed to compete successfully with the new entrants in the 1960s and 1970s.

When the government's proposals for regulation of the life assurance industry were first announced in 1985, the smaller linked life assurance companies shouted 'foul' and complained that the Government had bowed to pressure to protect the majors from competition. What no one realised at the time was that the government had also bowed to pressure to relieve insurance companies of the necessity to compete with one another through independent intermediaries.

As a consequence of the government accepting the case for a reduction in domestic competition, an industry which in the past had sufficiently terrified its European competitors to cause them to attempt to protect their markets by infringing EEC law, has been emasculated by a maximum commissions agreement and plethora of rules, regulations and annual reporting requirements. Whether or not such self-regulation will put an end to the excesses observed within the industry over the past 20 years, or will be circumvented in precisely the same way as all commission agreements have been circumvented in the past, it is still too early to tell. Whether or not such regulation will inhibit the growth of the industry by discouraging competition and encouraging inefficiency is more predictable. None of these regulations will protect consumers from fraudulent or predatory agents or from their own ignorance – if indeed that was ever anyone's intention – but they will protect the major established companies from domestic competition and remove the necessity for insurers to respond to the needs of consumers as expressed through their independent advisers. It was the innovatory, highly competitive nature of the UK market which terrified the Europeans. The industry, with the able assistance of government, has successfully ensured that the competitive impetus to innovate will, in the medium if not the short-term, wither away.

THE SALE OF ALCOHOLIC DRINKS

The sale of alcoholic drink in England and Wales provides a telling, if complex, example of the interaction of social and legal rules and economies of scale in severely constraining competition.

1. There is a web of licensing legislation, much of it stemming from the First World War, with some minor reforms in the early 1960s. These laws not only strictly limit the hours in which it is permitted to sell drink, but also regulate on grounds of 'need' the

number of licensed premises in any one area, thus creating local monopolies.

2. There are strong social and legal rules and pressures concerning the use of drink and its effect on the physical, mental and spiritual health of the drinker and his or her family and work colleagues, including questions of drinking and driving.

3. There is an exceptionally high degree of vertical integration linking brewers and public houses and of horizontal concentration, with the brewers supplying or controlling around 75 per cent of the drinks trade, mainly through the 'tied house' system.

From time to time concern is expressed on grounds of lack of competition as a result of these three areas of constraint. The Monopolies and Mergers Commission in 1986 re-opened its files on the brewing industry to take another look at the whole question. The previous 1969 MMC inquiry, which concentrated on vertical integration, had found that the 'tied house' system operated against the public interest. It recommended that drinking hours should be made more flexible and that 'need' should no longer be a criterion in granting a licence. Despite backing for the MMC from the Erroll Committee no action was taken by successive Labour and Conservative governments.

A subsequent investigation by the Price Commission in 1977 (pp. 44–5) came to a similar conclusion:

When one looks not at the detail but at the picture as a whole, the most striking point is the degree of horizontal and vertical integration in the industry. Horizontally, the industry is dominated by six concerns who over the years have pursued an aggressive policy of amalgamation and acquisition. Vertically it is highly integrated from brewery to the public house. Not only is brewing a highly concentrated industry, but there are significant barriers to entry and virtually no competition from imports.

These are the classic conditions for a monopoly which is likely to operate to the detriment of consumers. Legislation over a long period of time has contributed to the present situation. Nevertheless, the simple truth is that the way this trade is organised and run has a profound effect on prices and profits.

In England and Wales, beers and other alcoholic drinks are sold for consumption on or off the premises. The most familiar form of on-sales is the traditional public house. To obtain a licence to trade the licensee must be deemed by the local Justices of the Peace to be a fit and proper person with adequate premises and operating in a place where there is, in the opinion of the Justices, sufficient 'need' to justify the opening of another pub. 'Need' often appears as much a moral as a commercial issue, with a strange alliance of existing publicans and temperance workers arguing that there is no need for additional supply.

The majority of the public houses are owned by the breweries, who 'tie' most of the sales of drinks to their own brands. The non-brewery-owned outlets are known as 'free houses', which in principle are free to sell whatever beers they wish, but are often tied in some informal way, through brewery loans for improvements, for example. Such loans may not be a strict tie, but may impose costs in switching from one supplier to another.

The main alternative for the drinker to the public house is the club, where the property and stock of liquor belong jointly to the members. Clubs are for this reason exempt from many of the licensing conditions and are normally outside the brewer's tie, although, as with free houses, there are numerous informal ties.

Apart from public houses and clubs, alcoholic liquor is also sold in restaurants and hotels. In recent years this has been a growth area, as the licence conditions are less constricting and do not require proof of need in the way that public houses do.

The other main form of liquor sales is for consumption off the retail premises, normally at home. While there has been a marked decline in traditional specialist off-licences, there has been a growth in off-sales departments within general grocery shops, especially at the level of the supermarket, where beers have to compete against all other products for space. The brewers have managed to maintain their own share in their own off-licences.

The changing pattern of licences in England and Wales is complex. Total on-licences have fallen throughout this century, until the early 1970s when, in response to a partial liberalisation of the law in the 1960s, some new and additional outlets were opened. Clubs have revealed a perceptible if erratic growth throughout the period. Off-licences showed a slow decline to the early 1960s since when there has been fairly steady growth, as there has for licensed restaurants.

The traditional pub has thus faced increasing competition from restaurants, licensed guest houses, clubs and especially from supermarkets selling beers for drinking at home. It is difficult to isolate profitability at the level of the public house given the high degree of vertical integration in the drinks industry. One indicator is the sale price of public house premises which appears to be falling relative to catering and other retail outlets, presumably indicating lower profitability, which may point to the brewers taking super-normal profits further back in the distribution channel.

Another possible indicator of the changing fortunes of the beer industry is that volume sales have been fairly flat, with possibly 1 per cent annual growth over the period 1969 and 1985. Within these flat sales there has been a strong growth in lager: up from 10 per cent to 40 per cent over the 15 years from 1970 to 1985. Packaged beer sales in the on-trade have fallen away.

Price presents a similarly complex picture. While competition appears to have pushed down the price of beers in the free off-sales market, beer prices in the tied estates have over the last 25 years either kept pace with or moved ahead of inflation. Where groups of free houses or clubs have grouped together to establish joint buying operations, as has the National Union of Students, substantial price reductions are obtained.

One hesitates to estimate the price premium achieved as a result of restricted competition in the on-sales arena, but it could be as high as 20 per cent. Competition would, however, be unlikely to realise the full price saving as owners of bars would want to improve their offering to customers in terms of range of drinks offered and variety of types of bar tailored to the needs of market segments.

In other words we might expect some bars to offer a narrow range and minimalist facilities at rock bottom prices, where others would provide more choice and more comfort at a higher price. This pattern of a spread of prices and offerings can be observed in much of mainland Europe.

During the whole of this century concentration has increased. The big six (Bass Charrington, Allied Breweries, Whitbread, Watney/ Grand Metropolitan, Scottish & Newcastle, Courage) increased their control of public houses from around 65 per cent of trade in 1967 to about 75 per cent in 1985, mainly by acquisition.

Translating ownership of pubs into control of on-sales is hazardous, but it seems likely that 50 per cent by volume of sales of beers is covered by direct ties, with a further 25 per cent covered by indirect ties. The big six are responsible for around 80 per cent of beer production.

The brewery response over the past 20 years to competition from non-traditional outlets has been to concentrate investment on their larger outlets typically by adding fun facilities. These appear to enjoy a brief vogue then sales seem to fall away to pre-improvement levels. The other strategy has been to sell off the more marginal outlets to private buyers, who are possibly investing redundancy or retirement pay.

Part of the indictment against the present system is that pubs have found it difficult to respond to changing consumer preferences away from the male-dominated traditional stand-up and drink type bar. The public house's freedom of action is constrained in two directions – legal and licensing restrictions and the pubs' close relationships with the manufacturing brewers, ranging from full ownership with a salaried manager, to a more informal tie, based on a loan or other special long-term relationship.

There are currently around 70,000 on-licence premises – about 65,000 pubs and 5,000 hotels, railway stations, dance halls, etc. In addition there are some 30,000 clubs of one kind or another. This gives 100,000 conventional bars. To these should be added 15,000 restaurants and 10,000 residential licences, some with own restaurants, where the sale of drink is an ancillary activity. There are also 40,000 off-sales outlets. (The Brewers' Society Statistical Handbook.)

In Scotland there have been considerable changes in the powers of the licensing authorities, who have wide discretion to vary opening hours. Broadly speaking this more flexible approach to licensing hours appears to have led to less drunkeness.

In England and Wales, the law has remained virtually frozen for 70 years. However of late, due to EEC intervention, the nature of the tie between brewer and tenant has been modified in favour of the tenant, making it, in theory, easier to obtain a wider range of packaged beers.

On 1 July 1983, two new EEC block exemptions covering exclusive purchase and supply agreements came into force; the second included special clauses for beer supply and service station agreements. These appear to have been inserted at the behest of the British government to protect the tied house arrangements of the brewers and the exclusive arrangements between petrol companies and services stations, both of which are, within the EEC, unique to Britain.

EEC Regulation 84/83 appears to be a clear example of the power of vested interests to influence actual legislation. During the re-negotiation of the block exemption to Article 85(1) of the Rome Treaty, which 83/83 and 84/83 represent, advocates of greater competition had hoped that the new regulation would open up the beer market. Even if the tie itself was left untouched, brewers would at least, they hoped, be forced to open up their houses to a range of competing products.

However, in its general conclusions to the regulations, the Commission made it clear that it upheld the principle of exclusive purchasing agreements within beer markets. It stated that the tied system led to improvements in distribution at lower costs. It stimulated competition and helped the small and medium sized firms. It made it easier to establish, modernise, maintain and operate premises used for drinks consumption. Finally and improbably the Commission accepted that consumers benefited from goods of satisfactory quality and fair prices.

While these are early days yet, by 1985 there were signs that competition within the UK was declining. Brewers continued to move their larger and more successful houses from the tenanted estate to place them under direct management. This had been expected since the EEC attempt to restrict horizontal agreements was always likely to lead to an increase in vertical integration as a brewery counter-measure.

Despite fears that regulation will drive the anti-competitive practices within the vertically integrated firm, there may still be scope for further liberalisation through changes in UK and EEC law. However, in the end, the client relationship between brewer and tenant probably renders the freedom something of an illusion.

Another approach to facilitating change, which could be accomplished in an England and Wales context, would be to remove all questions of 'need' from decisions concerning the granting of licences, the magistrates being restricted to considerations of the fitness of the licence holder and the premises. This would transfer much of the control on the number of public houses in a district from magistrates to market forces operating within the constraints set by the local planning authorities.

A far more radical way of introducing competition to the drinks market, which is not on the current EEC agenda, would be to require the brewers to sell off their public houses. There might be a case for some upper limit on the number of multiple licences which could be held by any individual or corporate body. Breaking the tie would be likely to lead to a far more genuine competition between pubs for customers and between brewers and other suppliers for the landlords' orders, than would changes in legal relationships.

More competition, theory and experience tells us, is likely to lead to a better match between consumer demands and the supply of bars with different types of offerings. However, more inter-pub competition, coupled with a relaxation of laws concerning the permitted hours, would also be likely to lead to the elimination of those pubs offering limited and inflexible services in areas of weak demand or excessive supply. This could produce a small efficiency gain, although there might be a danger of remote areas being unable to support a pub. The solution here might be for an entrepreneur to combine on-sales with a retail business.

In practice the on-sales drinks market has been moving away from a competitive solution. In the years between the 1969 Monopolies and Mergers inquiry and the re-opened inquiry of 1986, we have seen the brewers increasing their control through horizontal concentration, through the equity control of small 'independent' brewers and through the growth of informal 'ties' in the free trade.

One of the most potent forces in this process of concentration has been a switch in public taste away from bitter beers to the relatively more expensive draught lager. Lager offers opportunities for economies of scale and raises the minimum efficient size for a plant to something in excess of 1.5 million barrels per annum. Regional brewers have found that while demand for their own local ale remains strong, they have had to tie themselves to one of the majors for lager supplies, thus reducing their freedom to compete.

Within the public house trade there has also been a switch from bottled to draught beers, releasing space and reducing the need for cooled shelves, thus making it more difficult for a bar to stock non-brewery packaged beers. Pubs have a relatively low minimum efficient size and there is thus little incentive to increase the selling area. None the less a normal busy public house could profitably carry a choice of seven or eight draught beers, stouts and lagers.

The current situation in the beer and other drinks market is one of highly structured competition, with the six big brewers, aided and abetted by the legal system, determining the rules of the game. Within the brewing industry itself, there are substantial economies of scale in production, high levels of concentration and limited rivalry. Some observers suspect a high level of gentlemanly collusion in price movements and other competitive acts.

It seems as though the brewers use their managed houses to act as price leaders for a district, with tenants following. Genuine free houses, by offering a better mix of beers and facilities, are able to command a small premium price. Price variations by region are, however, considerable, suggesting that the brewers have between them segmented the market on a spatial basis.

The big brewers, through control of the channel of distribution, are able to restrict entry into the market by other brewers from other countries who are forced to buy distribution, rather than win sales through competition. The brewers also own much of the production and distribution of substitute products, such as wines, spirits, cider and soft drinks, so that they can supply their own tied estates with their own products, making it difficult for new suppliers and new products to enter the market.

The result is limited consumer choice, minimal price competition and little or no entry of new products or new owners of public houses with new ideas. The only substantial free competitive market is in off-sales, principally in the supermarket chains, where there is wide choice, price competition and the enlivening effects of new entrants. One reason for competition prevailing in the supermarkets is their unwillingness to trade their buying power for soft-loans, which would be permitted under EEC Regulation 84/83.

The alternative to competition at the point of sale is to leave improvements to the producer brewers, who argue that over the years they have correctly interpreted consumer taste and ensured that there has been sufficient investment in licensed premises to maintain and improve the quality of the drinking environment. They might also wish to point to the way they have encouraged foreign beers, in the early days importing lagers helping to develop an alternative consumer demand to their own main product.

Breaking the tie might lead to the rise of half a dozen large retailers, replacing the brewers as owners and controllers of outlets. The brewers might argue that would have little effect on increasing competition, as they already compete between each other for customers.

The arguments have traditionally been stacked against competition in the drinks trade, both through the legal framework and through the close relationships between the great brewing families with each other and with the Conservative Party. It may be that the new style Tories, who have come to the fore under Mrs Thatcher, will be less impressed by traditional arguments.

The EEC's main interest appears to be in ensuring that drinks from one country can be sold in another and to this end it is willing to support inter-brewery licensing agreements. It is however, hostile to agreements which bind individual distributors but have the cumulative effect of closing off a market to new entrants.

The EEC appears to be taking the view that, if demand for a product can be demonstrated in the relatively open and competitive supermarket off-sales trade, and the brewers prevent its sale in their tied estates, then there would be grounds for investigation.

POSTSCRIPT ON BEER

The Monopolies and Mergers Commission in 'The Supply of Beer' (1989), reviewed the situation outlined in the above section of our book. The MMC report found that beer sales accounted for just over 2 per cent of Gross National Product or £9 billion in 1987, with lager taking a growing 45 per cent share, suggesting that the (inter)nationally promoted lager brands were stealing sales from the more local and regional bitter beers.

The strength of the big six brewers – Bass Charrington, Grand Metropolitan, Allied Breweries, Whitbread, Courage and Scottish Newcastle – has continued to increase with their beer sales rising from 68 per cent in 1967, at the time of the last MMC report, to a current 75 per cent. Beer drinking remains predominantly draught beer (75 per cent of all sales) consumed in public houses and other licensed premises (85 per cent against 15 per cent sales through off-licences). Again the dominance of the majors is sustained through their ownership of 75 per cent of the country's tied estate and their extensive use of tied-loans within the 'free' trade.

The report observes that the total number of licences has increased by 40 per cent since 1966 to 192,000, mainly in the form of restaurant, club and off-licences, since it remains rare for full licences to be granted for new public houses.

In addition to the six national brewers (75 per cent of beer sales and 75 per cent of the tied public houses), there are 11 regional brewers with 11 per cent of sales and 15 per cent of houses and 41 local brewers, with 6 per cent of production and 10 per cent of tied outlets. In addition there is a long tail of 160 small brewers producing in all 1 per cent of beer sold and no associated tied estates. Three brewers with no tied estate – Carlsberg, Guinness and Northern Clubs Federation – produce a further 8 per cent.

The Commission concluded that a complex monopoly existed which operated in favour of the larger producers, raising prices above what might be expected, especially for lager, and in many instances reducing consumer choice. The Commission recommended an upper ceiling of 2000 tied houses for any brewer, requiring disinvestment by the big six of 22,000 premises, but leaving the other tied estates intact. The MMC report also proposes an end to loan ties and the introduction of guest beers into tenanted houses.

The brewers, who are complimented in the report for the cogency and vigour of their evidence, responded to the MMC proposals with a strong defensive campaign. 'There is no doubt in our minds that the

(Brewers') Society is formidably effective in championing its members' interests', comments the report.

At the time of writing, March 1990, it is not yet clear the extent to which Government and industry will in practice implement the MMC proposals, although there are indications that the preferred solution will be to separate ownership of the old tied estates away from production, which, while presumably reducing the degree of vertical integration, may or may not increase the level of effective competition in what seems likely to remain a highly concentrated industry.

8 Competition Theory Revisited

Our discussion of the theory of competition set out within Chapters 1 to 4, and our review of the practice in Chapters 5 to 7, offers only one possible conclusion: that both the theory and the practice are riven with contradictions.

In all definitions of competition there exists a notion of an ethic, playing by some predetermined set of rules. Competitive sports, academic examinations, love and indeed war – as long as the winners achieve their position without bending or breaking the terms of the competition 'society admits no right, either legal or moral, in the disappointed competitors to immunity from this kind of suffering' (Mill, 1974, p. 164). Yet clearly the resultant suffering can be absolutely appalling. If we accept Freud's assertion that individuals are inherently aggressive, we are forced to accept that without rules of competition we have Hobbes' 'war of all against all' and the necessity for government to lay down rules, without which social relations will be defined by conflict and anarchy. While Locke may have expressed a somewhat more optimistic view of society, he also perceived a necessity for state regulation to ensure the continuance of 'the natural order'. Durkheim, as the sociological correlate of Hobbes, held that in order for societies to sustain themselves they must generate norms and values, the maintenance of which demands the creation of institutions of state to constrain individual behaviour. In asserting that rules of just conduct have gained wide acceptance 'because they impartially improved the chances of all individuals to obtain a larger command over the worldly goods for which they strive', Hayek places responsibility for an ordered society upon the legal enforcement of such rules and individual honesty. And, in asserting that competition is a game, Hayek states:

. . . the outcome of the game, the rules of which require people to take the fullest advantage of the opportunities that come their way to serve both themselves and others, can be no more 'just' than that of any game of chance. All we can ask is that the players behave honestly and do not cheat, and that the rules are the same for all (Hayek, 1980, p. 45).

The list of eighteenth, nineteenth and twentieth-century philosophers who have claimed the existence of an ethical relationship between competition and rules and the necessity for those rules to be adhered to honestly if society is not either to move towards totalitarianism (Hayek) or anarchy (Hobbes), is not infinite. However it is of sufficient length and authority for us to at least question the philosophical antecedents of the nihilistic, libertarian schools of economic thought which place such a very substantial emphasis upon the ability of market forces to regulate competitive behaviour but only in the *absence* of rules imposed by the state. As L. von Mises has said:

It is customary to speak metaphorically of the automatic and anonymous forces actuating the 'mechanism' of the market. In employing such metaphors, people are ready to disregard the fact that the only factors directing the market and the determination of prices are purposive acts of men. There is no automatism; there are only men consciously and deliberately aiming at ends chosen. There are no mysterious mechanical forces; there is only the human will to remove uneasiness. There is no anonymity; there is I and you and Bill and Joe and all the rest. And each of us is both a producer and a consumer . . . There is nothing inhuman or mystical with regard to the market. The market process is entirely a resultant of human actions. Every market phenomenon can be traced back to definite choices of the members of the market society (von Mises, cited in Taylor, 1980, p. 35).

Thus the denial of the necessity for any intervention in the market, as promulgated by Chicago and the new right can logically be extended to a denial of the theoretical basis for state intervention at any level within society. Yet any presumption that firm behaviour and market forces operate in the best interests of the collectivity rather than in the interests of the most powerful group, denies the self-evident truth that markets are only the sum of their constituent parts. Those parts are individuals who may be expected to operate in their perceived best interests rather than the interests of society as a whole. If firms were 'their brothers keepers' in fact, Chicago economists would be amongst the first to suggest that such collusive behaviour militated against the efficient allocation of resources.

As outlined in Chapter 2, Smith's 'invisible hand' – which libertarians assert must not be constrained by government intervention – referred only to the fact that industrialists may find themselves engaging in unintended behaviour in the pursuit of personal gain. If industrialists are prey to such unintended activity, it might be more properly associated with the psychological and game theoretical approaches than market forces; particularly if we accept that these forces are merely those factors determining movements in supply, demand and price. Referring again to Hayek, prices are the 'indispensable signals' that communicate the effects of events with which individuals cannot be directly acquainted. But:

> Only prices at which everyone is free to buy and sell as much as he wants and his means allow can operate as reliable guides. Only if all owners or users of goods can take part in the dealings will all requirement and all opportunities be taken into account. Prices fixed by political authority, or prices influenced by controls on demand and supply – such as rationing, subsidies, special taxes – do not guide in the right direction but generally mislead because they distort the information about supply and consumer demand and, moreover, add a political element that has little to do with reflecting technical possibilities or satisfying consumers.
>
> Prices may, for a time, be fixed by a monopolist who owes his position not to privilege conferred upon him by government, but to his superior efficiency which nobody else can equal . . . Contrary to a widespread belief, unless it is sheltered from competition by government protection, a big business has no more power than anyone else to fix prices arbitrarily. It is subject to the same disciplines of supply and demand. And if such a firm mistakes the signals, it will, fortunately, fail . . . (Hayek, 1980, pp. 32–3).

It is this naive belief in freedom of information and the dogmatic faith in the ability of the market to force failure upon the monopolist, which the new right has taken upon itself as the essence of contemporary economic thought on competition. Hayek's clear analysis of the need for and assumption of compliance with game rules is representative of his integrity as a philosopher. The omission of such central assumptions to any application of his theory, represents the corruption of one theory set in ideological concrete to support another.

The central core of libertarian thought as expressed in relation to anti-trust, parallels the observations of Marx and Engels. However, their observation that: 'Competition makes the immanent laws of capitalist production to be felt by each individual capitalist as external coercive laws' (Marx, Vol.1., p. 603), has been repeated by writers such as Bork and Posner, as fact rather than as a feeling. Baumol and Ordover (1985) have in fact gone so far as to show not simply how successful attempts to intervene in the operation of markets misallocates resources, but how the very existence of such law causes misallocation. By encouraging firms to think they may be able to disable or remove competitors, anti-trust regulation encourages the wasteful application of legal processes, lawyers' time and bureaucratic processes. The existence of coercive laws and the knowledge that they can be used against them, encourages firms to opt for second best solutions and sub-optimal business strategies. Add to this Bork's contention that no activity by a firm can be regarded as anti-competitive, and the costs associated with such regulation are unsupportable.

Yet there can be no doubt that these rules of competition were initiated by the capitalist class, those owners of capital who the Chicago School, at least, seeks to protect. The traditions of the Samurai warriors, Harvard, Eton and European aristocracies were, until only very recent times, the preserve of the capital-owning classes, who have always relied for their existence and the maintenance of their position upon rules and self-discipline. Of equal importance to these groups was co-operation for mutual gain, a fact to which we shall return again later. The changing nature of those who are the aristocracy in the 1980s and the changing nature of their commercial interests – bankers, financiers and owners of industrial manufacturing capacity rather than landed gentry – has given rise to a change in emphasis in ideology, and to the creation of factions within the capitalist class rather than the propagation of one unified ideological position.

One such faction has added weight to the arguments in favour of a non-interventionist anti-trust policy by encouraging a quiet, but sure-footed, revival of protectionism. Patriotism may be 'the last refuge of the scoundrel' (Samuel Johnson, 1775, p. 348) and the greatest enemy of international trade, but as a defence of a non-interventionist anti-trust policy it has few equals. Whilst its historical role in creating war and famine may have tarnished its popular image somewhat, its currency amongst the ruling classes has remained undimmed. Most significantly, it is embraced by those on the far right and left of the political spectrum who see the necessity to preserve national income, national pride, national industry, national jobs and national security, as the primary role of government and by extension, anti-trust enforcement agencies.

If we refer back to Scruton (Chapter 3), we find that his emphasis upon the right of government to govern, and the importance of the stable nuclear family as the central pivot of national economic growth, has echoes throughout Western capitalist society. Notable examples are the difficulties associated with the 1987 round of GATT negotiations and the gathering pace of the US EEC trade conflict; the pre-eminence of the Star Wars programme, and the decision of the UK government to establish a new 'Defence Engineers Service'; the AIDS epidemic being vaunted as the 'wrath of God' upon the promiscuous, whose sexual activity ought, by implication, to have been contained within a nuclear family for the good of America; the increasing contempt expressed for peace studies, sociology and any other academic subject which seeks to encourage students to question rather than simply to accept the *status quo*; and the increasing emphasis upon material goods as the route to perfect happiness. Any suggestion that such emphasis is in fact causing increasing levels of consumer indebtedness and a diminution of personal well-being is blamed again upon the breakdown of the family.

Yet there is a second grouping who perceive protectionism as not playing by the rules. There is a synthesis of competition and trade theory, which the EEC has conflated within the competition rules of the Rome Treaty. In its emphasis upon the free movement of goods, services, labour and capital within a highly regulated framework, there is an essential codification of free trade which mirrors the ideological framework to which in theory, at least, the more liberal conservative and social democratic elements of the ruling classes have some allegiance: playing *laissez-faire* capitalist economics by the book. For the EEC, this has also meant seeking to ensure that while the rights of companies to compete freely in the marketplace are relatively well protected, the rights of workers and consumers are protected too. Thus, for example, toxic food colourings, discrimination on grounds of sex, and unreasonable laboratory experimentation on animals are prohibited, while member states are now required to include consumer education within school curricula. The fact that member states don't always implement the rules means neither that the rules are unnecessary nor that they are unwelcome, simply that within many member states the political will is lacking.

Of greater significance than these two factions, therefore, is that faction which holds political power. Within the greater part of continental Europe, the UK, the USA, and (to a far lesser extent)

Japan, the political power elite has relinquished sovereignty over national economic policy, and protection of the consumer, by accepting that governmental regulation of the economy and corporate behaviour should be weak or absent. The reassertion of Mill's philosophy, the rediscovery of John Locke, and the revival of the Spencerian belief in the survival of the fittest to propagate a non-interventionist anti-trust policy, has resulted in a reification of the needs of the individual at the expense of the needs of society as a whole.

And because of this ideological posture, there is almost everywhere a prohibition upon horizontal collusion. Firms must stand on their own two feet, for if only the fittest company is to survive, it must do so alone, without the assistance or co-operation of any other actor in the marketplace. Co-operation, indeed, is seen as a greater evil than the vertical concentration of power: the UK's Restrictive Trade Practices Act outlaws information-sharing between horizontal competitors yet makes no reference to collusion between producers and distributors. Horizontal collusion within both the EEC and the US is subject to the *per se* rule. Thus within all of these areas, one firm controlling a chain of manufacture and distribution from the most basic initial input through to retail distribution, is unfettered by government regulation unless some substantive proof of abuse of that power within one of these many markets can be proven within a court of law.

In reality, all of these various state legislatures have provided a political framework within which the demands of your initial nationalistic faction are met. When the need arises they pass legislation nodding in the direction of free trade, and in continuing to support the institutions of the GATT and EEC they provide a substantive impression of seeking greater co-operation. There are, however, many examples of their hypocrisy, prime amongst which are 'voluntary export restraints', which are most frequently imposed by European and American nations upon South East Asian exporters. Ball-bearings, zip fasteners, televisions, video recorders and motor cars are just some of the examples where South East Asian exporters have accepted 'voluntary' quotas and reduced their levels of penetration within the major GATT member states – or face the consequences. The quotas are imposed purely because the importing states wish to protect national industries. The ultimate irony for the UK at least, has been that Japanese companies in particular have established factories on UK soil and use British workers as assemblers. That is, the number of goods which the Japanese would have wished to have exported direct now enter in kit form, and the UK offers tax incentives *et al.*, to encourage assembly on British soil.

Essentially, what we find in late twentieth-century Western capitalist economies is that firm behaviour considered to militate against the best interests of the nation state in the nineteenth century, has been de-criminalised and hailed as the new orthodoxy. Vertical restraints, from tie-in sales to refusal to supply to exclusive distribution contracts, and much more besides, are claimed to be the wealth generating, growth inducing panaceas of our age. Firms know what is best for them, and '. . . what's good for General Motors is good for the country' (Charles E. Wilson to a Congressional Committee, 1952). There are a few instances where the European Commission may have shown itself able to withstand the pressure against intervention, but this has more to do with its special remit, its particular set of powers, and its position of supra-nationality, than any substantial urge to back the philosophical trend.

Applying that analysis further, standard economic theories of the firm seeking to explain business strategy (Chapter 4) have a somewhat tired and jaded appearance in the latter part of the 1980s. While sophisticated models of profit maximisation may still be highly relevant, theories which fail to discuss growth maximisation within the context of corporate power, satisficing behaviour within the context of political influence, sales maximising behaviour within the context of conglomeracy, the rise of employee share ownership and 'management buy-outs', fail to acknowledge important structural changes within the global economy as a whole. Added to which neither Marris, Baumol or Cyert and March operated within a paradigm which took account of the importance and influence of information technology upon a firm's ability to adopt and change corporate strategy. The development of technology which allows firms to receive and communicate price decisions within microseconds has, with those other changes, dramatically altered the relevance of these theories, and equally significantly has disturbed much of the rationale underlying theories relating to investment decisions.

To summarise this first part of the chapter, it is evident that the necessity for the existence of rules and government institutions is clearly established within the ideological framework adopted by Western capitalist ruling oligarchies. It is also clear that while they may accept the necessity for rules to defend the state from external incursions and internal malcontents, there is no evidence to suggest that they regard domestic firms to be amongst those ranks, even where such firms may, by dint of size and annual turnover, hold substantial economic power. If this is the case, what then is the purpose of anti-trust or competition policy?

There are, as we have said, those who consider competition policy vital to police 'allocative efficiency', but as we have also said, allocative efficiency is almost impossible to quantify. Harberger (1954) developed his rather well-known model in the 1950s, Cowling and Mueller (1978) went to great lengths to measure welfare loss triangles in the 1970s. Tullock identified wealth transfer and allocative efficiency losses in the 1960s and welfare economics was subject to 'Liberal Restatement' by Rowley and Peacock in 1975. Sadly, each of these economists relies upon our accepting that they know what the level of distribution would have been had the allocation been optimal in the absence of monopoly, or regulation, or criminal acts. That is, all calculation of welfare loss is retrospective and income distribution levels are given (there are other assumptions, such as an absence of externalities which causes concern at some levels, plus the all-pervasive nature of second-best solutions, but an in-depth debate about the value of welfare economics is not our purpose at this juncture). Our contention is that the acceptance of allocative efficiency type arguments is essentially an act of faith. There are a number of writers who have identified what inefficiency probably is – notably X-inefficiency – but the approximation of allocative efficiency *per se* has proved more elusive. What is more frequently suggested, (notably in the UK, but less often within the US) is that if nations are experiencing balance of payments deficits this is a result of a misallocation of resources – or inefficiency. And that, very often, is as far as the economic analysis goes.

In having placed such heavy emphasis upon the ability of market forces to control the unquantifiable god of allocative efficiency, governments have failed to consider other possible rationales for competition policy. Perhaps most respectable of these amongst legislators and the nationalistic lobby, is the notion that decreasing levels of control over competition gives rise to increasing levels of concentration. By definition, concentration denotes the concentration of economic power within fewer and fewer hands.

Attempting to provide support for the theory of allocative efficiency and show that increasing moves towards deregulation are correct, Audretsch and Woolf (IIM/IP 85–38) seek to contradict the theory of collective action (Mancur Olson, 1965). This suggests that,

> if the number of sellers in the market is sufficiently small, and if information is widespread among those firms, the organisational costs of obtaining a restrictive policy will be relatively small. And if a few parties stand to gain from the transfer of a large amount of

wealth, the value of seeking restrictive policies to each member is high. The parties losing from that policy, on the other hand, especially consumers, tend to suffer from high organisational costs and a deficient distribution of information.

Essentially, the theory suggests that there may well be occasions when dominant firms within an industry find it in their interests to encourage the introduction of government regulation. In its most extreme form, it contends that there is some conspiracy being played out by industrialists against consumers – a theory frequently vilified by both left and right of the political spectrum. While we would not wish to expose ourselves to such criticism, it does appear from some of the cases we have investigated, and scandals uncovered within the City of London and Wall Street at the time of writing (Ivan Boesky, Morgan Grenfell, Guinness, etc.), that there is a degree of justification for the view that the structure of capitalist economies provides an environment where collective action is accepted as a norm of behaviour amongst those who hold economic and political power.

That is that we hope to draw out from the analysis of anti-competitive practices and our four case studies, evidence to support our view that while norms and values or game rules exist to regulate society as a whole, they are rarely if ever understood by the central economic and political players to apply also to them. Equally significantly, we hope to show that while the referees or representatives of state may understand the rules, they have no idea what, if anything, is their purpose, or indeed the real aim of the game. They know they have to have some sort of competition policy, but they don't really know why and in an attempt at justification have concocted a view which accords with the prevailing ideological orthodoxy. The contradictions inherent within the theory of competition are of substantial importance to certain economists, but are frequently too complex to be understood by the majority of state representatives. In offering contradictory motivations and policy prescriptions the theories encourage an emphasis upon ideological dogma, without which officials within national regulatory authorities would have little to justify their existence.

Regulation of the UK life assurance industry is a prime example of Olson's theory in practice. Unable to compete effectively with new products and modern marketing methods, the old established companies joined together to demand government regulation of their industry in a form which most nearly matched their needs. Yet regulation of that sector conflicted with the then government's declared intention of reducing its control over markets. Unable to rationalise the demands of the country's most important financial sector with political dogma, the government pulled the lever marked 'consumer protection' and opened the way to the introduction of collusive agreements aimed primarily at foreclosure of markets for independent advice. Had the government genuinely sought consumer protection, the most obvious approach would have been the prohibition of self-employed tied agents (as explained in Chapter 7). But the government was merely engaging in a knee-jerk response to demands from an extremely powerful group – one frequently responsible for advising government, and one which benefited greatly, not simply from consumers' ignorance about its activities, but also from substantial levels of ignorance on the part of politicians and bureaucrats.

Our study of the insurance industry highlights the relationship between politicians and financiers and emphasises the potentially damaging impact upon any single economy of regulators having no clear guidance as to the purpose of competition policy. Economists within the OFT are required to ensure that the rules laid down by the Self-Regulating Authorities do not distort competition, whatever that may mean. Within the Chicago School paradigm, consumer protection has no clear role. Within an Austrian framework, any regulation of this type is entirely reprehensible. The search for Pareto optimality requires efficiency in distribution and exchange and assumes perfect information – yet none of these variables are sought or attained as a result of these new regulations. Allocative inefficiency, economic power and structural inequalities in information and income are rewarded; price and non-price competition are actively banned.

Having outlined the ways in which the regulation of the insurance industry contravenes Article 85(1) of the Rome Treaty in a previously published article (Genn-Bash *et al.*, 1985, 1985a, p. 1), it is sufficient here to re-state only that state backing for regulation of the UK life assurance sector exhibits all the manifestations of regulation by an interest group. By presuming that the leaders of the British insurance industry understand and thus play by sportsmanlike rules, the government has ceded control over its activities to the industry's more powerful members. The only possibility of damage limitation – damage to the industry, consumers and the economy as a whole – is the supranational authority of the European Commission: 'foreigners' who neither play by nor understand the rules of cricket, and benefit greatly from the clear delineation of their role as protectors of the common market.

Unfortunately, the Commission's ability to perform that function effectively is constrained by the necessity to maintain a working relationship with its counterparts within the member states. Those bureaucrats may understand national game rules, but certainly in the case of the UK have an imperfect understanding of the structure of economic relations and the purpose of anti-trust. As a consequence they face substantial difficulties in their attempts to exercise control over market conduct and provide little support for the Competition Directorate in Brussels.

The dual role of the OFT as protector of competition policy and consumer affairs permits regulators the opportunity to take refuge in the somewhat nebulous notion of consumer protection where the contradictions within the government's approach to competition policy (arising from electoral constraints as outlined within Chapter 3), are simply too great. Self-regulation of the insurance industry is a prime example of those responsible for anti-trust enforcement finding themselves manipulated by business interests and political apathy. The overtly anti-competitive nature of the regulations proposed and supported by the industry can only be justified by insisting that they promote consumer protection – a suggestion as unrealistic in this case as any notion of increasing competition. The problem is that the left don't care because the Financial Services Act refers to money markets, and politicians on the left are never prepared to concern themselves with the operation of such unclean acts. Politicians on the right know that the legislation is simply a chimera – there has never been, nor will there ever be, any attempt to regulate financial markets because obviously the best people to regulate such behaviour are the actors themselves. The regulators find themselves being asked to engage in activity which in all other markets and at all other times would be criticised as unnecessary government intervention, and suffer an uncommon degree of ignorance about the operation of the market they are to regulate. Thus the reins are held by the industry's most powerful members because it is they who have immediate access to the regulators and upon whose advice the regulators must rely for information about the market. The fact that a highly competitive market has been made restrictive as a direct result of government intervention is testimony to the absence of any understanding, intellectual justification of or rationale for competition policy within the UK.

If we look at the case study of retailing, we find first of all that the titles of both the MMC and OFT reports are misleading. 'Discounts to Retailers' and 'Competition and Retailing' suggest that a wide analysis of the entire retailing sector was undertaken. In reality, both investigations were motivated by a large number of complaints from small, independent grocers, who claimed that they were being denied the opportunity to compete with the multiple supermarket chains on price. The independents believed that the multiples could only sell at prices below that at which they were having to buy, because they were receiving substantial discounts from the food manufacturers. Indeed, the independents claimed that the manufacturers' ability to offer these discounts was dependent upon their forcing the independents to cross-subsidise them.

Both the OFT and the MMC found that the countervailing power and scale economies enjoyed by the multiples resulted in efficiency gains which were passed on to consumers in the form of lower prices. The multiples were thus perceived to be increasing social welfare and operating in favour of the public interest.

Yet the OFT was not asked to investigate in its role as consumer protection agency, but as competition authority. As such it was required to search out activity which had, or was likely to have, the effect of restricting or distorting competition. Only the MMC may determine the public interest. The independents were not demanding to know whether or not consumers paid lower prices in supermarkets – their success determined that they must. The independents required an investigation of the extent to which their ability to compete was specifically reduced by food manufacturers raising prices to the independents to cover the costs of discounts to the major multiples. That possibility was never seriously investigated. Binding itself to the notion that competition authorities exist as the guardians of allocative efficiency, the OFT considered the superior efficiency and popular appeal of supermarket multiples as proof against anti-competitive behaviour.

Here of course is the essential core of Chicago School theory and the primary source of the theoretical contradictions: If firm A is more profitable than firm B it has to be because firm A is more efficient than firm B. If firm A offers lower prices than firm B, in all cases this denotes an increase in competition and resultant improvements in allocative efficiency. While in many cases this may be true, it must also be acknowledged that the theory provides an apology for rent-seeking behaviour and suggests a substantial lack of understanding of real-world conduct. It also assumes that consumers have perfect information and free access to all outlets within the distribution chain.

In its report, the OFT makes no reference to the impact upon total allocative efficiency of relatively high prices for food faced by consumers unable to visit supermarkets (most frequently the disadvantaged and those in low-paid jobs). If corner shops are unable to offer low prices because they are forced to subsidise discounts for the benefit of their rivals, any potential increase in allocative efficiency resulting from the rise of the 'pile it high, sell it cheap' school of retail practice is lost in the aggregate.

If we add to this the very high levels of multiple supermarket chain profitability, the contradictions inherent within both the theory and practice of competition policy become clear. On the one hand, we have considerations of allocative efficiency, on the other, some notion of consumer sovereignty, the public interest, and equitable distributions of income and power. In the case of competition in retailing, it is clear that the rise of the multiples has to a very large extent provided an illusion of increased allocative efficiency. If this is the only goal of anti-trust regulators, then multiples present an increase in social welfare where it is possible for some consumers to be made better off without making others worse off. Unfortunately, however, that final part of the equation – the truth of whether or not any consumers are made worse off – appears to be regarded as irrelevant, or simply too difficult to test. Whilst we would suggest that the calculation of gains is as unreliable as any empirical calculation of losses, the fact remains that adherence to an ideological construct appears to have blinkered regulators to the necessity to perform the second part of their test of allocative efficiency.

The absence of any outcry either by consumers or retailers on publication of the OFT's report may suggest that the original hypothesis predicting cross-subsidy and benefits to certain consumers at the cost of detriment to others, was false. Alternatively it may suggest that levels of disillusionment with anti-trust regulation, and governmental pronouncements in support of the self-employed, are such that only very few people expect the UK competition authorities to correct any significant examples of market failure.

And yet investigation of the Ford Motor Company is regarded by some observers as a major example of the OFT's readiness to defend consumers from the power of the multinationals (see Chapter 7). In our view the case study highlights the influence of Chicago School thinking. Taking government regulation as the only major source of entry barrier, the OFT made a sound case for the repeal of design copyright laws on the grounds that the law permitted rent-seeking behaviour and in so doing misallocated resources. The MMC's follow-up report agreed with that analysis and recommended reform of the law. The government's White Paper offered that reform at the beginning of 1986, but then drew back from the opportunity by failing to include reform of the intellectual property laws within its table of proposed legislation for 1987. What does all this suggest?

Essentially it suggests that the OFT welcomed and took hold of an opportunity to test government regulation as an entry barrier. The existence of efficiency losses directly resulting from legislation, provided the OFT with a justification for its ideological position. If, as a Chicagoan, one claims that there are no anti-competitive practices and no barriers to entry, one denies the necessity for a regulatory framework. However, highlighting barriers created through government regulation allows regulatory bodies back into story. Some of the most recent MMC reports have provided evidence of that body's equally unshakable faith in the free market mechanism. (See, for example, the Tampons report, which preferred to rely on supernormal profits acting as a 'magnet to attract new suppliers' rather than risk the possibility that regulation would inhibit new entry. MMC, 1986, p. 41).

Most significant, however, was the government's initial acceptance of the need to reform the law (presumably as we suggest in Chapter 7, greatly encouraged by the EEC's insistence that it do so urgently or find itself faced with infringement of the Treaty), and then its sudden about face. With two Green Papers providing intellectual support, the OFT and MMC calling for reform, a White Paper published and civil servants engaged on the process of refining and honing the terms to ensure its passage as a bill, the government simply dropped it without warning. For a government committed to increasing competition such an example of legislative barriers must be unpalatable. And indeed it probably is. But reforming the law and denying large companies a continuing product monopoly when they believe they are entitled to one requires more courage and less acceptance of the needs of business than most twentieth-century governments are able to exhibit. Equally, having found the Law Lords to be willing accomplices, the external imperative for reform was removed. With the British Leyland judgement any necessity for government intervention was mitigated by the creation of legal precedent. As discussed within Chapter 3, according to the legal model of competition, it is legal precedent alone which can and should guide the conduct of actors within the market.

Essentially the case studies would appear to suggest that firms have assimilated the need to co-operate. In the case of a multi-national, such as Ford, co-operation has taken the form of collusive agreements with its constituent parts to ensure the protection of its boundaries and extension of its monopoly into a secondary market. The protection of boundaries within the beer and insurance industries has resulted in co-operation to ensure the creation or continuance of restrictive regulation for the sole purpose of protecting positions of dominance within individual markets. And within the grocery sector, co-operation between manufacturers and major retailers, and implied agreement between the four major multiples, has ensured that the traditionally British concern for the underdog has been perverted.

And taking the particular analysis of game theory (as described in Chapter 1), such behaviour must surely be regarded as wholly rational. The lessons expressed within the Tragedy of the Commons, and the game theoretic approach provided within Axelrod's computer program 'Tit for Tat' (again described in Chapter 1), suggest that any society requires both competitive and co-operative strategies if actors within the economic sphere are to survive the drive towards any degree of economic growth. Thus the majors agreeing to co-ordinate their competitive conduct towards smaller companies suggests an implicit understanding of co-operative conduct rather than naked aggression as the optimal business strategy. Sweeping an eye across many of the most successful industries, it becomes apparent that such behaviour is indeed the norm rather than the exception, with the success of the Japanese economy based to a significant degree on acceptance of this self-evident truth. A rudimentary investigation of the chemical, pharmaceutical, non-metallic mineral, etc., etc., sectors provides further support.

Yet everywhere, regulatory authorities place greatest emphasis upon the prohibition of co-operation. Collusive behaviour, cartels, agreements to share information are all prohibited. Under Article 85(1) of the Rome Treaty, only certain types of joint ventures, and agreements aimed at rationalisation or restructuring have the potential for exemption, and then only where the agreements show potential economic benefits to consumers and can still prove the maintenance of competitive pressures (for example the agreement between ENI and Montedison). Throughout Europe, the US and Japan, the norm is that collusive agreements shall be outlawed.

If we accept that the theoretically most rational action for firms to engage in is expressly prohibited, is the inevitable conclusion that antitrust regulation forces firms to engage in irrational behaviour? Certainly there are examples of dominant firms engaging in behaviour which, with the benefit of hindsight, would appear at best to have been misjudged, at worst, irrational. If we take as one example the Raleigh case (OFT, 1981) we find that the dominant UK cycle firm cut its own throat by refusing to supply cheap distributors. Resorting to pleading a specialist product, with an attendant necessity for high levels of customer service, served only to ensure that a market, which until that point had experienced low levels of import penetration, was flooded with cheap imports. By 1987, Raleigh's share of the cycle market had been decimated to the point where the company and its debts were sold off by Tube Investments with an audible sigh of relief. And other firms appear to have taken no account of the possibility of being caught when steering their company in a direction which contravened anti-trust law.

Essentially the type of behaviour under discussion is the creation of vertical restraints. These are agreements which depend for their success upon imperfect information to consumers. Infrequently purchased goods (such as bikes, specialist cameras, hi-fi equipment, fine china, even car tyres), most commonly fall into this category, for essentially they are those goods which offer manufacturers the opportunity of indulging in strategies for maintaining outmoded images of 'specialist', 'luxury' and 'hi-tech'. If able to create or maintain such an illusion via selective distribution agreements *et al.*, companies establish a monopoly of 'the best' within a particular product group. The alternative to 'pile it high, sell it cheap' as a means of engaging in rent-seeking behaviour is 'severely restrict the number of distributors and raise the price'. With poor access to information, a period of rapidly changing technology, plus 'bandwagon, Veblen and snob effects' (Leibenstein, in Breit and Hochman, 1971, p. 111), manufacturers are able to create and maintain monopolies within markets no larger than the market for their particular brand of good.

Many economists believe that such behaviour must inevitably result in new firms entering the market, and in doing so implicitly reject any suggestion of single products holding a monopoly in the market for that single product. As a consequence any calculation of loss in allocative efficiency severely under-estimates the impact of vertical restraints upon national markets. The approach also underestimates the impact of time-lags, and the costs of new entry which must include the costs associated with establishing distribution outlets. Yet logic demands we accept either that the costs of creating and protecting vertical restraints are sufficiently offset by the potential gains to warrant their introduction; or, returning to our earlier hypothesis, that the desire to create a monopoly and remove competitive pressure is such that firms engage in vertical restraint despite the costs. Either they are engaging in rent-seeking behaviour, or the drive to win makes them ready to engage in an irrational strategy, whatever the cost.

By dismissing the possibility that vertical restraints may have any degree of economic impact, libertarian economists are rewarding the creation of monopolies in 'specialist' goods. They are encouraging misallocation of resources via wasteful indulgence in product differentiation (which creates the single-product monopoly in the first place) and encouraging firms to employ legal services to create and then protect any such monopoly – particularly to protect them from prosecution by the anti-trust authorities. Denial of such complicity suggests that libertarian economists believe firms engage in irrational behaviour. The Distillers' Company restricted the distribution of Red Label whisky in order to increase profits available in France, and the company was subject to take-over in 1986. The Wedgwood fine china company restricted distribution of its product to only high-priced, exclusive retailers and were taken over by Waterford Glass in 1986. Hasselblad severely restricted distribution of its cameras and was caned under EEC legislation. But these and many other instances are where vertical restraints have been emplaced to prevent or reduce the potential for new market entry and crucially, have become known to the competition authorities. The companies have suffered and monopoly profits have been reduced but not as a result of free market forces.

Our analysis suggests that dominant firms do not always achieve their positions of dominance by dint of greater efficiency and that any suggestion that they be regarded as the final arbiters of optimal business strategy, lacks credibility. The theoretical paradigm underlying the original hypothesis requires that individual nation states should accept a reduction in sovereignty over economic power to the point where, if appropriate, they cede power to supranational corporations. The very wide acceptance of libertarian theory with the attendant emasculation of the state's ability to protect its citizens from exploitation and colonisation by firms is neither Hobbes's war of all against all or Spencer's survival of the fittest. It is the game theoretic approach where co-operation is accepted as the norm amongst major non-competing groups: conglomerates agree to divide world markets between them, politicians and industrialists agree that the interests of the firm are synonymous with the best interests of the state. The co-operation for mutual gain which typified the old aristocratic order typifies the new, and late twentieth-century anti-trust economics has become the apologist of late twentieth-century political behaviour which is itself designed to protect and enhance the interests of large corporations rather than those of society as a whole.

9 Policy Conclusions

The creation and protection of monopolies within the UK has been perceived as the business of State certainly for the last 700 years with competition law – in the form of price control – dating at least from Saxon times. While the word 'monopoly' appears not to have been coined until 1516 by Sir Thomas More, royal monopolies were granted to individuals and guilds from the thirteenth century. The panoply of intellectual property laws, Labour government nationalisations and re-organisations, and present-day Conservative emphasis upon privatisations have ensured a continuity of privilege and bring that process up to date. The declared motivation for granting such rights has an equally unbroken lineage.

In the thirteenth century monopolies were granted to encourage the development and import of new trades. Under Elizabeth I, licences were granted as a matter of political expediency. But there was also some concern at the unfettered use of power so granted which mirrored the contemporary belief in the efficacy of social control to reap the benefits of economies of scale, without the social costs of private monopoly. From Tudor, through Elizabethan, Stewart and contemporary periods, there has also been a desire to raise money for the State through the sale of monopolies.

A more modern form of concern over commercial behaviour began to emerge in the 1920s and 1930s with the Wall Street Crash and Great Depression providing strong motivation for a rather more serious analysis of commercial relations. While the 1929 Balfour Committee on Trade and Industry argued that central intervention would simply inhibit growth, the UK's 1944 White Paper on Employment Policy made an explicit link between unemployment and monopoly. The White Paper's underlying rationale derived directly from economic theory, which showed that a profit maximising monopolist would restrict output, and hence jobs, in order to raise prices. In contrast, competition tended to raise output and employment and lower prices. Vigorous competition was perceived as a solution to the problems of poor export performance, the immobility of labour and the potential for profiteering.

Despite a presumption for competition on employment grounds, since 1948, in the UK there has been a powerful alternative political view that size of itself can bring great benefits of growth through economies of scale and the ability to invest in research and development. However, the correlation between large size and potentially undesirable market power has increasingly forced public policy to become a balancing act between control of market power and consequent restraints on competition, and a desire to foster the healthy growth of the economy on a 'bigness is best' principle.

Winthrop (see Chapter 5) argued that public policy should attempt to ensure that plant size is sufficiently large to exhaust all possible scale economies and that a sufficiently large number of competing firms exist in the industry to prevent welfare loss to society. He went on to point out that these two criteria are not necessarily attainable simultaneously, thus suggesting that a trade-off between efficiency and equity considerations may arise. Winthrop also presented evidence to suggest that UK plant sizes were inefficiently small while levels of firm concentration were unduly high. Because a single firm can own several plants, firm concentration levels tend to be much higher than plant concentration levels. Hence, economies of scale are not exhausted at the plant level and at the same time an insufficient number of firms exist in many industries to ensure effective competition. A loss of efficiency occurs and society suffers a welfare loss.

But the nature of the relationship between competition and technological change is a source of fierce debate among industrial economists. The Schumpeterian hypothesis is that technical progressiveness increases directly with firm size, which suggests that monopoly may have at least one virtue (and several more if Baumol's 'contestable markets' hypothesis is accepted). Galbraith, has reinforced this view: 'a benign Providence – has made for modern industry of a few large firms an almost perfect instrument for inducing technological change' (Galbraith, 1952, p. 86).

The counter view is provided by writers such as Arrow (1962), Scherer (1967) and Rosenberg (1976). Scherer has argued that R & D input, as measured by the number of scientific and technical personnel employed, increases at low levels of concentration but changes at medium to high levels. Specifically, when CR4 (4-firm concentration ratio) exceeds 50–55 per cent there is no longer a positive correlation.

The advantages of scale economies and technological progressiveness are often given in support of merger activity. Yet the case that large firms produce benefits from greater technological change is far from proven. Instead the counter view that competition is vital for successful research and development appears most plausible especially if we accept the findings of J. B. Rosenberg who found a significant negative relationship between employment of R & D personnel and the market share of large firms.

Indeed growth of firms through mergers and amalgamation, has on the evidence, failed to produce much in the way of growth for the economy as a whole (Cooke, 1986, pp. 44–5).

Strongly rising stock markets provide an apparent fount of wealth with which to purchase other firms. Managers, on grounds of risk averseness, prefer growth by acquisition to growth by investment and competition. The truth has all too often been that a firm which cannot compete on the international market by production, marketing and cost control, has bought its way out of trouble by acquiring its rivals.

The City of London's fondness for mergers arises from the generation of substantial fee and other incomes and from gains for the shareholders in the company which loses its identity – even if, in the longer term, shareholders in the acquiring company may tend to lose out.

Mergers are also encouraged by UK Government taxation policies and by the endemic weakness, in this country as opposed to the USA, of the anti-monopoly legislation. The take-over process is defended as part of the competitive process by which weak and sleepy management is eliminated. Managers in the successful predator company enjoy the activity as they automatically gain in power and status.

However, doubts have been expressed. Success in take-overs reflects more the ability of the predator to raise money and to invest expensive managerial time in the bid, than the relative efficiencies of the two firms. There is also concern that the constant threat of take-over, far from building efficiency, locks managers into short-term perspectives.

As the former Conservative Prime Minister Edward Heath expressed it in the House of Commons on 19 January 1987:

Finance takes the short-term view and allows three months only. If the results after that time do not seem satisfactory, the management is changed and somebody takes over the firm. There is no interest whatever in the long-term point of view. For those who are working in the markets, it is not even a three month view, it is three seconds, and if the answer is not up on the screen in front of them in three seconds they must do something about it.

Sir Gordon Borrie, the UK's Director General of Fair Trading has also expressed a 'heretical' concern with the rational expectations hypothesis of capital markets.

Using the discretionary or case-by-case approach adopted in the UK, the regulators are charged with implementing merger qua competition policy using a cost-benefit analysis of changes in industrial performance resulting from a change in structure. The public interest criteria to be applied under the Fair Trading Act requires a calculation of social costs and benefits, but without clear public policy guidelines, these can be difficult to define and indeed to measure. However, the 1984 introduction of the 'Tebbit doctrine' provided a partial solution to that problem by requiring that decisions be made with reference only to the effect on competition.

Sawyer (p. 255) makes the following important point in a discussion of such a cost-benefit approach:

The assessment of costs and benefits of changes in industrial performance arising from changes in industrial structure would generally lead to proposals for changes in the structure. These changes may involve the break-up of existing firms or the encouragement of mergers. Thus the existing level of industrial concentration may be judged too high or too low. The basis of any judgement is the *social* costs and benefits of a change in structure, whereas the firms are presumed to be interested in the difference between *private* benefits and costs (i.e. profits). If social benefits and costs coincide with private benefits and costs, there is little problem in persuading the firms involved of the benefits of the change. But such a coincidence could often lead the firms to make the change anyway. Where there are differences between social net benefits and private net benefits, difficulties of implementation arise. For example, it is difficult to imagine firms merging in the 'public interest' if the merger were believed by the participants to be unprofitable.

Hence any firm faced with an investigation into a proposed merger bid, or indeed an alleged anti-competitive practice, would rationally compare the costs and benefits of compliance with non-compliance. Unless the legislative body charged with implementing competition policy is able to impose a sufficiently onerous penalty on the firm for non-compliance that offsets the benefits to the firm from continuing the practice, public policy will be ineffective.

The deep problem for public policy over competition everywhere bar Japan, is that there is no agreement on the nature of competition nor on its part in the overall strategy for the national economy. The rationale provided in 1948 is no longer considered relevant thus while there are rules which perhaps might be tightened to good effect in some areas, the power of the rules is weakened by political interference and a lack of the political will to back the regulatory bodies.

Apart from issues of electoral interest, politicians have only their general principles to guide them. At various stages in this book we have argued that both competitive and co-operative strategies are available to firms and other organisations. There is no a priori reason for assuming a competitive route will be chosen – in fact much of the evidence points in the other direction. Competition is no more, or less, 'natural' than co-operation.

The existence of rules concerning competition involves a double trade-off between, on the one hand questions of personal freedom and the collective good, and on the other between economic efficiency and social equity. The simplistic view is that more competition will mean more freedom, more efficiency, more human happiness, and that under a regime of competition, each will be rewarded according to their value to their firm. The likely outcome of competition, should the competitive process ever be established, is however, far more ambiguous.

Marx, for one, saw capitalism driven by competition to a crisis based on an overaccumulation of capital. Others saw the outcome not as crisis, but as a stationary state in which all possibilities had been exhausted. Still others saw competition as distributing rewards from the poor, who work, to the rich, who own.

Collusive and monopoly behaviour leads, as stated above, to reduced output and to fewer jobs and also to higher prices and profits, gained by managers enjoying an easier life than they would under real competition. In contrast, co-operation probably produces considerable psychic income for those involved.

The centre of our policy prescription – which every concluding chapter is required to provide – rests upon a synthesis of competition theory and the theory of international trade. But before we begin to develop such a paradigm it is important to state clearly the conclusion that the previous chapters force us to draw. The most important aspect of market conduct overlooked by theoreticians is that for the firms functioning within separable markets there is a primary desire not to compete. Firms do not want to be required by law, forced by circumstance, or cajoled via government policy to engage in the process of competition. Whether such competition be dubbed 'rivalrous', 'workable', or 'monopolistic'; whether markets be described as 'frictionless', 'contestable', 'perfect' or 'oligopolistic', the reality as we now understand it is that the primary goal of business strategy is to negate the necessity to engage in the competitive process.

The position is exemplified by the existence of four basic size categories of firm:

1st tier: Giant diversified multinationals – those which represent the top 100 of any rank ordering of the world's top companies.

2nd tier: The second half of such a rank order – companies whose profits have yet to reach the heights of those within the first group and whose position is somewhat less inviolate.

3rd tier: Major national firms with limited or no overseas interests.

4th tier: Small to medium-sized businesses whose share of the market might be as little as 5 per cent or less.

At the first tier, the giant multinationals have substantial global power. They face little or no threat of takeover and because of their economic importance may have substantial power over nation states. It is rare to see such firms the subject of takeover battles and to see any effective action taken against them by national governments. The fear is that the multinational may transfer part or all of its operations to another country if put under pressure by a particular government to comply with local rules of conduct. Since multinationals employ 30 million of the 90 million manufacturing workers in OECD countries, the scale of their power and influence is apparent.

The suggestion that at the first level, threat of takeover is minimal arises from the high incidence of information sharing or joint venture agreements, the existence of international cartels, and the establishment of co-operation agreements which exist between them. In reality many, if not all of these companies (plus certain of those within the second tier) exist within supra-national space – their continuing ability to do what they do is wholly independent of national or international legislation, and indeed national or international capital markets. Where they consult with regulatory authorities, such consultation often amounts to little more than a public relations exercise to ensure that their preferred joint strategy does not become subject to an annoying and costly series of anti-trust investigations. The ten-year European investigation of IBM provided major companies with a salutary lesson in how not to ignore the regulators. The inability of both the US and the EC anti-trust agencies to prove a case against the company however, provides further evidence to support the notion that essentially, the self-sufficiency of this group of companies, their effective emergence as independent nation states (often with turnover greater than individual nation's GDP), and their ability to recover from dips in profitability sets them apart from puny attempts at national anti-trust enforcement.

Firm behaviour is based upon nothing more rarified than a simple desire to make as much money as possible in the easiest – least competitive – way. Strategies towards the achievement of that end are numerous. If an appropriate means at a particular time is indulgence in predatory behaviour (and a resultant short-term loss) to clear the market of smaller competitors, pockets are deep enough, and in-house lawyers and accountants adept enough to ensure that such activity will become part of corporate strategy. Any attempt by regulators to protect the interests of their small domestic concerns from such activity will be regarded as unwarranted interference and dealt with from a position of superiority – one often not very far removed from contempt. Alternatively or simultaneously, the pursuit of wealth may result in companies regarding co-operation as the most appropriate route to achieving that end. Whatever the preferred strategy, it will be based upon the attempt either to preserve or to increase autonomous control over a substantial proportion of the world's wealth.

The slavish pursuit of intellectual property rights, the frequent recourse to anti-dumping procedures, the insistence that Governments introduce voluntary export restraints, and substantial involvement in various forms of market-sharing or price-fixing agreements, provide clear evidence of real-world attempts by firms to establish unbreachable boundaries around themselves specifically to avoid the unpalatable necessity to compete.

That conclusion leads us into international trade theory, for each of the first three forms of conduct just described are frequently and clearly understood to be protectionist measures. What is not as frequently perceived as such, but essentially takes precisely the same form, are all forms of collusive conduct, all forms of vertical restraint, vertical price squeezing, price discrimination *et al*.

Anti-competitive practices are used for the purpose of compartmentalising sections of national markets, and removing rivals from the arena. Where such practices are successfully emplaced and targeted at inter-industry trade they isolate regions and partition markets from competition or, as it ought more properly be regarded, free trade. Where they are specifically required simply to protect an industry from any competition they more insidiously prevent the growth of intra-industry trade.

Such an analysis ought to be regarded as obvious yet the compartmentalisation of economics within academia frequently isolates students of industrial economics from a study of international trade, and vice versa.

Yet Lipsey claims that:

Economists have long recognised that the principles governing the gains from trade apply equally well to foreign trade as to domestic trade.

The question of the advantage of trade is usually referred to as that of the gains from trade . . . Trade between individuals allows each person to specialise in things he can do well, and buy from others the things he cannot easily produce for himself . . . The same principles apply to regions. Without interregional trade, each region would have to be self-sufficient . . . the living standards of the inhabitants of all regions can be made higher if the inhabitants of each specialise in producing the commodities in the production of which they have some natural or acquired advantage, and obtain other products by trade, than when each region is self-sufficient (1976, p. 636).

But if we look back to the theoretical works on competition referred to in earlier chapters, for example, Marvel's (1982) essay on vertical restraints, Littlechild's work (1978) on mergers, or Cowling and Mueller's (1978) work on the welfare effects of concentration, nowhere do we find any reference to the potential detriment to inter-industry, interpersonal, interregional or international trade. Thus there may still be many who are asking, 'what has the theory of international trade to do with competition policy?' The answer is: everything.

If exclusive agreements, intellectual property rights or collusive behaviour, permit only one region to specialise in the production or supply of a particular commodity, other regions which may have equal or comparatively superior ability to produce or supply that good, are denied the opportunity to take advantage of that ability. They must either concentrate upon the production or supply of other goods that they are possibly less well-equipped to produce or accept under-employment – the misallocation of resources.

The essential premise upon which the establishment of the European Economic Community was based, emanates from the notion that interregional free trade is as important as its international counterpart. Thus criticism of the EEC's competition policy for its attachment to the creation of a 'common market', misunderstands the rationale underpinning its establishment. The creation of a free trade area within Europe was intended as the means by which European nations would grow in wealth and stature to take their place, as a single entity, beside the United States. The growth of EEC trade to the point where it now represents one third of all world trade is regarded by some as testimony to the resounding success of the experiment.

However, our role is not to support or deny such a hypothesis. At this juncture our purpose is to show that political commitment to rigorous anti-trust enforcement is essential if development of the national economy, and consequently the international economy as a whole, is to be regarded as a priority.

The late twentieth century economic reality is that in seeking to avoid competition, many companies co-operate with one another and collude with Government in an attempt to guarantee maximum returns for minimal levels of effort. Their ability to do so is greatly enhanced by the political process which, within Western democracies at least, is wholly chauvinistic and heavily dependent upon the success of the domestic economy. Thus multinational companies can prey upon fears of 'flights of capital', and by presenting themselves as guardians of national employment, gain acceptance of agreements to co-operate with one another to share markets across the rest of the world. The important point to note here is not that co-operation itself necessarily results in a waste of resources. Rather, as described earlier, co-operation may be the best solution in certain circumstances. Problems with cartelisation and so on, arise because co-operation is used, not as a means to enhance total economic growth or social welfare, but to enhance the power and profitability of certain groups at substantial cost to others. As a consequence the gains available both from co-operative and from competitive conduct are often illusory.

Even where the behaviour of a firm or firms is found to be anti-competitive it may be difficult for regulatory bodies charged with implementing policy to ensure that greater competition takes place in the market. Sir Gordon Borrie, UK Director General of Fair Trading wrote in 1982 (1982, p. 141):

> Government intervention may be able to clear away the restrictions on competition that are constituted by cartels and various kinds of anti-competitive practices; but it cannot compel businessmen to compete if they do not wish to do so . . . Competition policy cannot make people compete – it can only create the conditions in which they are able to do so.

The depression of the 1930s provided stark evidence of the

detrimental impact of protectionism – or refusal to compete. The economy of the UK in the 1980s suggests that little has been learned from that experience. Perhaps it is because it was Karl Marx who declared that 'those who do not remember their history are condemned to relive it', that certain entrepreneurs and conservative legislations have made a point of taking a wholly ahistorical approach to the present re-run of that international recession and have sought to forget, distort or discredit lessons to be drawn from it.

If we look very superficially at those industries which have shed most workers since 1979, it becomes clear that the reasons for their decline – their role as 'sunset' industries – are not as clear cut as some commentators would have us believe. Rather, each has been subject to a greater or lesser form of protectionism gained within the immediate post-war period and retained in one form or another until the present day. That protection has succeeded only in reducing their competitive thrust to the point where many have been all but destroyed by the experience. The textile industry blames foreign competition for its troubles yet the international Multi-Fibre Agreement has protected that industry since its inception in 1974, as have numerous forms of Government subsidy. Equally, the less than buoyant British car industry has 'enjoyed' Government subsidy throughout the period and in its absence, voluntary export restraints currently perform precisely the same purpose – but at less obvious cost to the British taxpayer. Steelworkers and shipbuilders have gained and lost in much the same way – with shipbuilding first being protected by public procurement contracts and then suddenly required to face international competition. There are of course, other factors which have contributed to the decline of Britains' heavy industrial base but a most important, imponderable question must be: would the pace of technological advance have been so slow and the race to find substitute goods have been as hectic had a prohibition upon protectionism forced traditional industries to compete? Tolerance of anti-competitive practices, or non-tariff barriers to trade, removes a most important force to retaining a competitive edge over one's rivals – just as the theory of monopoly predicts. Firms who do not face real competitive pressure are rarely the first to innovate, they become sluggish, unresponsive to change in consumer demand and complacent. As a result they fail over time to retain their position within existing export markets and fail to win new ones, and expose their domestic markets to import penetration.

It may thus be considered that one of the primary reasons that areas of the UK are now industrial wastelands is because the notion that firms are the best judge of what is good for the economy has been allowed to take hold. Large firm preference for protectionism has had to be less overt since development of the GATT and UK membership of the EEC, but their access to the ear of government has meant that the circumvention of free trade posturing via non-tariff barriers and careful subsidy has achieved the desired result.

The standard alternative explanation for the UK's relative economic decline holds trade union monopoly practices responsible for all of UK industry's ills. Yet trade unions have substantial power within many European nation states who appear not have suffered a recession of the order of that experienced within the UK – West Germany being a prime example. Equally, more recent UK experience suggests that while unions may have short periods of monopoly power, such power is only exercised with the permission of the ruling hierarchy. When it no longer suits their purpose, any power the unions may have can and will be taken away.

Protectionism by definition amounts to protection of firms from the necessity to compete. Within the UK at least, that refusal has resulted in retarded technological change, lack of investment in research and development, scant regard for quality or design, and refusal to acknowledge change in consumer taste. The result for the British economy has been equally predictable. Historically high levels of unemployment, historically low levels of manufacturing output, a decline in the manufacturing and industrial base, an inrush of imports, and a reduction in living standards for all bar the top 10 per cent of the population.

To have expected an alternative result is to deny the simple truth that trade protection is protection of producer profits. There are no controls to guarantee even partial reinvestment of those profits within the UK economy, nor are there regulations to protect the economy from multinational corporations' ability to manipulate their published accounts and hide their heavy indulgence upon disingenuous transfer pricing (a system designed to lower total taxes paid by international firms wherein intracorporate sales and purchases of goods and services are artificially invoiced so that profits accrue to branches located in low tax countries, while offices in high tax countries show little or no taxable profits). Such protection of producer profits cannot be equated with protection of national income. All that is protected is share prices and the concentration of wealth within the hands of the producers.

As Todaro suggests:

By focusing on the atomistic behaviour of competitive firms in the context of different commodities being produced . . . standard trade theory has ignored the crucial role governments play in international economic affairs . . . [It] . . . neglect[s] the crucial role national governments can and do play in the international economic arena. Governments often serve to reinforce the unequal distribution of resources and gains from trade by differences in their size and relative economic power. Rich-country governments can influence world economic affairs by their domestic and international policies. They can resist countervailing economic pressures from weaker nations and can act collusively and often in conjunction with their powerful multinational corporations to manipulate the terms and conditions of international trade to their own national interests (1982, pp. 355–6).

However, the experience of the 1980s at least suggests, that in agreeing to protect domestic firms and the multinationals, Governments collude in activity which they mistakenly perceive as intended to serve the needs of national economic policy – particularly if such policy aims to increase economic growth via increased competition. Add to this the substantial weight of evidence suggesting that no good ever came of protectionism (see for example, Soderstern, 1981, Greenaway, 1983 and Caves and Johnson, 1968), and the sporting analogy that has featured throughout this work makes one last important appearance.

Competitive team sports require that members of the team co-operate fully with one another in beating the other side. Competition is thus fully fledged but within a context of full co-operation. Within an international framework we have for example, pharmaceutical companies, chemical fertiliser companies, cement manufacturers playing together as a team to maximise producer profits at a very substantial cost to the rest of the world. The analogy extends across the Standard Industry Classification wherever a cohort of the 'Fortune 500' are represented. The result of such team sports is writ large across the international economy which suffers greatly from the Third World's retarded development – development retarded by the actions of these companies, which may range from price fixing agreements, through market sharing agreements, to agreements on types of technology which will, and will not, be transferred.

The dangers for regional, national and indeed the global economy of retarded Third World development are exemplified by the current 'debt crisis' of the 1980s. Debtor and creditor nations are locked into a most brutal form of mutual dependency. If debtor nations simply refuse to re-pay their debts, the international banking system, would on a good day, fall into disarray. Or more obviously, the retardation of Third World development caused by anti-competitive firm behaviour at the level of national, regional and international markets, must first slow and then damage growth within developed market economies. If continuing economic growth is as closely related to international trade as all the theory supposes it to be, each nation requires the maximum access to other markets as cultural, and transport barriers will allow. Such access permits specialisation in areas where each economy has a natural or acquired advantage and prevents the wasteful misallocation of scarce resources to inappropriate activity. In an ideal world, where all trade was unrestricted, the international economy would develop and begin to shift back upon an even axis rather than remaining tilted towards the developed market economies.

However, in the real world, players cheat, with short-term national considerations everywhere perceived to be more pressing than guaranteeing a secure, long-term future for the international economy as a whole. That reality does not deflect us from the necessity to call for vastly increased regulation at the level of individual nations – for each nation to grow, as for example, the US has done, there has to be free trade within the nation state to ensure development of industry at national level. Only pre-eminence within national markets gained by matching high-quality goods with the demands of the final consumer can encourage intra-industry trade. Only if competition is rigorously enforced among and between a group of nations can the benefits of intra-trade be achieved. And then only if trade can be free and fair between these trading blocks will the international economy grow for the benefit of all. Intra- and inter-industry trade can create the framework for a more equitable distribution of wealth and power on a global scale but only if both are rigorously enforced at a national, regional and international level.

That has to be the primary purpose of competition policy and Governments have to be convinced of the rectitude of supporting vigorous anti-trust enforcement. Late twentieth century economic relations in no sense parallel those of Saxon or Tudor times. The practice of conferring monopoly power upon individuals or companies is entirely inappropriate to current concerns, particularly as contemporary history suggests that companies cannot be trusted to do anything other than improve their particular position.

Advocacy of such a policy prescription, requires an acknowledgement of the main public policy questions arising from it, viz.:

1 Who is to set the rules and in whose interest?
2 Who is to police the rules and with what powers?
3 How are the rules to be related to society's overall goals?

There has been a tendency in the United Kingdom at least to allow the main players, in the name of self-regulation, to determine the rules. As a consequence they have frequently been written to the advantage of the strongest (as outlined in Chapter 3). In practice the rules set and enforced by government have, as a result of lobby pressure, also tended to favour the stronger players rather than the newcomers, potential entrants, and consumers, who find it much harder to apply parliamentary pressure.

If we feel that the setting and policing of rules should not be left to the players, then we require an effective political process to set and police the rules. The worry, for some, is that an imperfect political process may not produce rules which are markedly superior to those of the player-rulemakers.

However, the balance of advantage seems to lie with the political process being used to set rules in line with more general political objectives and in establishing an effective policing body. This being done, it is the job of parliament to oversee the operation and from time to time to review the rules and powers of the enforcement agency.

Business people often relish the rhetoric that competition is all about winners and losers, while the reality is that the winners plan to fix the game, so that they stay at the top. If we leave it to the players to set the rules, it will only be by accident that interests wider than those of the top players are considered. To avoid such an unpalatable possibility we turn to those regulatory structures already in place, plus certain of those already proposed for the UK, to provide our policy prescription.

Perhaps the most important and urgently need change relates to mergers. Merger activity in 1986 was at a record level in the UK, despite substantial economic research suggesting little evidence that mergers lead to either greater efficiency or profitability. Approximately 12 per cent of corporate Britain changed hands over the period 1983–6 in almost 400 takeover deals, worth in total, over £27 billion. In 1986 alone, there were 184 successful takeover attempts worth more than £16 billion. In a 1987 survey of British industry, Lloyd and Munchau (*Financial Weekly*, 12.2.87) discovered that most of the senior executives of Britain's largest companies, believed that existing rules and regulations governing mergers and acquisitions take insufficient account of an industry's long-term interests. Furthermore, only 38 per cent considered the 'so-called takeover boom good for British industry'.

High levels of industrial concentration are much harder to reduce than to prevent. Hence a firm check on merger activity is urgently required if society is concerned at the concentration of wealth and power over markets within few hands. On those grounds, this should not only apply to horizontal mergers but to vertical and conglomerate mergers as well. A most popular current suggestion is to reverse the burden of proof in proposed mergers (as discussed in Chapter 5).

Equally therefore, while companies must be required to show how the proposed change will have either a neutral or positive impact upon the competitive nature of the market in question, companies should be required to show that the criteria established for the protection of the public interest are acknowledged and upheld.

Restrictive Agreements, anti-competitive pricing and distributive practices, or non-tariff barriers to trade are in theory at least, well covered by national, and regional laws. The General Agreement on Tariffs and Trade (GATT) is currently seeking to establish a new round of talks dependent upon an agreement to reduce non-tariff barriers, particularly in the market for services. At a time when the United Nations Council for Trade and Development (UNCTAD) reports (*Financial Times*, 25.3.87) that 80 per cent of developing country trade and 30 per cent of developed country trade faces non-tariff barriers, it is not surprising to find that developing countries regard the developed world's commitment to tariff disarmament with not a little scepticism.

However, national governments are in a position to improve the situation. Within Japan, the US, the UK and the EEC, policy exists to prevent the erection of anti-competitive barriers to market entry. Laws to prevent the establishment of restrictive agreements, anti-competitive practices, are already in place. The problem, is simply a lack of political will. In the US that lack of will to enforce the law arises from the primacy of Chicago School economics and a belief in the free-market mechanism. Coupled with this is the emphasis upon law suits brought by and against individuals rather than corporate bodies and triple damages, which tends to ensure that anti-trust cases are vigorously defended. In Japan, the reluctance to enforce a policy of free trade, arises in part, from the unreasonable non-tariff barriers it is forced to accept in the form of voluntary export restraints. In the EEC the political will to create a truly common market exists but the Community's budget is simply the total of contributions agreed by the Member States. In consequence its administration is tiny, with just 80 people policing competition policy across a region which now encompasses 12 nation states. While the UK's Office of Fair Trading employs more people, it is required to administer consumer protection policies as well as those aimed at protecting competition. However, it is not a lack of staff which restricts the OFT's ability to fulfil its function as competition authority, but a severely restricted level of power.

The UK's competition policy is badly in need of reform. It is emasculated by a reliance on gentlemanly conduct in a period when such conduct is long out of fashion. As a member of the EEC it has finally succumbed to the need to look across the water at the relative triumphs of the Commission's Competition Directorate and bring its policy, procedures and powers into line with Articles 85 and 86 of the Rome Treaty.

Before politicians representing constituencies apparently decimated by the ravages of free trade recoil in horror from such a prescription, they should investigate the historical realities of industries that have died and consider the investment patterns that prevailed. They might also consider the relevance of the European equivalent of the 'public interest criteria'. In being required to publicise the basis for exempting or refusing to exempt an agreement or practice from the competition rules, the European Commission is forced to clarify the relevance of the community's goals to competition policy. The Monopolies and Mergers Commission, on the other hand, pays no more than lip service to the requirement that it clarify the basis for its decisions. Thus without any necessity to return to Parliament for approval, it is able to ignore, reinterpret or distort the public interest criteria in line with the preference of whoever is in power at any one time, rather than the general will, as indeed can the Secretary of State for Trade and Industry.

The introduction of genuine and clearly enforced prohibitions upon protectionism at national and regional level, would improve and enhance the ability of international agencies to police collusive, anti-competitive conduct at an international level. The ability of multi-national companies to play one nation off against the interests of another would, in time, be curtailed, and the ability of the world economy to grow would be properly assisted by stable growth emerging at the level of the individual nation state.

That reality was accepted at the end of the Second World War and provided the rationale for the first major wave of anti-trust legislation which hit the Western world. The primary difference between that period and UK experience in the late 1980s is that many of the goals then considered appropriate for an ordered, civilised society have been removed from the political agenda and replaced by a presumption in favour of market forces.

UK experience shows that it is not enough to have in place a legislative framework capable of protecting and enhancing a nation's economic performance. The legislation governing the protection of competition must be rigorously enforced by politicians and regulators ready to divorce the need to guarantee the efficient allocation of scarce resources through a dynamic competitive process from sectional interests and the pressures they may bring to bear.

Bibliography

Aaronovitch, S. and Sawyer, M. (1975) *Big Business*, Macmillan: New York.

Allen, G. C. (1978) *How Japan Competes*, Hobart Paper 81, IEA.

Amin, S. (1978) *Unequal Development*, Harvester: Brighton.

Areeda, P. and Turner, D. F. (1975) 'Predatory Pricing and Related Practices', *Harvard Law Review*, Vol. 88.

Arrow, K. J. (1984) The Economics of Agency, Technical Report No. 451, Centre for Research on Organisational Efficiency, Stanford University.

Arrow, R. (1962) *The Rate and Direction of Inventive Activity*, Princeton University Press: Princeton, NJ.

Auerbach, P. (1988) *Competition: The Economics of Industrial Change*, Basil Blackwell, Oxford.

Axelrod, R. (1984) *The Evolution of Co-operation*, Basic Books: New York.

Baba, M. (1976) 'Industrial concentration in Japan: The economic background to the revision of the antimonopoly laws', *Internationales Asienforum*, Vol. 7, pp. 54–74.

Bain, J. S. (1949) 'A note on pricing in monopoly and oligopoly', *American Economic Review*, Vol. 39, pp. 448–64.

——— (1956) *Barriers to New Competition*, Harvard University Press: Cambridge, Mass.

——— (1966) *International Differences in Industrial Structure: Eight Nations in the 1950s*, Yale University Press.

Balfour Committee on Trade and Industry (1929) Cmnd. 3282. HMSO: London.

Baran, P. and Sweezy, P. (1967) *Monopoly Capital*, Penguin: Harmondsworth.

Bator, F. M. (1957) 'The simple analytics of welfare maximisation', *American Economic Review* (reprinted in Breit, W. and Hochman, H. (eds) (1968), *Readings in Microeconomics*, Holt, Rinehart and Winston.

Baumol, W. J. (1959) *Business Behaviour, Value and Growth*, Macmillan: London.

———, Panzar, J. C. and Willig, R. D. (1982) *Contestable Markets and the Theory of Industry Structure*, Harcourt Brace: New York.

'Contestable Markets: An uprising in the theory of industrial structure',

American Economic Review, Vol. 72, No. 1.

—— and Ordover, J. A. (1985) 'Use of Antitrust to subvert competition', *Journal of Law and Economics*, Vol. XXVIII.

Benton, S. (1987) 'The hardening on the Right', *New Statesman*, 6 March 1987.

Berle, A. and Means, G. (1932) *The Modern Corporation and Private Property*, Macmillan: London.

Bertrand, J. (1883) Book review of Cournot's work, *Journal des Savants*, pp. 499–508.

Blair, J. M. (1972) *Economic Concentration*, Harcourt Brace: New York.

Bork, R. H. (1954) 'Vertical integration and the Sherman Act: the legal history of an economic misconception', *University of Chicago Law Review*, Vol. 22, pp. 157–201.

—— (1978) *The Antitrust Paradox*, Basic Books: New York.

Borrie, Sir, G. (1982) 'Competition policy in Britain: retrospect and prospect', *International Review of Law and Economics*.

Bothwell, J. L. (1980) 'Profitability, risk and the separation of ownership from control', *Journal of Industrial Economics*, Vol. XXVII, pp. 303–11.

Breit, W. and Hochman, H. (eds) (1971) *Readings in Microeconomics*, 2nd edn, Dryden Press: Hinsdale, Illinois.

Burton, J. (1983) Picking losers . . .? Hobart Paper 99, IEA: London.

Caves, R. E. and Johnson, H. G. (1968) *Readings in International Economics*, Vol. XI, Richard D. Irwin: Homewood, Illinois.

—— *Readings in International Economics*, George Allen & Unwin: London.

—— and Vekusa, M. (1976) *Industrial Organisation in Japan*, Brookings Institution, Washington DC.

Cecchini, P. (1989) *The European Challenge 1992: The Benefits of a Single Market*, Wildwood House: Aldershot.

Chamberlin, E. H. (1933) *The Theory of Monopolistic Competition*, Harvard University Press: Cambridge, Mass.

Chandler, A. (1977) *The Visible Hand*, Balknap Press: Harvard.

Chard, J. S. (1980) 'The economics of exclusive distributorship arrangements with special reference to EEC competition policy', *Antitrust Bulletin*, Summer.

Chomsky, N. (1965) *Language and Mind*, MIT Press: Cambridge, Mass.

Clark, J. M. (1940) 'Towards a concept of workable competition', *American Economic Review*.

Colman, A. (1982) *Game Theory and Experimental Games*, Pergamon: Oxford.

Comanor, W. and Wilson, T. (1967) 'Advertising market structure and performance', *Review of Economics and Statistics*, Vol. 49, pp. 423–40.

Cooke, T. E. (1986) *Mergers and Acquisitions*, Basil Blackwell: Oxford.

Cotterrell, R. B. M. (1984) *The Sociology of Law*, Butterworth: London.

Cournot, A. A. (1838) *Researchers into the Mathematical Principles of the Theory of Wealth*, trans. by N. T. Bacon (1927), Macmillan: New York.

Cowling, K. and Mueller, D. C. (1978) 'The social costs of monopoly power', *Economic Journal*, Vol. 88, pp. 727–48.

Curran, J. and Stanworth, J. (1984) 'Beware the talk of panacea', *Guardian*, 3 August.

———— Stanworth, J. and Watkins, D. (1986) *The Survival of the Small Firm*, Gower: Aldershot.

Cyert, R. M. and March, J. G. (1963) *A Behavioural Theory of the Firm*, Prentice-Hall: Englewood Cliffs, NJ.

Darwin, C. (1859) *Origin of Species*, Dent: London, 1972.

Dawkins, R. (1976) *Selfish Gene*, Oxford University Press: Oxford.

———— (1986) *The Blind Watchmaker*, Longman Scientific and Technical: Harlow.

Demsetz, H. (1969) 'Information and efficiency: another viewpoint', *Journal of Law and Economics*.

Director General of Fair Trading (1986), *Annual Report of the Director General of Fair Trading 1985*, HMSO: London.

Dore, R. (1986) *Flexible Rigidities; industrial policy and structural adjustment in the Japanese economy, 1970–80*, Athlone Press: London.

Downs, A. (1957) *An Economic Theory of Democracy*, Harper and Row: New York.

DTI (1978) *A Review of Monopolies and Mergers Policy: a Consultative document* (1978) Cmnd. 7198, HMSO, paras 30 and 33 of Annex A.

DTI (1988) *Mergers Policy*, HMSO: London.

Edgeworth, F. Y. (1897) English translation appeared as *The pure theory of monopoly in Papers relating to Political Economy*, Macmillan: London, 1925.

Ehrlich, I. (1936) *Fundamental Principles of the Sociology of Law*, trans. by W. L. Moll, Arno Press: New York, 1975.

Engels, F. (1844) *Outlines of a Critique of Political Economy*, Collected Works, Laurence & Wishart: London, 1975.

European Commission (1983) Commission Decision of 14/12/83 relating to a proceeding under Article 86 of the EEC Treaty (IV/30.698–ECS AKZO) OJL374, 31/12/85.

Evely, R. and Little, I. M. D. (1960) *Concentration in British Industry*, Cambridge University Press: London.

Ferguson, C. E. (1969) *The Neoclassical Theory of Production and Distribution*, Cambridge University Press: Cambridge.

Freud, S. (1930) *Civilisation and its Discontents*, trans. Joan Riviese, London: Hogarth Press and the Institute of Psychoanalysis Library.

Friedman, M. (1953) *Essays in Positive Economics*, University of Chicago Press (reprinted in Breit, W. and Hochman, H. (eds) (1968)), *Readings in Microeconomics*, Holt, Rinehart and Winston: New York.

Fromm, E. (1979) *To Have or to Be?* Penguin: Harmondsworth.

Galbraith, J. K. (1952) *American Capitalism*, Hamish Hamilton: London.

———— (1969) *The New Industrial State*, Penguin: Harmondsworth.

———— (1981) *A Life in our Times*, André Deutsch: London.

Genn-Bash, A., Burke, T., Haines, B. and Killick, G. (1985a) 'The applicability of Articles 85 and 86 to the UK insurance industry',

European Competition Law Review, 1985.

—— (1985b) 'Ford in UK car-tel?', *Economic Affairs*, Vol. 5, No. 3.

George, K. D. (1985) *Monopoly and Merger Policy*, University of Wales, discussion paper.

Gerth, H. H. and Mills, C. Wright (eds) (1974) *From Max Weber, Essays in Sociology*, Routledge & Kegan Paul: London.

Gibrat, R. (1931) *Les Inegalités Economiques*, Recueil Sirey: Paris.

Giddens, A. (ed.) (1977) *Emile Durkheim: Selected Writings*, Cambridge University Press: Cambridge.

Gouldner, A. W. (1960) 'The norm of reciprosity: a preliminary statement', *American Sociology Review*.

Gower, L. E. B. (1984) *Review of Investor Protection*, Cmnd. 9125, HMSO: London.

Greenaway, D. (1983) *International Trade Policy: From Tariffs to the New Protectionism*, Macmillan: London.

Hague, D. C. (1971) *Pricing in Business*, George Allen and Unwin: London.

Haldi, J. and Whitcomb, D. (1967) 'Economies of scale in industrial plants', *Journal of Political Economy*, Vol. 75, pp. 373–85.

Hall, R. L. and Hitch, C. J. (1939) *Price Theory and Business Behaviour*, Oxford Economic Papers, vol. 2, pp. 12–45.

Hannah, L. and Kay, J. (1977) *Concentration in Modern Industry*, Macmillan: London.

Harberger, A. C. (1954) 'Monopoly and resource allocation', *American Economic Review*, Proceedings, Vol. 44, pp. 73–87.

Hardin, G. (1968) 'The tragedy of the Commons', *Science*, 162.

Harris, J. W. (1980) *Legal Philosophies*, Butterworth: London.

Hart, I. E. (1985) *Recent Trends in Concentration in British Industry*, NIESR discussion paper No. 82: London.

Hartley, K. (1975) 'Industry, labour and public policy', in Grant, R. M. and Shaw, G. K. (eds) (1975), *Current Issues in Economic Policy*, Ch. 2, Philip Allan: Oxford.

Hay, D. A. and Morris, D. J. (1979) *Industrial Economics: Theory and Evidence*, Oxford University Press: Oxford.

Hay, G. (1985) *Vertical Restraints*, Cornell University, discussion paper.

Hayek, F. A. (1978) *Competition as a Discovery Process. New Studies in Philosophy, Politics, Economics and the History of Ideas*, Routledge & Kegan Paul: London.

—— (1980) *1980's Unemployment and the Unions, The Distortion of Relative Prices by Monopoly in the Labour Market*, Hobart Paper 87, IEA: London.

Hirst, P. (1987) 'Can Socialism live? ', *New Statesman*, 6 March.

Hobbes, T. (1651) *Leviathan*, Dent: London, 1973.

Holland, S. (1975) *Strategy for Socialism*, Spokesman Books: London.

House of Commons (1982), Restriction on Agreements (Manufacturers and Importers of Motor Cars), Order (Statutory Instrument 1982, No. 1146), HMSO: London.

Hughes, A. and Kumar, M.S. (1984) 'Recent trends in aggregate concentration in the UK Economy', Cambridge Journal of Economics, Vol. 8, September.

Hunter, A. (1966) *Competition and the Law*, George Allen and Unwin: London.

Importers of Motor Cars Order (1982) (Statutory Instrument No. 1146), HMSO: London.

Institute of Directors (1986) *IOD Business Leaders' Manifesto*, IOD Policy Unit: London.

Jensen, M. C. and Meckling, W. H. (1976) 'Theory of the firm: managerial behaviour, agency costs and ownership structure', *Journal of Financial Economics*, Vol. 3, pp. 305–60.

Johnson, G. and Scholes, K. (1984) *Exploring Corporate Strategy*, Prentice Hall International: London.

Kaldor, Nicholas (1950) 'The economic aspects of advertising', *Review of Economic Studies*.

Kirzner, I. M. (1973) *Competition and Entrepreneurship*, University of Chicago Press: Chicago.

––––– (1980) *The Primacy of Entrepreneurial Discovery*, IEA: London.

Knight, F. (1921) *Risk, Uncertainty and Profits*, Houghton Mifflin: Boston.

––––– (1923) 'The ethics of competition', *Quarterly Journal of Economics*, Vol. XXXVII.

Korah, V. (1982) *Competition Law in Britain and The Common Market*, 3rd ed., Martinus: Nijhoff.

Koutsoyiannis, A. (1982) *Non-price Competition – the Firm in a Modern Context*, Macmillan: London.

Larner, R. J. (1966) 'Ownership and control in the 200 largest non-financial corporations, 1929 and 1963', *American Economic Review*, Vol. 56.

Laughlin, P. R. and Jacquard, J. J. (1975) 'Social facilitation and observational learning of individuals and co-operative pairs', *Journal of Personality and Social Psychology*.

Legrand, J. (1987) 'The market: workers, capital and consumers', *New Statesman*, 6 March.

Leibenstein, H. (1950) 'Bandwagon, snob and Veblen effects in the theory of consumer demand', *Quarterly Journal of Economics*, May, pp. 183–207.

––––– (1966) 'Allocative efficiency vs. x-efficiency', *American Economic Review*, Vol. 56.

Lewin, K. (1951) *Field Theory in Social Science*, Harper: New York.

Lipsey, R. (1976) *Positive Economics*, Weidenfeld & Nicolson: London.

––––– (1983) *Positive Economics*, Weidenfeld & Nicolson: London.

Littlechild, S. C. (1978) *The Fallacy of the Mixed Economy*, Hobart Paper 80, IEA: London.

––––– (1981) 'Misleading calculations of the social costs of monopoly power', *Economic Journal*, Vol. 91, pp. 348–63.

Lloyd, T. and Munchau, W. (1987) 'Do infected waters make for a fit economy?', *Financial Weekly*, 12 February.

Locksley, G. and Ward, T. (1979) 'Concentration in manufacturing in the EEC', *Cambridge Journal of Economics*.

Lorenz, K. (1966) *On Aggression*, Harcourt, Brace & World: New York.

Luce, R. and Raiffa, H. (1957) *Games and Decisions*, John Wiley: New York.

Machlup, F. (1967) 'Theories of the firm: marginalist, behavioural, Managerial', *American Economic Review*, Vol. 57.

Malthus, T. (1798) *Essay on the Principle of Population as it Affects the Future Improvement of Society*, Macmillan: London, 1926.

Marris, R. (1964) *The Economic Theory of 'Managerial' Capitalism*, Macmillan: London.

Marshall, A. (1977) *Principles of Economics* (8th edn), Macmillan: London.

Marvel, H. P. (1982) 'Exclusive dealing', *Journal of Law and Economics*, April.

Marx, K. and Engels, F. (1844) *Communist Manifesto*, Progress Publishers, Moscow, 1973.

Marx, K. (1973) *Grundrisse*, Penguin: Harmondsworth.

—— (1918) *Capital*, C. Kerr (ed.), Chicago.

—— (1979) *The Letters of Karl Marx*, S. K. Padoven (ed.), Prentice Hall: New Jersey.

Mason, E. S. (1939) 'Price and production policies of large-scale enterprise', *American Economic Review*, Supplement 29, pp. 61–74.

Maynard Smith, J. (1982) *Evolution and the Theory of Games*, Cambridge University Press: Cambridge.

McGee, J. S. (1958) 'Predatory price cutting: the standard oil (N.J.) case', *Journal of Law and Economics*, 137.

—— (1980) 'Predatory pricing revisited', *Journal of Law and Economics*, October.

Menge, J. A. (1962) 'Style change costs as a market weapon', *Quarterly Journal of Economics*, November.

Merkin, R. and Williams, K. (1984) *Competition Law; Antitrust Policy in the United Kingdom and the E.E.C.*, Sweet and Maxwell: London.

Mill, J. S. (1974) *On Liberty* (1859), Penguin: Harmondsworth.

—— (1924) *Autobiography*, J. J. Cross (ed.), Columbia University: New York.

Monopolies and Mergers Commission (1973) Chlordiazepoxide and Diazepam, HC197, HMSO: London.

—— (1975–6) Contraceptive Sheaths (No. 1), HC135, HMSO: London.

—— (1976) Indirect Electrostatic Reprographic Equipment, HC47, HMSO: London.

—— (1980) Credit Cards, Cmnd. 8034, HMSO: London.

—— (1981) Discounts to Retailers, HC311, HMSO: London.

—— (1981–2) Car Parts H.C.422, HMSO: London.

—— (1985) Ford Motor Company Limited, Cmnd. 9437, HMSO: London.

—— (1985) Supply of Animal Waste, DTI Press Notice: 3 April.

—— (1986) Tampons, Cmnd. 9705, HMSO: London.

—— (1989) The Supply of Beer, HMSO: London.

Netter, J. M. (1982) 'Excessive advertising; an empirical analysis', *Journal of Industrial Economics*, June.

von Neumann, J. and Morgernstern, Y. (1944) *Theory of Games and Economic Behaviour*, Princeton University Press: Princeton, NJ.

Office of Fair Trading (1981) T1 Raleigh Industries Limited, T1 Raleigh Limited, OFT: London.

—— (1982) British Railways Board: Admission of Hackney carriages to Brighton Central Railway Station to ply for hire, OFT: London.

—— (1984) Arrangements for the provision of Chauffeur-Driven Hire Car Services at Gatwick Airport, OFT: London.

—— (1984) Ford Motor Company Limited, Licensing for the manufacture or sale of replacement body parts, OFT: London.

—— (1985) Competition and Retailing, OFT: London.

—— (1986) Ford Motor Company Gives undertaking on Vehicle Body parts, Press Release, 15 December, OFT: London.

Ornstein, S. I., Weston, J. F., Intriligator, M. D. and Shrieves, R. E. (1973) 'Determinants of market structure', *Southern Economic Journal*, Vol. 39, pp. 612–25.

Parry, L. J. (1985) *Freedom to Drink*, IEA Hobart Paper: London.

Preston, M. H. (1959) 'On the sales maximisation hypothesis', *Economica*, Vol. 26.

Phillips, J. (1986) *Introduction to Intellectual Property Law*, Butterworth: London.

Porter, M. E. (1980) *Competitive Strategy: Techniques for Analysing Industries and Companies*, Free Press: New York.

Posner, R. A. (1976) *Antitrust Law, an Economic Perspective*, University of Chicago Press: London.

—— (1977) 'The rule of reason and the economic approach, reflections on the sylvania decision', *University of Chicago Law Review*, Vol. 45, No. 1, Fall.

Price Commission (1977) *Beer and Margins* No. 31, HMSO: London.

Ricardo, D. (1951) *On the Principles of Political Economy and Taxation*, 3rd ed., 1821, Royal Economic Society, CUP edition.

Ritson, C. (1977) *Agricultural Economics*, Granada: London.

Robbins, Lord (1932) *The Nature and Significance of Economic Science*, Macmillan: London.

Rosenburg, J. B. (1976) 'Research and market share – a reappraisal of the Schumpeter hypothesis', *Journal of Industrial Economics*, December.

Rosenham, D. L. (1978) 'Towards resolving the altruism paradox: affect, self-reinforcement and cognition', in *Altruism, Sympathy and Helping; Psychological and Sociological Principles*, L. Wisp (ed.), Academic Press: New York.

Ross, S. A. (1973) The economic theory of agency: the principals problem, *American Economic Review*, Vol. 62, pp. 134–9.

Rowley, C. K. and Peacock, A. T. (1975) *Welfare Economics, A Liberal*

Restatement, Martin Robertson: London.

Sawyer, M. C. (1979a) *A Note on Recent Trends in Industrial concentration in the U.K.*, Discussion paper No. 41, University of York, Dept. of Economics and Related Studies.

—— (1979b) *Theories of the Firm*, Weidenfeld and Nicolson: London.

—— (1981) *The Economics of Industries and Firms*, 2nd ed., Croom Helm: Beckenham.

Scherer, F. M. (1967) 'Market structure and the employment of scientists and engineers', *American Economic Review*, June.

—— (1980) *Industrial Market Structure and Economic Performance*, 2nd ed., Rand McNally: Chicago.

Schumpeter, J. A. (1942) *Capitalism, Socialism and Democracy*, Harper and Row: New York, first ed.

Schwartz, M. and Eisenstadt, M. (1982) *Vertical Restraints*, Economic Policy Office Discussion Paper, EPO 82–8, US Department of Justice: Washington, DC.

Scitovsky, T. (1943) 'A note on profit maximisation', *Review of Economic Studies*, Vol. 11, reprinted in Boulding, K. E. and Stigler, G. J. (eds) (1953), *Readings in Price Theory*, Allen and Unwin: London.

Scruton, R. (1980) *The Meaning of Conservatism*, Penguin: Harmondsworth.

Secretary of State for Trade and Industry (1981) *Reform of Copyright and Design Law: A Consultative Document*, Cmd. 8302, HMSO: London.

—— (1983) *Intellectual Property Rights and Innovation*, Cmnd. 9117, HMSO: London.

—— (1985) *Financial Services in the UK: A New Framework for Investor Protection*, Cmnd. 9432, HMSO: London.

—— (1986) *Intellectual Property and Innovation*, Cmnd. 9712, HMSO: London.

Seldon, A. and Crozier, B. (1983) *Socialism Explained*, Sherwood Press: London. Republished New York (1986) as *Socialism, The Grand Delusion*, University Books: New York.

Seta, J. J. (1982) 'The impact of comparison processes on co-actors' tasks performance', *Journal of Personality and Social Psychology*.

Sherif, M. (1966) *In Common Predicament: Social Psychology of Intergroup Conflict and Co-operation,* Boston: Houghton Mifflin.

Shubik, M. (1982) *Game Theory in the Social Sciences*, MIT Press: Cambridge, Mass.

Simmel, G. (1950) *The Sociology of George Simmel*, K. H. Wolff, Free Press: Glenco, Ill.

Simon, H. A. (1959) 'Theories of decision-making in economics and behavioural science', *American Economic Review*, Vol. 49.

Smith, A. (1896) *Lectures on Justice, Police, Revenue and Arms delivered in the University of Glasgow by Adam Smith, reported by a student 1763*, E. Cannon (ed.), Clarendon Press: Oxford.

—— (1976) *An Inquiry into the Nature and Causes of the Wealth of*

Nations, 1776, R. H. Campbell and A. S. Skinner (eds), Clarendon Press: Oxford.

Sodersten, B. (1981) *International Economics*, 2nd ed., Macmillan: London.

Sorenson, R. (1974) 'The separation of ownership and control and firm performance: an empirical analysis', *Southern Economic Journal*, Vol. 40, pp. 145–8.

Spence, A. M. and Zeckhauser, R. (1971) 'Insurance, information and individual action', *American Economic Review*, Vol. 61, pp. 380–7.

Stano, M. (1976) 'Monopoly power, ownership control, and corporate performance', *Bell Journal of Economics and Management Science*, Vol. 7, pp. 672–9.

Stelzer, I. M. (1987) 'Changing antitrust standards', comments at Workshop on Antitrust Issues in Today's Economy, sponsored by The Conference Board, 5 March, New York City.

Stevens, R. B. and Yamey, B. S. (1965) *The Restrictive Practices Court*, Weidenfeld and Nicolson: London.

Stigler, G. (1958) 'The economics of scale', *Journal of Law and Economics*, Vol. 1, pp. 54–71.

—— (June 1961) 'The economics of information', *Journal of Political Economy*.

—— (1968) 'Competition', *International Encyclopaedia of the Social Sciences*.

—— (1968) *The Organisation of Industry*, Richard D. Irwin: New York.

Storey, D. *et al.* (1987) *The Performance of Small Firms*, Croom Helm: Beckenham.

Strong, N. and Waterson, M. (1987) 'Principals, agents and information', in Clarke, R. and McGuinness, A. *The Economics of the Firm*, Basil Blackwell: Oxford.

Taylor, T. C. (1980) *The Fundamentals of Austrian Economics*, 2nd edn, Adam Smith Institute: London.

Todaro, M. R. (1982) *Economic Development in the Third World*, Longman: New York and London.

Triplett, N. (1897–9) 'The dynamogenic factors in pacemaking and competition', *American Journal of Psychology*.

Tsurata, T. (1985) 'Japan's industrial policy', in Thurow, L. C. (ed.), *The Management Challenge*, Ch. 9, MIT Press: Cambridge Mass.

Von Stackelberg, H. (1934) *The Theory of the Market Economy*, trans. Peacock, A. T. (1952), William Hodge: London.

Walshe, G. (1975) *Recent Trends in Monopoly in Great Britain*, Cambridge University Press: Cambridge.

Waterson, M. (1984) *Economic Theory and Industry*, Cambridge University Press: Cambridge.

White Paper on Employment Policy (1944), Cmnd. 6527, HMSO: London.

Williamson, O. E. (1964) *The Economics of Discretionary Behaviour: Managerial Objectives in a Theory of the Firm*, Prentice Hall: Englewood Cliffs, NJ.

——— (1972) *Corporate Control and Business Behaviour*, Prentice Hall: Englewood Cliffs, NJ.

Wilson, S. O. (1975) *Sociobiology, the New Synthesis*, Belknap Press, Harvard UP, Cambridge, Mass.

Winthrop, J. R. (1976) 'Monopoly around the world: a comparative study of concentration and efficiency in other countries', *Antitrust Law and Economic Review*, Vol. 8, pp. 91–100.

CASES REFERRED TO IN TEXT (with page numbers in *italics*)

A. E. G. Telefunken. 107/82 (1983) ECR 3151 *76, 136, 137, 138.*

Aluminium Company of America (1945) Anti-trust case 148, Fed. 2d. *139.*

Bourgoine v. Maff (1985) ICMLR 528 (1986) & ICMLR 267; (1985) 3 All ER 585 (HC & CA) *135.*

British Leyland Motor Corporation Ltd. v. Armstrong Patents Co. Ltd. Court of Appeal (Civil Division) (1984) FSR 591, (1984) 3 CMLR 102. House of Lords. 136 NLJ 211, *The Times*, 28 Feb. 1986 *171, 172, 178, 215.*

Cassis de Dijon *see* Rewe v. Bundesmonopolverwaltung.

Centres Leclerc v. Au Ble Vert (229/83); (1985) 2 CMLR 286; CMR 14.111 *135.*

Ceramic Tiles, Glazed and Floor Tiles Home Trade Associations Agreement, Re (1964) LR, 2RP 239 *137.*

Consten/Grundig (1964) CMLR 89, OJ 2545/64 *76, 137.*

Continental TV Inc. v. GTE Sylvania Inc. (1977) 97 S. C. + 2549 *72, 142.*

Dassonville *see* Procureur du Roi v. Dassonville.

Distillers (1978) OJ1978 L50/16; on appeal, 30/78 (1980) ECR 2229 *76, 136.*

Dutch Cement Dealers – Cement Cases (1973) CMLR D257, OJ 1972, L22/16 *137, 152.*

ECS/AKZO (1983) 3 CMLR 694, final decision OJ 1985, L374/22 *76,137, 158.*

ENI/Montedison, Commission Decision of 4/12/86: OJ L5/13 7.1.87 *216.*

Ex-parte Island Records (1978), Ch. 122 *70.*

Garden Cottage Foods v. Milk Marketing Board (1983) 2 All E R 770 *136.*

Hasselblad v. Commission Case 86/22 (1984) ICMLR 559 *138, 218.*

Hoffman-La Roche (1973) *See* Monopolies and Mergers Commission, Chlordiazepoxide and Diazepam *136, 155.*

Lonrho v. Shell and British Petroleum (No. 2) (1981) WLR 33 (H. L.) *72.*

Michelin OJ 1981, L353/33; on appeal (322/81) (1983) ECR 3461 *76, 137.*

Mogul S. S. v. McGregor Gow (1892), (A. C.) 25 *70–1.*

Procureur du Roi v. Dassonville (8/74) (1974) 2 CMLR 436 *147.*

Rewe v. Bundesmonopolverwaltung Case 120/78 (1979), ECR 649 *135.*

Schroeder Music Publishing v. Macawlay (1974), 3 All ER 616 *70.*

Stanley Adams v. Commission of the European Communities. European

Parliament Resolution 23/5/80, OJ No. C 147, 16/6/80, p. 137. Appeal of 18 July 1983, Case No. 145/83. Court of Justice Case No. 145/83 dated 7 Nov. 1985. Joint answer to written questions OJC72, 20/2/87, p. 45, *155*.

Topliss Showers v. Gessey (1982) ICR 501 *137*.

United Brands, OJ 1985, L95/1, on appeal 27/76 (1978) ECR 207 *76, 136*.

Warnink v. Townsend (1979) A. C. 731, (1980) RPC 31, (1979) F. S. R. 397, (1979) W. L. R. 68, (1979) 2 All ER 927, 123 SJ 472 (H. L.) *73*.

Windows – Standard Metal Window Group Associations Agreement, Re (1962) LR 3RP 198 *140*.

Index

Aaronovitch, S. 86–7, 89
Abbey Life 189, 191
acquisition 114; *see also* mergers
Adams, Stanley 155
advertising 52, 60, 113, 165
AEG Telefunken 76, 136, 138
AFBD 186
aggression 44–5
agreements, trade 216–17; *see also
    under* anti-competitive practices
Agriculture, Fisheries and Food,
    Ministry of 135
AIDS 206
AKZO 76, 137, 158
alcohol *see* beer
Allen, G. C. 146
Allied Breweries 195, 200
Allied Dunbar 189, 191
allocative efficiency 209–10
altruism 4, 28, 46
Aluminium Company of America
    139
Amin, S. 16
anti-competitive practices 151–69;
    distribution 161–9; and
    international trade 225–8; pricing
    151–61
anti-trust laws 119, 204–5; and
    Conservative Party, UK 80–1;
    Japan 145; USA 73–4, 89, 139–41,
    159; *see also* legislation
arbitrage 65–6
Areeda, P. 158–9
Arrow, K. J. 69
Arrow, R. 220
Audretsch, D. B. 209

Auerbach, P. 70
'Austrian' School 64–8
Axelrod, Robert 24, 216

Baba, M. 144
Bain, J. S. 55, 62–3, 120–1
Balfour Committee on Trade and
    Industry (1929) 219
Baran, P. 85
bargaining 13, 47
barriers, entry and exit 9, 55, 106–9
Bass Charrington 195, 200
Bator, F. M. 51
Baumol, W. J. 56, 68, 93, 96–9, 120,
    156, 205, 208, 220
beer 192–201; differential pricing
    153–4
behavioural theory 97–9
Benton, Sarah 78–9, 80
Berle, A. 92–3
Bertrand, J. 54
Black Bolt & Nut 152
Blair, J. M. 141
Bork, R. H. 142, 164, 205
Borrie, Sir Gordon 126, 130, 222, 227
Bothwell, J. L. 94–5
Bourgoine v. *Maff* 135
boycotting 70
Breit, W. 217
brewing *see* beer
British Leyland v. *Armstrong
    Patents* 171, 172, 178, 215
British Rail (BR) 153
British Telecom 167
Burton, J. 146
Business Start-Up and Expansion

Schemes 79
businesses *see* firms

Canada 120–1
capital 41–3, 223; competition for
102–4; and entry 106–7
Capital Asset Pricing Model
(CAPM) 94
capitalism: development of 48, 85–6;
and marxist theory 40–3, 223;
monopoly 85–6; theory 28–33
car industry 9; *see also* British
Leyland; Ford
Carlsberg 200
cartels 54, 145, 151–2, 162, 227
Cassis de Dijon 135
Caves, R. E. 152, 230
Cecchini, P., Report 148–9
Celler-Kefauver Act (1950), USA
140
Cement Makers Federation 152
Centres Leclerc 135
Ceramic Tiles, Re 137
Chamberlin, E. H. 51–2
Channel Tunnel 108
Chard, John S. 163, 164
Chemical Fertilizers 154
'Chicago' School 62–4, 74–5, 184,
203–4, 213
choice xi
Chomsky, Noam 12
Clayton Act (1914), USA 140, 163
Cockfield, Lord 148
coercion x–xi, 205
collective action, theory of 209–11
collusion 19, 207, 215–18, 223;
oligopoly 54–5, 60–1; *see also* co-
operation
Colman, Andrew 24
Comanor, W. 60
Comparative Advantage Principle
14–15, 32
competition 1–2; alternatives to x–
xi, 10–11; anti-competitive
practices 151–69; business model
of 100–16; and business strategy 3,
8–10, 85–117; classical views of
27–48; costs of 2–3, 4–6, 222;
ethics ix–xi, 202; and happiness
xi, 2, 3–4, 6–8, 34; and marxist

theory 40–3; modern models 49–
84; monopolistic 51–3; paradoxes
2–11; perfect 50–1; policy 206–7,
219–35; and politics 3, 10–11, 77–
84; rules 118–50 (*see also*
legislation); structured and
unstructured 86; theory (*q.v.*) 27–
84, 202–18
Competition Act (1980) 128–9, 151,
155, 178–9
Competition Directorate, EEC 132–
4, 138, 172, 234
concentration, industrial 86–9, 233
Conservative Party, UK 10, 78–81;
and anti-trust laws 80–1;
competition policy 128–9;
deregulation policies 170; and
design copyright 179; and small
businesses 79, 90–1, 184
conspiracy 70, 111
Consten/Grundig 65, 137
consumers 4, 9, 64–5; information
50; interests of 60, 111–12, 184–5,
222; loyalty 8, 52, 106, 113; and
prices 60, 152, 157; protection of
170, 211
Consumers' Association 188, 190
control *vs.* ownership 93–5
Cooke, T. E. 221
co-operation x–xi, 40, 101, 207, 215–
18; and oligopoly 54–5, 61; *see
also* collusion
Copyright Act (1956) 171, 178
costs of competition 2–3, 4–6, 222
Cotterell, R. B. M. 74
Counter-Inflation Act (1973) 126
Courage 195, 200
Cournot, A. A. 54
Courtaulds 160
Cowling, K. 122, 209, 226
Crown Life 189
Curran, J. 89–90
Cyert, R. M. 93, 97–9, 208

Darwin, Charles 7, 27, 35, 37–9, 48
Dawkins, Richard 40
'debt crisis' 230–1
Delors, Jacques 148
demand 53–6
Denning, Lord Chief Justice 72

deregulation 170, 209–10
design *see* intellectual property rights
DGIV *see under* EEC
differential pricing 153–4
differentiation, product 8, 9, 66, 106, 115
Diplock, Lord Justice 72, 73
Director General of Fair Trading (DGFT) 129–30, 152
discounts 155–6
discrimination, price 153–6; differential pricing 153–4; discounts and rebates 155–6; level pricing 154–5
Distillers' Company 76, 136, 218
distribution practices 9, 161–9; exclusive arrangements 162–6; refusal to supply 161–2; tie-in sales 166–8
diversification 114, 116
Dore, R. 144
Downs, A. 122
Dresher, Melvin 23
drives 7–8, 25, 44–7, 48
DTI 87
duopoly 57–60
Durkheim, Emile 71, 202
Dutch Cement Dealers 137, 152

economies of scale xi, 105–6, 220–1
ECS 76, 137, 158
Edgeworth, F. Y. 54
efficiency x, 4, 73–4, 86; allocative 209–10; monopoly 73–4, 75; and profit 62, 184, 213
Ehrlich, I. 74
Eisenstadt, M. 156, 162, 168
Engels, Friedrich 5, 41
ENI 216
Enterprise Allowance Scheme 79
entrepreneurism 65–7
entry barriers 106–8, 109
equilibrium 64–5
Erroll Committee 193
ethics ix–xi, 202–3
European Commission (EC) 75–6, 211–12, 234; and Ford Motor Company 76, 172–3, 177–8
European Economic Community

(EEC): and beer 196–7, 199; Competition Directorate (DGIV) 132–4, 138, 172, 234; and exclusive dealing 164–5; and free trade 226–7, 233–4; legal systems 74–6; legislation 130–9, 147–50; predation 158–9; and price fixing 152; and protectionism 206; single European Market 147–50
Evely, R. 86
evolution 37–40
exclusive dealing arrangements 162–6
exit barriers 108–9

Fair Trading Act (1973) 126
family 206
Federal Trade Commission Act (1914), USA 140
Ferguson, C.E. 49
feudalism 4, 30, 41
FIMBRA 185–6, 190, 191
Finance Act (1983) 79
Financial Services Act (1986) 185
firms 3, 8–10; behaviour of 225; business strategy 85–117; competition for capital 102–4; competitive choices 112–14; competitive strategy 114–16; entry and exit barriers 106–9; extension *vs.* diversification 116; intensity of rivalry 111–12; interactive game 100–2; and market structure 85–91; model of competition 100–16; product life-cycle 109–11; size of xi, 51, 85, 89–91, 104–6, 224; small 79, 90–1, 184; theory of 91–9, 208
fixing, price 151–3
Flood, Merrill 23
food retailing 180–5, 212–14
Ford Motor Company 76, 170–80, 214
France 120–1
'free riders' 161–2
free trade 13–17; classical theory 28–33; EEC and 226–7, 233–4
freedom: economic 5; individual 4, 34–5
Freud, Sigmund 44, 48, 202
Friedman, Milton 21, 78, 96

Fromm, Erich 7

Galbraith, John Kenneth 61, 85–6, 175, 220
games x–xi, 17–25, 202–3; and oligopoly 57–61; rules of 19–20, 26; theory 21–5, 216
Garden Cottage Foods v. *Milk Marketing Board* 136
'gateways' 123–4
General Agreement on Tariffs and Trade (GATT) 13, 74, 207, 233
Genn-Bash, A., *et al.* 176, 211
George, K. D. 125–6
Gibrat, R. 89
Gouldner, Alvin W. 46
government: collusion against competition 227–30; intervention rationale 202–18; *see also* legislation; policy
Gower, L. E. B. 186–7
grammars 12–13, 25
Grand Metropolitan/Watneys 195, 200
Greenaway, D. 230
Grey Green Coaches 160
grocery retailing 180–5, 212–14
groups 46–7
Guinness 200

Hague, D. C. 95–6
Haldi, J. 118
Hall, R. L. 95–6
Hambro Life (Allied Dunbar) 189, 191
Hannah, L. 141
happiness xi, 2, 3–4, 6–8, 34
Harberger, A. C. 122, 209
Hardin, G. 22
Harris, J. W. 71–2
Hartley, K. 122
'Harvard' School 62–4
Hasselblad 138, 218
Hattersley, Roy 81, 127–8
Hay, D. A. 118
Hay, George 142–3
Hayek, Friedrich A. 64, 71–2, 74, 78, 202–3, 204
Heath, Edward 221–2
Hirst, P. 81

'hit and run' entry 56–7, 68–9
Hitch, C. J. 95–6
Hobbes, Thomas 28, 48, 202
Hochman, H. 217
Hoffman-La Roche 136, 155, 160
Holland, Stuart 81
homo oeconomicus 20
horizontal price fixing 151–2
Hughes, A. 86–7
Hunter, A. 123

IBM 224
Imperial Trident 189
IMRO 186
India 120–1
individuals 25; happiness 6–8; rights of 4, 34–5, 81; and society 64–5
Industrial Reorganisation Corporation 145
industrialisation 3–4; Japan 143–4
industries, concentration 86–9, 233
information: access to 70, 204; consumers 50; sharing of 207, 216; technology 208
innovation 9, 66–8, 103–4
Institute of Directors 79
insurance 185–92, 210–12
Insurance Companies Act (1980) 186
intellectual property rights 73, 170–80
international trade 14–17, 225–31
Intriligator, M. D. 88
'invisible hand' 29, 204
Island Records, Ex Parte 70
Italy 120–1

Jacquard, J. J. 45
Japan 120–1, 207, 233; industrial policy 143–5; legislation 143–6; MITI 145, 146; price fixing 152
Jefferson, Thomas 12
Jensen, M. C. 69
Johnson, Gerry 100
Johnson, H. G. 230
Johnson, Samuel 205

Kay, J. 141
Kirzner, Israel M. 65
Knight, Frank ix–x, xi
Korah, Valentine 70

Koutsoyiannis, A. 9
Kumar, M. S. 86-7

labour 29-31
Labour Party, UK 81-3;
    competition policy 127-8
laissez-faire capitalism 13, 206
Lamarck, J. B. A. P. de Monnet 39
Larner, R. J. 93
Laughlin, P. R. 45
LAUTRO 186, 189-90, 191
legislation 70-7; case decisions 72-3;
    and economic theory 71-2, 73-4;
    EEC 130-9, 147-50; insurance
    185-92, 210-12; Japan 143-6;
    patents 68, 171-2, 178; and power
    74; UK 121-130, 233-5; USA 139-
    43
Legrand, J. 82
Leibenstein, H. 120, 217
level pricing 154-5
Lewin, Kurt 44
Lewis, W. A. 16
licensing *see* beer
Liesner, H. H. 127
life assurance 185-92, 210-12
life-cycle, product 109-11
limit of market size (LMS) 105-6
limit pricing 55
Lincoln, Abraham 12
Lipsey, R. 226
List, Friedrich 15-16
Little, I. M. D. 86
Littlechild, Stephen C. 67, 122-3,
    226
Lloyd, T. 232
Locke, John 28-9, 48, 202, 207
Locksley, G. 86
long-run average cost (LRAC) 55-6,
    118
Lonrho v. *Shell and BP* 72
Lorenz, Konrad 44
low-cost strategy 114-15
Luce, R. 60
luck x

McGee, John S. 156-7
McGuire Act (1952), USA 140
Machlup, Fritz 96
Malthus, Thomas 35-6, 40, 48

management, and ownership 92-5
March, J. G. 93, 97-9, 208
markets 3; and business strategy 85-
    91; laws of 78-9; 'mechanism' of
    203; power 62-3; structure of 49-
    62, 85-91
Marris, R. 93, 208
Marshall, Alfred 4-5, 43
Marvel, Howard P. 163-4, 226
Marx, Karl 5, 28, 40-3, 48, 205, 223,
    228
Mason, E. S. 62
Maynard Smith, John 24
Means, G. 92-3
Meckling, W. H. 69
Menge, J. A. 9, 175
Menger, Carl 64
mergers 89, 232; Japan 145-6; policy
    221-2; UK 141, 145; UK
    legislation 124-5; US legislation
    140-1
Merkin, R. 71, 155, 164
Michelin 76, 137
Mill, John Stuart 27, 34-5, 202, 207
minimum efficient size (MES) 104-
    6, 118-19
minimum feasible size (MFS) 104-6
Ministry of International Trade and
    Industry (MITI), Japan 145, 146
Mises, Ludwig von 64, 65, 78, 203
Mogul S. S. v. *McGregor Gow* 70
monetarism 75
Monopolies and Mergers Act (1965)
    124-5
Monopolies and Mergers
    Commission (MMC) 124-7, 130,
    133-4, 215, 234; and 'Austrian'
    School 67; criticism of 75; and
    food retailing 180-2, 185, 212-14;
    and pricing 154, 155, 160-1; and
    tie-in sales 167, 168
Monopolies and Mergers
    Commission Reports: Car parts
    173-7; Chlordiazepoxide and
    Diazepam 136, 155, 160;
    Contraceptive Sheaths 160; Credit
    cards 160; Discounts to retailers
    180-2, 185; Ford Motor Company
    Ltd 171-7, 214; Photocopiers 167;
    Supply of animal waste 160;

Supply of asbestos 163; Supply of beer 193, 200–1; Tampons 215
Monopolies and Restrictive Practices Act (1948) 121
monopolistic competition 51–3
monopoly xi, 33, 219–23; and 'Austrian' School 66–8; classical criticism of 31–3; efficiency 73–4, 75; neo-classical theory 61–2; pricing 73–4; and 'public interest' 121–3; trade unions 229
monopsonism 62, 83, 160
Montedison 216
More, Sir Thomas 219
Morgernstern, Oskar 21
Morris, D. J. 118
Mueller, D. C. 122, 209, 226
Multi-Fibre Agreement 83, 228
multinationals 224–5, 227, 229
Munchau, W. 232

nationalism 15–16
negotiation 13, 47
neo-classical theory 49–64; of the firm 91–3; and industrial economics 62–4; monopolistic competition 51–3; monopoly 61–2; oligopoly 53–61; perfect competition 50–1
'Nim' (game) 21–2
Nippon Steel Corporation 145
non-price competition 9, 52
Northern Clubs Federation 200

Office of Fair Trading (OFT) 75, 129, 132–4, 234; and anti-competitive practices 155, 163; and food retailing 181–2, 185, 212–14; and Ford Motor Company Ltd 171, 214; and insurance 211
oligopoly 53–61, 63
Olson, Mancur 209–10
Opium Wars 13
Ordover, J. A. 205
Ornstein, S. I. 88
ownership, *vs.* control 93–5

Padover, S. K. 43
Paley, Bishop William 38

patents, law of 68, 171–2, 178
patriotism 205
Peacock, A. T. 209
Peston, M. H. 97
Phillips, J. 77
photocopiers 167
Pilkington Glass 80
policy 107, 206–7, 219–35; Conservative 128–9; Japan 143–5; Labour 127–8; mergers 221–2; monopolies and mergers 127–8; UK 233–5; *see also* legislation
politics 3, 10–11, 77–84; goals 83–4; UK 78–83
population 35–6, 49
Porter, Michael E. 61, 100
Posner, Richard A. 72, 73–4, 157–8, 167–8, 205
power: buying 61; and legislation 74; market 62–3; multinationals 214–15; political 78
predatory pricing 60, 76, 156–60
Price Commission 193, 126
pricing ix–x, 29, 204; anti-competitive 151–61; beer 195; competition 9; discrimination 153–6; fixing 151–3; limit 55; monopoly 73–4; predation 60, 76, 156–60; vertical squeezing 160–1
principal-agent model 69–70
'Prisoners' Dilemma' 23–4, 60, 101
privatisation 10, 69, 101, 128
Procter & Gamble 57
profit 3; and efficiency 62, 184, 213; maximisation 92–7; motive 66; and oligopoly 54; tendency to fall 42–3; and trade protection 229–30
Prosper de Mulder Ltd 160
protectionism 31–2, 205–6, 228–9; theory 15–17
psychology 43–7
'public interest' 61–2, 121–3, 156, 160, 222
pubs *see* beer

Raiffa, H. 60
rebates 155–6
reciprocity 46
Red Label Whisky 154, 218
Rees, Peter 125

refusal to supply 161–2
resale price maintenance (RPM)
123–4, 152–3, 180
Resale Prices Act (1964 and 1976)
124, 153, 180
Restrictive Practices Act (1968) 125–
6
Restrictive Trade Practices Act
(1956) 123, 135, 152–3, 207
Restrictive Trade Practices Court
75, 127, 131, 137, 152
retailing, grocery 180–5, 212–14
Ricardo, David 14, 32
rights: individual 4, 34–5, 81;
intellectual property 73, 170–80;
to free trade 13–17
Ritson, C. 50
rivalry 111–12, 113
'Robbers Cave' experiment 47
Robinson-Patman Act (1936), USA
140
ROLAC 189–90
Rome, Treaty of 130–2, 172, 216
Rosenberg, J. B. 220–1
Rosenham, D. L. 46
Ross, S. A. 69
Rowley, C. K. 209
rules x, 18–20, 26, 202–3, 223, 232;
see also legislation

'satisficing' 99
Sawyer, M. C. 86, 87, 89, 93, 105,
222
scale, economies of xi, 105–6, 220–1
Scherer, F. M. 164–5, 166–7, 178,
220
Scholes, Kevan 100
Schroeder v. *Macawlay* 70
Schumpeter, Joseph A. 64, 65
Schwartz, M. 156, 162, 168
Scitovsky, T. 93, 95
Scottish & Newcastle 195, 200
Scruton, Roger 79, 206
Securities Association 186
Securities and Investment Board
(SIB) 185, 188, 190–1
Seldon, Arthur 80
self-regulation 232; *see also*
insurance
selfishness 4, 28

Seta, J. J. 45
Sherif, Muzapher 46
Sherman, Senator John 139–40
Sherman Act (1890), USA 139–41
shipbuilding industry 228
Shrieves, R. E. 88
Shubik, M. 59
Simmel, Georg 46
Simon, H. A. 99
size of firms *see under* firms
small firms 79, 90–1, 184
Smith, Adam 4, 12, 15, 27, 28–33,
46, 48, 94–5
Social Democrats 83
'social facilitation' 45
socialism 81–2
sociobiology 39–40, 44–5, 48
Soderstern, B. 230
Sorenson, R. 95
Spence, A. M. 69
Spencer, Herbert 7, 39
sport *see* games
Stackelberg, H. von 54
Standard Industrial Classification
(SIC) 87
Stano, M. 95
Stanworth, J. 89–90
steel industry 228
Stelzer, Irwin M. 157
Stevens, R. B. 123
Stigler, G. 55, 85, 118
Storey, D., *et al*, 90–1
strategy: business 85–117; game 20–1
25–6
Strong, N. 70
Structuralist School 63, 141
structured and unstructured
competition 86
survival 29, 35–40
Sweden 120–1
Sweezy, P. 85
Sylos Postulate 55
Sylvania 72, 142

takeovers *see* mergers
Target Life 189
taxation 97, 221
Taylor, T. C. 203
'Tebbit doctrine' 222
technology 220–1; information 208

textile industry 228
Thatcher, Margaret 10, 78–9
theory 27–84; 202–18; allocative
efficiency 209–10; 'Austrian'
School 64–8; behavioural 97–9;
'Chicago' School 62–4, 74–5;
classical 28–35; collective action
209–11; Comparative Advantage
14–15, 32; evolution 37–40; of
firms 91–9, 208; games 21–5, 216;
'Harvard' School 62–4;
international trade 225–31; *laissez-
faire* 13; legal models 70–7;
marxism 40–3; neo-classical 49–
64; new developments 68–70;
oligopoly 53–61; political models
77–84; price 9; price leadership 56;
protection 15–17; psychology 43–
7; Structuralist School 63
Third World 230–1
TI Raleigh 161, 217
tie-in sales 166–8
'Tit for Tat' strategy 24, 216
Todaro, M. R. 229–30
Topliss Showers v. *Gessey* 137
Trade and Industry, Department of
(DTI) 87
trade, international 14–17, 225–31
trade unions 229
'Tragedy of the Commons' 22–3,
101, 216
Triplett, Norman 45
Tsurata, T. 143–4
Tucker, A. W. 23
Tullock, G. 209
Turner, D. F.158–9

unemployment 219–20
Unger, M. 72, 74
Unilever 57
United Brands 76, 136
United Kingdom (UK) 120–1; and
EEC legislation 132–9; legal
systems 74–5; legislation 121–30,
233–5; mergers 124–5; 141, 145;
monopoly and 'public interest'
121–2; politics 78–83
United Nations Council for Trade
and Development (UNCTAD) 233
United States of America (USA):

anti-trust laws 73–4, 89, 139–41,
159; car industry 9; legal systems
74–5; legislation 139–43;
monopoly and 'public interest'
122; predation 159; price
discrimination 156
Usher, James, Archbishop of
Armagh 37

values ix–xi, 202
Vekusa, M. 152
vertical price fixing 152–3
vertical price squeezing 160–1
vertical restraints 141–2, 208
von Neumann, John 21

wages 29–30
Walras, Leon 43
Walshe, G. 87
Ward, T. 86
Warnink v. *Townsend* 71
Waterford Glass 218
Waterson, M. 70
Watkins, D. 90
Watneys 195, 200
Weber, Max 71
Wedgwood 218
welfare economics 61–2, 121–3, 156,
160, 222
Weston, J. F. 88
Wheeler-Lea Act (1938), USA 140
Whitbread 195, 200
Whitcomb, D. 118
Williams, K. 71, 155, 164
Williamson, O. E. 89, 93
Wilson, Charles E. 208
Wilson, S. O. 44
Wilson, T. 60
Wilson, President Woodrow 140
Winthrop, J. R. 119, 220
Wire Rope 154
Woolf, E. 209

X-inefficiency 120

Yamey, B. S. 123

Zeckhauser, R. 69
zero-sum games 57–60